Matthew's Gospel

A Study of the King and His Kingdom

M J Tiry

Matthew's Gospel

A Study of the King and His Kingdom

M J Tiry

Matthew's Gospel: A Study of the King and His Kingdom / M J Tiry

ISBN

Paper Back:	979-8-9903305-9-7
Hard Cover	979-8-9918240-0-2
ePub	979-8-9918240-1-9

Library of Congress Control Number 2025900225

Printed in the United States of America

Published February 2025

Published by M J Tiry Publishing
Chippewa Falls, WI 54729

DEDICATION

This Study is dedicated to you the student of the Word of God. May this it be edifying and encouraging to you as you engage yourself in the quest for Bible truth.

CONTENTS
TABLE OF CONTENTS

INTRODUCTION TO MATTHEW'S GOSPEL...11

MATTHEW 1:1-25 THE GENEALOGY OF THE KING...15

MATTHEW 2:1-23 THE BIRTH OF THE KING..19

MATTHEW 3:1-17 JOHN THE BAPTIST ANNOUNCES THE KING...............21

MATTHEW 4:1-25 THE TEMPTATION OF JESUS..27

MATTHEW 5:1-12 THE PLATFORM OF THE KINGDOM...............................31

MATTHEW 6:1-34 THE SERMON ON THE MOUNT CONTINUES..............45

MATTHEW 7:1-29 THE CITIZENS OF THE KINGDOM..................................49

MATTHEW 8:1-27 THE CREDENTIALS OF THE KING...................................53

MATTHEW 9:1-37 JESUS RETURNS TO CAPERNAUM..................................59

MATTHEW 10:1-42 THE KING'S REPRESENTATIVES......................................65

MATTHEW 11:1-30 THE KING IS REJECTED..73

MATTHEW 12:1-50 THE SON IS BLASPHEMED...79

MATTHEW 13:1-58 THE MYSTERIES OF THE KINGDOM OF HEAVEN...87

MATTHEW 14:1-36 THE KING'S FORERUNNER IS MURDERED..................97

MATTHEW 15:1-38 THE WOMAN OF CANAAN..101

MATTHEW 16:1-28 THE SIGN OF THE PROPHET JONAH.........................105

MATTHEW 17:1-27 THE TRANSFIGURATION...111

MATTHEW 18:1-35 CHILD-LIKE FAITH TO ENTER THE KINGDOM.....115

MATTHEW 19:1-30 BACK TO JUDEA..119

MATTHEW 20:1-34 THE LAST SHALL BE FIRST...123

MATTHEW 21:1-46 PASSION WEEK STARTS...127

MATTHEW 22:1-46 JESUS THE PASSOVER LAMB.......................................133

MATTHEW 23:1-39 JESUS, THE KINGDOM, AND THE LAW....................139

MATTHEW 24:1-51 THE DESTRUCTION OF THE TEMPLE FORTOLD .143

MATTHEW 25:1-46 THE JUDGE AND THE JUDGMENTS...........................155

MATTHEW 26:1-75 THE FEAST OF THE PASSOVER....................................159

MATTHEW 27:1-66 THE COUNSEL OF THE ELDERS OF ISRAEL.............165

MATTHEW 28:1-20 THE EMPTY TOMB...171

CONCLUSION..173

Tables:

1. Threefold Temptation ....Page 27
2. The Beatitudes Page33
3. Deuteronomy 30 and Romans 10 ....Page 37
4. The Law Fully Filled ....Page 38
5. Three Bible Churches ....Page 107
6. The Blessing and the Woes...Page 141
7. Satan and Christ Compared ....Page 146
8. From History to Prophecy it is all His Story ....Page 181
9. Prophecy and the Mystery..Page 183

Abbreviations used:

c.	circa ("about/Approximately")
cp	Compare
e.g.	exampligratia ("for example")
et. al.	Et allii ("and others")
etc.	Et. cetara ("and so forth")
ff	and the following (verses, pages, etc.)
i.e.	id. est. (that is)
vas, vv	verse (s)
viz.	Videlicet ('namely")

Notes to the Reader:

A word is in order here on how to study the Bible and actually how to approach the Bible. Some basic principles to hold in our study of Scripture then are:

1. Understand that all of scripture came from the mouth of God and it fully equips the man of God to do anything that God would have him do. "All scripture *is* given by inspiration of God, and *is* profitable for doctrine, for reproof, for correction, for instruction in righteousness: That the man of God may be perfect, throughly furnished unto all good works." (2 Timothy 3:16-17) The term "inspiration of God" means that it was breathed out of God's mouth. It is truly as the Lord tells the devil in Matthew 4:4 "It is written; Man shall not live by bread alone, but by every word that proceedeth out of the mouth of God."

2. Scripture must be studied in its context in order for it to make sense. There are two contexts: the immediate context in which the passage is set and there is the remote context that looks at the Bible as a whole. That concept is what Peter is communicating when he said in 2Peter 1:20 & 21 "Knowing this first, that no prophecy of the scripture is of any private interpretation. For the prophecy came not in old time by the will of man: but holy men of God spake *as they were* moved by the Holy Ghost." No passage of scripture is intended to stand by itself but rather each passage actually relates to every other passage of scripture. One of the greatest tools to Bible study is a good cross reference. By comparing scripture with scripture the Bible teaches itself. The Bible itself is its greatest and best teacher.

3. While all of scripture is written for our learning, not every passage of scripture is addressed specifically to us who live in the dispensation of grace. The word of truth then must be rightly divided. Paul tells us this in 2Timothy 2:15 saying "Study to shew thyself approved unto God, a workman that needeth not to be ashamed, rightly dividing the word of truth." We trust that appendix 2 of this book will be very helpful in seeing this concept.

4. Another key to understanding the Bible is simply to let it say what it clearly says. It is a major mistake to spiritualize scripture. The Bible is written to be taken literally. There are times when the Bible uses figures of speech (figurative language) but when it does it is apparent that such is the case. Basically, we must remember the adage "if the literal sense makes perfect sense, seek no other sense."

5. There is yet another key to an effective study of the word of God. That is the heart attitude of the Bereans of Acts 17:11. They received the Word with and open mind but they did not just take any man's word for truth or error of what was said until they searched it out in the scripture. That approach gave them protection from error for they made the Word of God their final authority and examined what everyone said based on the Word of Truth – the Bible.

6. One final thing regarding the Bible having the impact in our lives that God intended it to have is the simple matter of believing it. Paul tells the Thessalonians that they received the word of God, they received it not as the word of men but as it is in truth the word of God, which "...effectually worketh in you that believe." It is not just the understanding of it that makes it effective but applying it by faith to one's life that makes it effective to give spiritual strength and vitality.

The author has a series of four books in what is called the Prophecy Series. This book is the third in the series. The first in the series is "*A Study in Daniel – The King and the Kingdom in Prophecy.*" The second of this series is "*Matthew's Gospel- Study of the King and His Kingdom.*" The fourth and last in the series is "*A Study in the Revelation—the End Times Fulfillment of Bible Prophecy.*"

PREFACE

The Bible is laid out in clearly defined sections that show the dispensations as they unfold in time. The two-fold purpose of God is presented in a sequence that was determined by God and sequentially revealed to man. The revelation of the Word of God was revealed as it was needed for man to respond in faith to what God was telling him to do. There are two programs whereby God interacts with man. The majority of the Bible is involved with the program that is called Bible Prophecy. That program centers in the nation of Israel and concerns a kingdom that God will one day set up on earth under the reign of the promised Messiah. That kingdom is called the Kingdom of Heaven in Matthew's gospel. The other program is called "the Mystery" and involves a body of believers called "the church which is His Body." The program called the Mystery is revealed in the Bible in the Pauline epistles and is referred to as "The Dispensation of the Grace of God."

To understand the Bible, it is helpful to see that the two programs are revealed in the five sections of the Bible as shown bellow. The Old Testament presents the promise of the Kingdom of Heaven in prophecy. The four gospels (and particularly Matthew's gospel) present the Kingdom of Heaven as being "at Hand" – it was ready to be set up. The Book of Acts presents the offer of the Kingdom of Heaven to Israel and Israel's rejection of the offer when the nation rejected the resurrected King and thus also the Kingdom. The Book of Acts also reveals the sending of Paul to the world as the apostle of the Gentiles. The Pauline epistles then present the Dispensation of Grace as a temporary postponement of the establishment of the Kingdom of Heaven. Finally, Hebrews through Revelation present the establishment of the Kingdom on earth. There are four key books in the Bible that deal with the kingdom established on earth -- those being Daniel which sees the kingdom in prophecy, Matthew which sees the kingdom of heaven as being at hand, Hebrews which presents Jesus Christ as the High Priest of Israel who will return as Israel's redeemer, and the Revelation which finally presents the establishment of the kingdom.

Matthew's gospel presents the Lord Jesus Christ as the rightful king who will reign over Israel and the earth in the kingdom. It is called "The Kingdom of Heaven" in Matthew's gospel because when it is set up, God's will is going to be done in the earth as it is in heaven (Matt. 6:10).

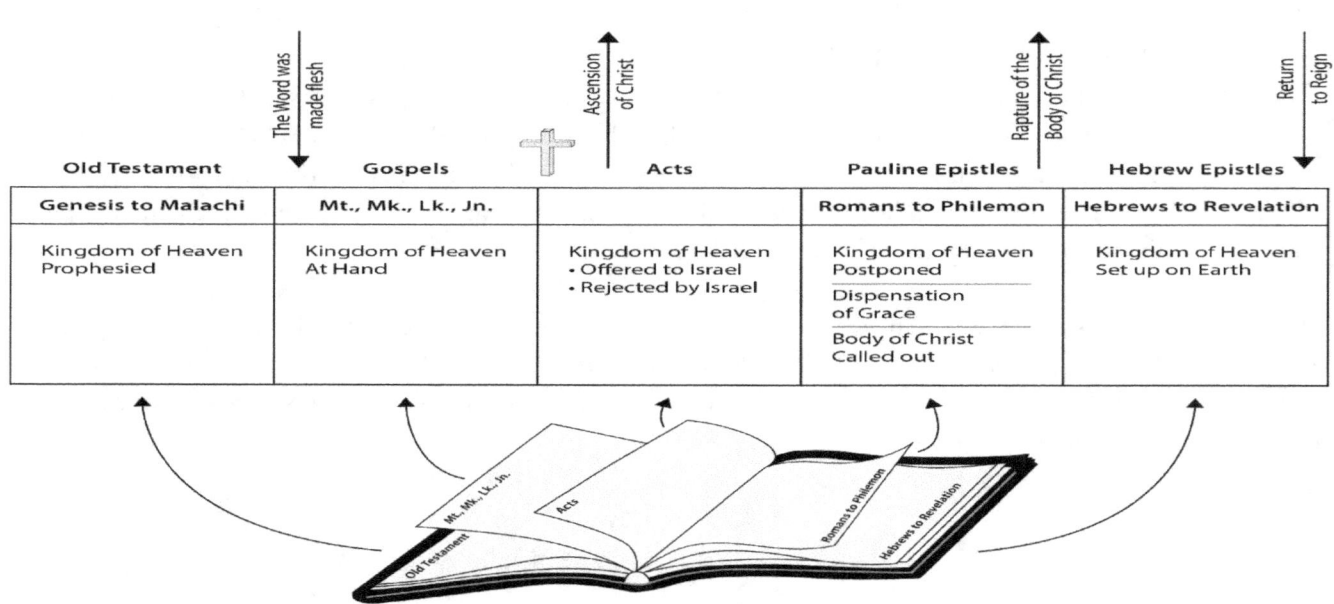

Old Testament	Gospels	Acts	Pauline Epistles	Hebrew Epistles
Genesis to Malachi	**Mt., Mk., Lk., Jn.**		**Romans to Philemon**	**Hebrews to Revelation**
Kingdom of Heaven Prophesied	Kingdom of Heaven At Hand	Kingdom of Heaven • Offered to Israel • Rejected by Israel	Kingdom of Heaven Postponed — Dispensation of Grace — Body of Christ Called out	Kingdom of Heaven Set up on Earth

The Progression of Revelation to Man

ACKNOWLEDGMENTS

I thank the Lord Jesus Christ for redeeming my soul and the souls of believers through the ages by His sacrifice of His perfect life at Calvary. I thank God also for the regenerating work of the Holy Spirit of God for quickening my spirit that I might understand the Word of God. I thank our heavenly Father for all He is and for the riches of His grace in which He has made us believers accepted in His beloved Son. I thank Him for the very Word of God that he has given to us and that we can study it in our own language. I appreciate the students of the Word with whom I share a great passion for study of the Bible to learn of the eternal blessings that are there for our learning and edification. I particularly appreciate the series of messages presented by Richard Jordan of the Grace School of the Bible for the insight that his diligent teaching on the book of Matthew has provided.

I thank my daughters for their help in putting this work together and for the publishing process. I would not be able to do it without their help. I thank Vince Kison and Diane Tiry for their work in review of this book.

INTRODUCTION TO MATTHEW'S GOSPEL

The four gospel accounts (Matthew, Mark, Luke and John) each present a particular view of the same person (the Lord Jesus Christ) and His ministry. Just as four different writers would describe a building from four different directions in different terms, so each of the writers describe the earthly ministry of our Lord from four different perspectives. Matthew describes Him as the king who will sit on the throne of David in a kingdom to be set up on earth. Mark describes Him as the Servant of the Lord. Luke describes Him as the perfect Man. John describes Him as the eternal Word (God) who was made flesh and dwelt among us men. The writers were apparently chosen by God because of their backgrounds. Matthew was a publican (a tax collector) and therefore interested in government. The Kingdom of Heaven is a term used only in Matthew's gospel. The term is a reference to the Kingdom in which God's will is going to be done in the earth as it is in heaven (Matt. 6:10).

Whenever the throne of God was described in scriptures (e.g. Rev. 4:6-8; Ezek. 1:10; 10:14; 41:20), there are seen four living creatures called cherubim around the throne. Each of the four creatures has four faces. The four views of the Messiah as presented in the four gospel accounts have a parallel to the four faces of the four creatures around the throne. The faces of the cherubim are: The face of a lion, the face of an ox, the face of man, and the face of an eagle. The lion is often thought of as the king of the beasts. This would correspond to Matthew's presentation of Jesus Christ as the king. The ox is a beast of burden to serve mankind. This would correspond to Mark's presentation of Jesus as the Servant of the Lord. As we read Mark's gospel we see fast paced action without much detail as a servant would be involved in action (getting the work done without looking into the details). Luke (the physician) looks at the humanity of Jesus Christ. He presents Christ as the perfect man. This corresponds to the face of the man on the cherubim John presents Jesus Christ as God. This corresponds to the face of the eagle – the eagle being a creature that flies high in the sky over all things in earth.

The genealogies that we find in the gospels are significant to each of these presentations of the nature of Christ as well. Matthew's genealogy is traced back through Joseph (the husband of Mary) to David the king. Jesus Christ is to sit on the throne of David in the kingdom. Mark presents no genealogy but then no one is interested in the genealogy of the servant. John's gospel goes back to God with the opening words "In the beginning was the Word and the Word was with God and the Word was God." This takes us to passages such as Hebrews 11:3 "Through faith we understand that the worlds were framed by the word of God, so that things which are seen were not made of things which do appear." As we study creation in Genesis Chapter 1 we see that creation was brought in to existence by the Creator's words "And God said…" the eternal Word who created all things.

Four Behold statements regarding the branch:
There are four presentations of the coming Messiah as "…the Branch"

- **Matthew's Gospel – the Branch of David the King** "[5] Behold, the days come, saith the LORD, that I will raise unto David a righteous Branch, and a King shall reign and prosper, and shall execute judgment and justice in the earth." (Jer. 23:5) This is the view of Messiah as presented in Matthew's gospel as the king who will sit on David's throne.

- **Mark's Gospel – My Servant the Branch** "[8]Hear now, O Joshua the high priest, thou, and thy fellows that sit before thee: for they *are* men wondered at: for, behold, I will bring forth my servant the BRANCH." (Zech. 3:8) This is the presentation of Messiah as the Servant of the LORD (Jehovah) as He is presented in Mark's gospel.

- **Luke's Gospel – the Man who is the Branch** "[12] And speak unto him, saying, Thus speaketh the LORD of hosts, saying, Behold the man whose name *is* The BRANCH; and he shall grow up out of his place, and he shall build the temple of the LORD:" (Zech. 6:12)

- **John's Gospel – the Branch of the Lord** [2] In that day shall the branch of the LORD be beautiful and glorious, and the fruit of the earth *shall be* excellent and comely for them that are escaped of Israel." (Isa. 4:2)

We find all four of these presentations of Messiah in Paul's epistles. Note:
Christ as the King has:
A realm over which he reigns (2Tim. 2:4)
Soldiers (2Tim. 2:3)
People who reign with him (2Tim. 2:12)
Ambassadors who represent him in foreign lands (2Cor. 5:20)
Christ is the pattern servant (Phil. 2:5)
Christ is a Man (1Tim. 2:5)
Christ is presented as God (Rom. 9:5; Titus 2:12 & 13; Acts 20:28))

The gospel of Matthew covers only the earthly ministry of Jesus Christ. The purpose for His earthly ministry is presented in Romans 15:8-12 "…to confirm the promises made unto the fathers." Matthew used the term "…the kingdom of heaven…" and presents the gospel of the kingdom (Matt. 3:1-3; 4:17-23). It is interesting to note that the gospel of the kingdom does not include the blood atonement (Matt. 16:15-28; 24:14). The presentation of the blood atonement is not given to the Hebrew people until the Book of Hebrews (Heb. 6:1-4). In fact, the disciples did not even understand His death (Luke 9:1-6 compared with Verses 43-45 of the same chapter; Matt. 16:21 & 22). The keeping of the Law of Moses was however a part of the program during the presentation of the gospel of the kingdom (Matt. 6:12; 18:21-35; 23:1-5; Acts 21:20).

The Gospel according to Matthew is divided conveniently into three sections as follows:
1. In Chapters 1 thru 11 the Lord addresses the nation at large with the simple message: "the kingdom of Heaven is at hand." The kingdom is "at hand" because the King is in their midst That is saying the kingdom of heaven is within you because the King is in your midst (Luke 17:20). However, the nation rejects the king and the preaching of the gospel of the kingdom. The transition starts in Matthew 11:20 – 26 where we will see Him focus not on the kingdom but on Himself.
2. In Chapters 12 & 13 we will see the nation rejecting the King and the message of the kingdom. There is a three fold rejection in Chapter twelve. They reject Him as the prophet (12:41) as the priest (12:6), and as the king (12:42). In Chapter 13 He talks about the mysteries of the kingdom. The mystery is that the kingdom will eventually be proclaimed without the King being present. This will happen in the early part of the Book of Acts.
3. In Chapters 14 thru 28 we will see the Lord focus His attention on preparing the little flock of believers to carry on their ministry without Him being present with them.

The first part of Matthew's gospel is laid out by chapters as follows:
Chapter 1 presents the genealogy of the king.
Chapter 2 presents the birth of the King.
Chapter 3 presents John the Baptist prepares the way for the King.
Chapter 4 presents the preparation of the King.
Chapters 5, 6 &7 lay out the platform of the Kingdom.
Chapters 8 & 9 present the credentials of the King.
Chapter 10 Present the Kings' representatives.
Chapters 11 & 12 reveal that the King is being rejected.
Chapter 13 presents the Mysteries of the Kingdom of Heaven.

The second part of Matthew's gospel goes on to cover His work in the preparation of the disciples to carry on their ministry to Israel in His absence.

The second part of Matthew's Gospel is laid out by chapters as follows:

Chapter 14 the Murder of John the Baptist
Chapter 15 the Woman of Canaan
Chapter 16 Peter's Confession and the Messianic Church
Chapter 17 the Transfiguration
Chapter 18 Lessons on Childlike Faith
Chapter 19 Jesus leaves Galilee; Ministers to the Twelve Apostles to the Twelve Tribes of Israel
Chapter 20 Jesus Informs the Twelve His Impending Death and Resurrection
Chapter 21 the Cursing of the Fig Tree
Chapter 22 the Examination of the Passover Lamb
Chapter 23 Teaching on the Kingdom and the Law
Chapter 24 Prophecy on the Mount
Chapter 25 the Judge and the Judgments
Chapter 26 the Last Supper
Chapter 27 the Crucifixion
Chapter 28 the Resurrection

MATTHEW 1:1-25

THE GENEALOGY OF THE KING

Matthew 1:1 .[1] The book of the generation of Jesus Christ, the son of David, the son of Abraham.

The name "Jesus Christ" is actually both a name and a title. The term "Christ" is a title for the Messiah. Peter's confession that Jesus is the Christ the Son of the living God is what will be the confession that would get an Israelite into the Kingdom of Heaven (Matt. 16:16 cf. John 6:69). The use of the title is clear from the high priest's statement "I ajure thee by the living God, that thou tell us whether thou be the Christ, the Son of God." Matthew's gospel shows Christ as the Son of David in the first 25 chapters and as the Son of Abraham in Chapters 26-28.

Matthew 1:2-16 "[2] Abraham begat Isaac; and Isaac begat Jacob; and Jacob begat Judas and his brethren; [3] And Judas begat Phares and Zara of Thamar; and Phares begat Esrom; and Esrom begat Aram; [4] And Aram begat Aminadab; and Aminadab begat Naasson; and Naasson begat Salmon; [5] And Salmon begat Booz of Rachab; and Booz begat Obed of Ruth; and Obed begat Jesse; [6] And Jesse begat David the king; and David the king begat Solomon of her *that had been the wife* of Urias; [7] And Solomon begat Roboam; and Roboam begat Abia; and Abia begat Asa; [8] And Asa begat Josaphat; and Josaphat begat Joram; and Joram begat Ozias; [9] And Ozias begat Joatham; and Joatham begat Achaz; and Achaz begat Ezekias; [10] And Ezekias begat Manasses; and Manasses begat Amon; and Amon begat Josias; [11] And Josias begat Jechonias and his brethren, about the time they were carried away to Babylon: [12] And after they were brought to Babylon, Jechonias begat Salathiel; and Salathiel begat Zorobabel; [13] And Zorobabel begat Abiud; and Abiud begat Eliakim; and Eliakim begat Azor; [14] And Azor begat Sadoc; and Sadoc begat Achim; and Achim begat Eliud; [15] And Eliud begat Eleazar; and Eleazar begat Matthan; and Matthan begat Jacob; [16] And Jacob begat Joseph the husband of Mary, of whom was born Jesus, who is called Christ."

There is an important and interesting point to be made here. In Verse 11 we find the godly king Josiah is the father of Jechonias (Jehoiakim) who is the father of Jehoiakin (Coniah) of whom the Lord said that no man of his seed will sit on the throne of David (Jer. 22:24-30). Joseph is of Coniah's seed but he is not the physical father of Jesus. The fact that Joseph is the husband of Mary enables Christ to sit on the throne of David as the seed of David by marriage of Mary to Joseph. Christ is the seed of David through the royal seed line through Solomon by the fact that Mary is the wife of Joseph. He is also of the seed of David through Mary through another son of David – Nathan (Luke 3:31). Christ had to be the virgin born son of David through a different lineage than Joseph's in order for Him to sit on the throne of David.

Matthew 1:17 "[17] So all the generations from Abraham to David *are* fourteen generations; and from David until the carrying away into Babylon *are* fourteen generations; and from the carrying away into Babylon unto Christ *are* fourteen generations.

The term "…the son of David, the son of Abraham…" in association with Christ draws our attention to three covenants. From Abraham to David (fourteen generations) the focus of scripture was on the Abrahamic Covenant. From David to the captivity of Israel (another fourteen generations), it was on the Davidic Covenant regarding a kingdom on earth. From the captivity to Christ (again fourteen generations), the focus of scripture is in the prophetic writings of prophets such as Jeremiah, Daniel, and Ezekiel in which the focus was on the New Covenant that God will make with Israel.

> **Matthew 1:18-21** "[18] Now the birth of Jesus Christ was on this wise: When as his mother Mary was espoused to Joseph, before they came together, she was found with child of the Holy Ghost. [19] Then Joseph her husband, being a just *man*, and not willing to make her a public example, was minded to put her away privily. [20] But while he thought on these things, behold, the angel of the Lord appeared unto him in a dream, saying, Joseph, thou son of David, fear not to take unto thee Mary thy wife: for that which is conceived in her is of the Holy Ghost. [21] And she shall bring forth a son, and thou shalt call his name JESUS: for he shall save his people from their sins.

Mary was betrothed to Joseph and as such he was regarded as her husband though they be not officially married yet. The fact that she was found to be with child left Joseph with two options. One option is that he could have her stoned according to Deuteronomy 22:23 & 24. The other option is the he could divorce her (Deuteronomy 24:1). Joseph was thinking that he would divorce her (Verse 19). Deuteronomy 23:2 states that "A bastard shall not enter into the congregation of the LORD…" Therefore, the Lord intercedes (Verse 20) and explains the situation to Joseph.

The name Jesus means "Jehovah Savior." The word "Christ" is His title as the Messiah of Israel. The name Lord is the position that He holds as Lord over all of creation. Therefore, His full name is the Lord Jesus Christ

> **Matthew 1:22-25** "[22] Now all this was done, that it might be fulfilled which was spoken of the Lord by the prophet, saying, [23] Behold, a virgin shall be with child, and shall bring forth a son, and they shall call his name Emmanuel, which being interpreted is, God with us. [24] Then Joseph being raised from sleep did as the angel of the Lord had bidden him, and took unto him his wife: [25] And knew her not till she had brought forth her firstborn son: and he called his name JESUS."

Joseph "knew her not" (he had no sexual relationship with her) until after she brought forth her first born Son (vs. 25). Mary and Joseph had children together after the Lord was born. We understand from scripture that the Lord had four half brothers and at least two half sisters (Matthew 13:55).

Chapter 1 Study Guide Questions:

1. Why does Matthew trace the genealogy of the Lord back to Abraham while Luke goes back to Adam?

2. Why does Matthew's genealogy go back through Joseph while Luke's goes back through Mary?

3. How many generations intervene from Abraham to David, from David to the captivity, from the captivity to Christ?

4. What were the options that Joseph was contemplated in Verses 18 to 21 regarding the fact that Mary his espoused wife was with child?

5. What does Verse 25 mean when it says that Joseph "Knew her not until after she brought forth her first born son?

6. Did Mary and Joseph have a normal marital relationship after the birth of Jesus?

Chapter 2
MATTHEW 2:1-23

THE BIRTH OF THE KING

Matthew 2: 1-6 "¹ Now when Jesus was born in Bethlehem of Judaea in the days of Herod the king, behold, there came wise men from the east to Jerusalem, ² Saying, Where is he that is born King of the Jews? for we have seen his star in the east, and are come to worship him. ³ When Herod the king had heard *these things*, he was troubled, and all Jerusalem with him. ⁴ And when he had gathered all the chief priests and scribes of the people together, he demanded of them where Christ should be born. ⁵ And they said unto him, In Bethlehem of Judaea: for thus it is written by the prophet, ⁶ And thou Bethlehem, *in* the land of Juda, art not the least among the princes of Juda: for out of thee shall come a Governor, that shall rule my people Israel."

Chapter 2 is interesting in that it presents intense interest from Gentiles in Israel's Messiah. These Gentiles from the East know more about Israel's Messiah than the man sitting on Israel's throne did. They came from the East where Babylon is located. They apparently have been studying the Book of Daniel. In Daniel Chapter 9 they would be able to determine that it was time for the Messiah to be born. At the end of the 69th week of Daniel Chapter 9 Messiah would come to Israel. Understanding that a priest would start his ministry at the age of 30, they could determine with great precision when Christ should be born. Both Anna and Simeon had figured this out as well (Luke 2:25, 36).

Balaam made an interesting prophecy in Numbers 24:17 regarding a star "…There shall come a star out of Jacob…" Balaam was from the same area in the East (Mesopotamia) as the wise men. This is probably the Shekinah glory of the Lord that had departed from Israel in the days of Ezekiel and it returns in the person of Christ. This will likely be the sign of the Son of Man that Matthew 24:30 speaks of that will appear in the tribulation period.

Matthew 2:7-11 "⁷ Then Herod, when he had privily called the wise men, enquired of them diligently what time the star appeared. ⁸ And he sent them to Bethlehem, and said, Go and search diligently for the young child; and when ye have found *him*, bring me word again, that I may come and worship him also. ⁹ When they had heard the king, they departed; and, lo, the star, which they saw in the east, went before them, till it came and stood over where the young child was. ¹⁰ When they saw the star, they rejoiced with exceeding great joy. ¹¹ And when they were come into the house, they saw the young child with Mary his mother, and fell down, and worshipped him: and when they had opened their treasures, they presented unto him gifts; gold, and frankincense, and myrrh"

This worship of Israel's Messiah is what the Gentiles will do in the Kingdom (Zech. 8:3). The gifts that they bring are interesting. They bring gold that one would bring to a king. They also bring perfumes that would be used in embalming.

Matthew 2:12-15 "¹² And being warned of God in a dream that they should not return to Herod, they departed into their own country another way. ¹³ And when they were departed, behold, the angel of the Lord appeareth to Joseph in a dream, saying, Arise, and take the young child and his mother, and flee into Egypt, and be thou there until I bring thee word: for Herod will seek the young child to destroy him. ¹⁴ When he arose, he took the young child and his mother by night, and departed into Egypt: ¹⁵ And was there until the death of Herod: that it might be fulfilled which was spoken of the Lord by the prophet, saying, Out of Egypt have I called my son.

In Exodus 4:22 God refers to Israel as His son and calls Israel out of Egypt. Christ who is the real Israel in that only those of the nation who will find their hope in Him is also called out of Egypt. (Hos. 11:1)

> **Matthew 2:16-18** "[16] Then Herod, when he saw that he was mocked of the wise men, was exceeding wroth, and sent forth, and slew all the children that were in Bethlehem, and in all the coasts thereof, from two years old and under, according to the time which he had diligently enquired of the wise men. [17] Then was fulfilled that which was spoken by Jeremy the prophet, saying, [18] In Rama was there a voice heard, lamentation, and weeping, and great mourning, Rachel weeping *for* her children, and would not be comforted, because they are not."

The Old Testament reference for Verse 17 is Jeremiah 31:15.

> **Matthew 2:19-23** "[19] But when Herod was dead, behold, an angel of the Lord appeareth in a dream to Joseph in Egypt, [20] Saying, Arise, and take the young child and his mother, and go into the land of Israel: for they are dead which sought the young child's life. [21] And he arose, and took the young child and his mother, and came into the land of Israel. [22] But when he heard that Archelaus did reign in Judaea in the room of his father Herod, he was afraid to go thither: notwithstanding, being warned of God in a dream, he turned aside into the parts of Galilee: [23] And he came and dwelt in a city called Nazareth: that it might be fulfilled which was spoken by the prophets, He shall be called a Nazarene."

Here again, Prophecy is being fulfilled to the finest detail. In Verse 19 we find an angel of the Lord appearing to Joseph in a dream providing him instruction. Hebrews 1:14 gives us a clue as to the interaction of angels with humanity saying of them: "Are they not all ministering spirits, sent forth to minister for them who shall be heirs of salvation?" This is what we see in those books of the Bible that pertain to Israel's future. However, when we are in the Pauline epistles we find a different role that angels play. There, in the Pauline epistles, we do not find angels ministering to believers who are members of the body of Christ. What we do find is that angels today are learning about the wisdom of God as they observe the life changing work that the Holy Spirit accomplishes in the edifying of believers under grace.

Chapter 2 Study Guide Questions:

1. Verse 1 speaks of wise men from the East who knew of the time of the birth of Israel's Messiah. Where would they have learned that?

2. What kind of a star was it that they followed?

3. Why would these Gentiles have such interest in Israel's Messiah?

4. What is the significance of the gifts that they brought?

5. What son does God call out of Egypt in Exodus 4:22? What Son is called out of Egypt in Hosea 11:1?

6. What prophecy is fulfilled in Verse 17?

Chapter 3

MATTHEW 3:1-17

JOHN THE BAPTIST ANNOUNCES THE KING

Matthew 3:1-4 "¹ In those days came John the Baptist, preaching in the wilderness of Judaea, ² And saying, Repent ye: for the kingdom of heaven is at hand. ³ For this is he that was spoken of by the prophet Esaias, saying, The voice of one crying in the wilderness, Prepare ye the way of the Lord, make his paths straight. ⁴ And the same John had his raiment of camel's hair, and a leathern girdle about his loins; and his meat was locusts and wild honey."

John's message to Israel is "Repent for the Kingdom of Heaven is at hand". To repent is to change one's mind about someone or something or to think differently than one did before. The Kingdom of Heaven is a reference to the rule of the heavens over the earth. The Lord describes this in what people call "the Lord's prayer" in Matthew 6:10 with the words "…thy will be done in the earth as it is in heaven…" Daniel 2:44 is referring to the ten toes on the great image representing the ten kings who will reign with the antichrist saying: "In the days of these kings shall the God of heaven set up a kingdom which shall never be destroyed." The God of heaven sets up that kingdom but it will be set up on the earth. Jeremiah 23:5 addresses this kingdom "Behold, the days come, saith the LORD, that I will raise unto David a righteous Branch, and a King shall reign and prosper, and shall execute judgment and justice in the earth." This kingdom will be vested in Christ as Luke 1:33 says: "He shall reign over the house of Jacob forever, and of his kingdom there shall be no end."

The Kingdom of heaven as being "at hand" is repeated often in Matthew's gospel up until Chapter 12. In this time period the kingdom is being proclaimed while the king is being present in the midst of the people. To understand this we need to understand that the King and the Kingdom are essentially one and the same. Consider Luke 17:20 in this light: "²⁰ And when he was demanded of the Pharisees, when the kingdom of God should come, he answered them and said, The kingdom of God cometh not with observation: ²¹ Neither shall they say, Lo here! or, lo there! for, behold, the kingdom of God is within you." He tells them that the kingdom of heaven is within you (i e. within Israel) because He was in the midst of them. We see this concept by comparing Mark 11:10 with Luke 19:38.

"¹⁰ Blessed *be* the kingdom of our father David, that cometh in the name of the Lord: Hosanna in the highest." Mark 11:10)

"³⁸ Saying, Blessed *be* the King that cometh in the name of the Lord: peace in heaven, and glory in the highest." (Luke 19:38)

The kingdom of heaven can be further defined by Matthew 12:46-50 as consisting of those who will do the will of the Father in heaven.

From Matthew Chapters 13 through 23 the Lord talks about the mysteries of the kingdom. In these chapters, He is preparing them for the time when they will be proclaiming the kingdom without the King being present. Going to Luke 17:22, ("²² And he said unto the disciples, The days will come, when ye shall desire to see one of the days of the Son of man, and ye shall not see *it*.") we see him preparing them for that experience of proclaiming the kingdom without the King being present.

"Esaias" in Verse 3 is Isaiah. The reference is to Isaiah 40:3. Isaiah speaks of going before to prepare the way of the LORD. In Malachi 3:1 we see the LORD speaking and saying "Behold, I will send my messenger, and he shall prepare the way before me…" We note from this the "me" in Malachi 3:1 is the LORD in Isaiah 40:3 and we understand that the messenger being sent is to prepare Israel for the Messiah. In Malachi 4:1-6 we see that the messenger is going to be Elijah the prophet. Luke 1:17 says of John "He shall go forth …in the spirit and power of Elijah…" In Matthew 11:14, the Lord tells Israel "And if ye will receive *it*, this is Elias which was for to come…" in speaking of John. In Matthew 17:12 He tells them that "Elias is come already, and they knew it not…" Had Israel repented and done the will of the Father, John , the Baptist would have been Elijah and the Lord would have Jesus would have been the prophet like unto Moses and the prophecy that Elijah had to come first would have fulfilled. John was a prophet and more than a prophet (Matt. 11:18).

However, there was a prophecy of another prophet that was to come. In John 1:21 the Jews sent messengers to John the Baptist asking him "Art thou Elias? And he saith, I am not. Art thou that prophet? And he answered, No." There was another prophet that they were looking for. The prophet is foretold in Deuteronomy.

> **Deuteronomy 18:15-19** "15 The LORD thy God will raise up unto thee a Prophet from the midst of thee, of thy brethren, like unto me; unto him ye shall hearken; 16 According to all that thou desiredst of the LORD thy God in Horeb in the day of the assembly, saying, Let me not hear again the voice of the LORD my God, neither let me see this great fire any more, that I die not. 17 And the LORD said unto me, They have well *spoken that* which they have spoken. 18 I will raise them up a Prophet from among their brethren, like unto thee, and will put my words in his mouth; and he shall speak unto them all that I shall command him. 19 And it shall come to pass, *that* whosoever will not hearken unto my words which he shall speak in my name, I will require *it* of him."

That prophet was to be the Lord Jesus Christ – Israel's Messiah. John's ministry was to call out the little flock of believers (Luke 12:32) who were to comprise the "Righteous nation" of which Isaiah 26:2 speaks.

> **Matthew 3:5-10** "5 Then went out to him Jerusalem, and all Judaea, and all the region round about Jordan, 6 And were baptized of him in Jordan, confessing their sins. 7 But when he saw many of the Pharisees and Sadducees come to his baptism, he said unto them, O generation of vipers, who hath warned you to flee from the wrath to come? 8 Bring forth therefore fruits meet for repentance: 9 And think not to say within yourselves, We have Abraham to *our* father: for I say unto you, that God is able of these stones to raise up children unto Abraham. 10 And now also the axe is laid unto the root of the trees: therefore every tree which bringeth not forth good fruit is hewn down, and cast into the fire."

The baptism of John is an important and significant event in Israel's History. Paul says of John's baptism "…John had first preached before his coming the baptism of repentance to all the people of Israel." (Acts 13:24) Mark writes "John did baptize in the wilderness and preach the baptism of repentance for the remission of sins." (Mark 1:4). Water baptism was required in Israel for the forgiveness sins at that time. We see the same thing in Peter's address in Acts 3:28 when his convicted hearers asked: "Men and brethren, what shall we do?" Peter's response was "Repent and be baptized every one of you in the name of Jesus Christ for the remission of sins…" The scribes and Pharisees asked John "Why baptizest thou then, if thou be not that Christ, nor Elias, neither that prophet?" We understand from their question that they understood what water baptism was and that they expected that water baptism would be associated with the arrival of the Messiah.

Water baptism is actually an Old Testament ordinance. We find it in Numbers 19 as the ordinance of the red heifer. It was a purification rite. It was administered in the induction of a man to the priesthood along with anointing with oil (Exodus 29:1ff). The oil is a type of the Holy Ghost. Israel is to be a kingdom of priests (Exodus 19:6). Peter says they are to be a royal priesthood (1Peter 2:9). While John's baptism brings the purifying of the water, Peter adds the Holy Ghost (Acts 2:38). John (the apostle) says in Revelation 1:6 that Jesus Christ "…hath made us kings and priests unto God and His Father…" Revelation 5:10 adds that as kings and priests "…we shall reign on the earth…" in the kingdom.

Verse 18 says: "The axe is laid to the root of the trees." The trees here refer to Israelites. Every tree (speaking of Israelites) that bringeth not forth good fruit is hewn down and cast into the fire. This is the harvest of the earth that Revelation 14:5 talks about. This is the legal ground of the Law of Moses. Israel was under the legal covenant of the law and will be until the New Covenant is presented to them in the seventieth week of Daniel (i.e. in the coming Tribulation Period). The believers who are in view in Verse 11 and also those who are baptized with the Holy Ghost (Acts 2:38) are Israelites. They will bring forth fruit meet for repentance, and will not be cut down.

In Judges 9 Verses 8 thru 15 four trees are used to represent Israel.
- The olive tree represents access to God (Gen 8:11; Ex. 17:20; 30:25; Lev. 24:2; 1Kings 6:32; Zech. 4:3; Rev. 11:3 & 4; 17-24). In the prophetic program, access to God was to be through Israel.
- The fig tree represents man's works righteousness or religious activity (Gen. 3:7; Matt. 21:19; 24:32). Israel had a God ordained religion in the Law of Moses.
- The vine represents Israel as a nation (Gen. 40:13; 49:10; John 15:1ff; Isa. 5:5; 27:2; Matt. 21:39).
- The bramble represent apostate Israel in rebellion (Judges 9:14; Luke 6:44).

Matthew 3:11-12 "¹¹ I indeed baptize you with water unto repentance: but he that cometh after me is mightier than I, whose shoes I am not worthy to bear: he shall baptize you with the Holy Ghost, and *with* fire: ¹² Whose fan *is* in his hand, and he will throughly purge his floor, and gather his wheat into the garner; but he will burn up the chaff with unquenchable fire."

John baptized Israel with water unto repentance. The Pharisees rejected the baptism of John because they viewed themselves as not needing repentance.

There are two baptisms in the New Testament involving the Holy Ghost. Jesus Christ will baptize Israel **with** the Holy Ghost and **with** fire. We today in the dispensation of grace are baptized by the Holy Ghost **into** a living spiritual union with Jesus Christ (Rom 6:1-4; 1Cor. 12:12 & 13; Gal. 3:27; Col. 2:10-12; et. al.).

The believers of Israel will be baptized with the Holy Ghost to bring them into the New Covenant that God will make with the nation. The unbelievers of the nation will be baptized with fire to purge them out of the nation. The illustration is that of the threshing floor. The fan creates the wind to separate the chaff from the grain. The wheat represents the believers of the nation. They will be gathered into the garner (the kingdom). The chaff will be burned with unquenchable fire.

Matthew 3:13-17 "¹³ Then cometh Jesus from Galilee to Jordan unto John, to be baptized of him. ¹⁴ But John forbad him, saying, I have need to be baptized of thee, and comest thou to me? ¹⁵ And Jesus answering said unto him, Suffer *it to be so* now: for thus it becometh us to fulfil all righteousness. Then he suffered him. ¹⁶ And Jesus, when he was baptized, went up straightway out of the water: and, lo, the heavens were opened unto him, and he saw the Spirit of God descending like a dove, and lighting upon him: ¹⁷ And lo a voice from heaven, saying, This is my beloved Son, in whom I am well pleased."

The question that John asks is the same question that we need to answer in order to understand how sin and guilt is transferred from the sinner to the Savior. John is confused. He is preaching the baptism of repentance for the remissions of sins in order to get Israel ready to receive her Messiah. However, here the Messiah comes to John's baptism having no sin of which to repent. To understand this, we go to an Old Testament prophecy in Isaiah 53:12 "¹² Therefore will I divide him *a portion* with the great, and he shall divide the spoil with the strong; because he hath poured out his soul unto death: and he was numbered with the transgressors; and he bare the sin of many, and made intercession for the transgressors."

Water baptism identified Israel's Messiah with the transgressors and also identified the transgressors with the Messiah. Thereby, water baptism with faith became the mode of salvation for Israel. That is why the formula for salvation in the commission that the Lord gave to Israel was: "He that believeth and is baptized shall be saved…" (Mark 16:16).

For us today living in the dispensation of grace, the formula for salvation is to simply believe the gospel that "…Christ died for our sins according to the scriptures; And that he buried and that he rose again the third day according to the scriptures." When a person believes that, the Holy Ghost baptizes the person into an eternal spiritual union with Jesus Christ in which Jesus Christ receives the believer to Himself and receives the believers' sin and guilt in the process. God then applied the merits of the cross of Christ to clear the believer's sin debt. In the same transaction, the righteousness of Christ is credited to the believer's account. All of this happens according to 2Corinthians 5:21 without water baptism entering into the chain of events.

Chapter 3 Study Guide Questions:

1. Who is John calling to repentance in Verse 2?

2. What is the Kingdom of Heaven?

3. What is the significance of the Kingdom being at hand?

4. Who is Esaias in Verse 3? What is the Old Testament prophecy in Verse 3?

5. Is John Isaiah?

6. Is there another prophet that was foretold who would come?

7. Verse 10 speaks of an axe laid to the root of the trees. Who is represented figuratively by the trees?

8. What is the baptism that John is performing?

9. Verses 11 and 12 speak of three different baptisms. Describe each and tell me what each accomplishes.

10. There is a baptism in verse 12 involving Jesus, the Holy Ghost, and believers of Israel. Who is doing the baptizing? What is accomplished by that baptism? Compare this with the baptism that involves Jesus, the Holy Ghost, and believers today in the dispensation of grace in 1Corinthians 12:13? Who is the baptizer in 1Corinthians 12:13? What is accomplished by that baptism?

11. In Verses 13 to 17 we see Jesus who had no sin to repent of comes to a baptism of repentance. Why did He do that?

Chapter 4

MATTHEW 4:1-25

Matthew 4:1-11 "[1] Then was Jesus led up of the Spirit into the wilderness to be tempted of the devil. [2] And when he had fasted forty days and forty nights, he was afterward an hungred. [3] And when the tempter came to him, he said, If thou be the Son of God, command that these stones be made bread. [4] But he answered and said, It is written, Man shall not live by bread alone, but by every word that proceedeth out of the mouth of God. [5] Then the devil taketh him up into the holy city, and setteth him on a pinnacle of the temple, [6] And saith unto him, If thou be the Son of God, cast thyself down: for it is written, He shall give his angels charge concerning thee: and in *their* hands they shall bear thee up, lest at any time thou dash thy foot against a stone. [7] Jesus said unto him, It is written again, Thou shalt not tempt the Lord thy God. [8] Again, the devil taketh him up into an exceeding high mountain, and sheweth him all the kingdoms of the world, and the glory of them; [9] And saith unto him, All these things will I give thee, if thou wilt fall down and worship me. [10] Then saith Jesus unto him, Get thee hence, Satan: for it is written, Thou shalt worship the Lord thy God, and him only shalt thou serve. [11] Then the devil leaveth him, and, behold, angels came and ministered unto him."

This is an amazing thing that the Messiah begins His earthly ministry by being tempted of the devil. He is tempted after 40 days of fasting. He is in a weakened state. Forty is the number for testing in the Bible. We are reminded of Israel being in the wilderness forty years. As we study the testing that the Lord suffered here we see a parallel with the temptation of Adam and Eve in the garden. There is also a parallel with the temptation that all men are subject to as we see it in 1John 2:16. The following table draws the parallel:

Table 1 the Threefold Temptation of Christ

1John 2:16	Gen 3:6	Mathew 4
The lust of the flesh	It was good for food	Command the rocks to be made bread
The lust of the eyes	It was pleasant to look at	The glory of the nations
The pride of life	It would make them wise	Demonstrate your royal privilege

The significance of this testing was that where Adam (the first man) failed, Christ the last Adam (1Cor 15:45) did not. He was tempted in all points like the first Adam was but He did not sin. He had to succeed in this in order to qualify as the redeemer of the man. The writer of Hebrews says that Christ "…was in all points tempted like as we are, yet without sin." (Heb. 4:15). All that is in the world is aimed at attacking man in these three areas (1John 3:16). The best definition of the "world" in scripture that I have heard is that it is the unified desire of the hearts of unregenerate men to create a culture that excludes God so that man can pursue ungodly conduct with impunity.

There are a number of interesting points of note in this temptation.

- Satan uses Scripture to tempt Christ (Verse 6). He did that with Eve as well by questioning it (Gen 3:1) and then denying it (Gen 3:4 & 5). Christ defeated the devil by quoting Scripture to him (Verses

4, 7, and 10). The scripture is our defense against the devil as well. Eve lost the battle against the devil because she did not accurately know the scripture (Gen. 3: 2 & 3).

- In Verse 8, the devil offered all of the kingdoms of this world to Christ. But all of the kingdoms of this world are created by Christ and for Christ (Heb. 1:2; 2:10; Rev. 4:10) as are all of the kingdoms of the heavens (Col. 1:16). But today, all the things in heaven (Eph 2:1-3) and the things in this earth (2Cor. 4:4) are in Satan's hands. Christ came into this world to reconcile all things to Himself (Col. 1:19). In the prophetic program as far as Satan could tell and all that he could figure out from what had been revealed so far was that the only things that were at stake here were the things of this world (Dan. 7:27). What Satan had no knowledge of was the mystery program by which Christ would reconcile all things to Himself including the things in earth and the things in heaven (Col. 1:20).

- Every time Satan uses Scripture, he is trying to question the provisions of God (e.g. "yea hath God said?" in Genesis 3:1) and attempts to sow doubts in the minds of people of the goodness of God. Satan uses scripture to try to trick us. Christ defeated Satan by using scripture making a wise use of it. Comparing Psalm 91:11-13 (which Satan quotes) with Matthew 3:6 & 7 we see that Satan misquotes the scripture by leaving important words out and adding other words. How important it is to quote the scripture correctly.

- There are three different tacks used by Satan in this temptation:
  o Take the matter into your own hands (turn the rocks into bread)
  o Make God do it for you (cast thyself down)
  o I will do it for you (I will give you…if…)

The Imprisonment of John

Matthew 4: 12-17 "¹² Now when Jesus had heard that John was cast into prison, he departed into Galilee; ¹³ And leaving Nazareth, he came and dwelt in Capernaum, which is upon the sea coast, in the borders of Zabulon and Nephthalim: ¹⁴ That it might be fulfilled which was spoken by Esaias the prophet, saying, ¹⁵ The land of Zabulon, and the land of Nephthalim, *by* the way of the sea, beyond Jordan, Galilee of the Gentiles; ¹⁶ The people which sat in darkness saw great light; and to them which sat in the region and shadow of death light is sprung up. ¹⁷ From that time Jesus began to preach, and to say, Repent: for the kingdom of heaven is at hand."

The imprisonment of John the Baptizer is a significant point in the Lord's ministry. The fore runner of the Messiah is rejected by Israel. Israel's guilt starts to accumulate here as the nation tolerates this mistreatment of John. It is at this point that Christ begins to pick up John's message "Repent for the kingdom of heaven is at hand." Had John's ministry had the effect in the nation as it should have, this would not have been necessary. John's ministry had failed to reach the whole nation because of the darkness of their hearts. This is the first of three crisis points in Matthew's gospel. Each of these crisis points are a turning points in the Lord's earthly ministry to Israel.

1. With the imprisonment of John, the Lord begins to pick up on the ministry of John and to preach "Repent for the Kingdom of Heaven is at hand."
2. Later we will see that Israel rejects Christ as the priest (Matt. 12:6), the prophet (12:41), and as the king (Matt.12:22). The preaching of the kingdom being at hand is rejected and he upbraids the cities for not repenting (Matt. 11:20). In Chapters 12 and 13 He begins to speak in parables and to focus on His disciples to prepare them to carry on in His absence.
3. In Matthew 16:21 He begins to tell them that He is going to die. From Chapter 16 to the end of the book, He is headed for the cross. In Matthew 17:5 we again see the Father's stamp of approval on the Lord's ministry "This is my beloved Son in whom I am well pleased."

With the imprisonment of John, the Lord goes to Galilee. Verses 15 & 16 is a quote from Isaiah 9:1 & 2 "[1] Nevertheless the dimness *shall* not *be* such as *was* in her vexation, when at the first *he* lightly afflicted the land of Zebulun and the land of Naphtali, and afterward did more grievously afflict *her by* the way of the sea, beyond Jordan, in Galilee of the nations. [2] The people that walked in darkness have seen a great light: they that dwell in the land of the shadow of death, upon them hath the light shined."

The area of Galilee was a mix of Jews and pagans from among the Gentiles – therefore its name Galilee of the Gentiles. The people in that area were not regarded as a part of the nation by the Jews in Judaea. He does not leave Galilee until Matthew 19:1. It is in Galilee that He calls his disciples. In fact all of the disciples were Galileans except Judas Iscariot. He is ministering among the men of low estate. It is clear that the Lord had a problem with pride and arrogance. The leaders of Israel regarded the disciples as lowly Galileans and called them "…ignorant and unlearned men." (Acts 4:13). Here, as is often the case, "…God chooses the foolish things of the world to confound the wise…" (1Cor. 1: 27). When the Lord finally returns to Jerusalem, he tells the leaders of Israel "The kingdom will be taken away from you and given to a nation bringing forth the fruits thereof…" (Matt. 21:43). He tells His followers "Fear not little flock, it is your Father's good pleasure to give you the kingdom." (Luke 12:32). This little flock is the group that Paul speaks of in Romans 10:19 "[19] But I say, Did not Israel know? First Moses saith, I will provoke you to jealousy by *them that are* not a people, *and* by a foolish nation I will anger you." (cf. Deut. 32:21) As far as God is concerned, the little flock is the real Israel. The rest will be rejected.

> **Matthew 4: 18-22** "[18] And Jesus, walking by the sea of Galilee, saw two brethren, Simon called Peter, and Andrew his brother, casting a net into the sea: for they were fishers. [19] And he saith unto them, Follow me, and I will make you fishers of men. [20] And they straightway left *their* nets, and followed him. [21] And going on from thence, he saw other two brethren, James *the son* of Zebedee, and John his brother, in a ship with Zebedee their father, mending their nets; and he called them. [22] And they immediately left the ship and their father, and followed him."

In Verses 18 thru 22 we see the call of Peter and Andrew. They are fisher men by trade. He calls them to be "fishers of men." This picks up on the theme of Habakkuk 1:13- 15 "[3] *Thou art* of purer eyes than to behold evil, and canst not look on iniquity: wherefore lookest thou upon them that deal treacherously, *and* holdest thy tongue when the wicked devoureth *the man that is* more righteous than he? [14] And makest men as the fishes of the sea, as the creeping things, *that have* no ruler over them? [15] They take up all of them with the angle, they catch them in their net, and gather them in their drag: therefore they rejoice and are glad." In Habakkuk, the angle, the net and the drag are the weapons of the Babylonians. The fish were the Israelites, There in Habakkuk; they caught the fish to destroy them. However, Peter and Andrew were to catch men to save them.

In Verses 21 & 22 we see Him call James and his brother John. James and John immediately leave their father's ship and their father and follow the Lord. This was a requirement for discipleship in the Kingdom of Heaven. The object of saving faith in the kingdom of heaven was to have faith in the provision of the Lord and what he would provide. We see this in the Lord's instruction to them in Matthew 6:25, 28, 30, 32-33, etc. We will see this requirement stated by the Lord in Matthew 19:16-26 (and Luke 12:31-33; 14:25-33) with the rich young ruler. This program would have worked had Israel repented and thus the Kingdom been established. God knew that the nation would not repent and the kingdom would not be set up yet. He knew too that He would interrupt the program with the dispensation of the grace of God which, at this point in time, was still a mystery hid in God (1Cor. 2:7; Eph. 3:9). However, God would none the less provide for the "poor saints at Jerusalem…" by means of a collection from the Gentile churches "whose debtors they are…" (Rom. 15:27).

> **Matthew 4: 23-25** "[23] And Jesus went about all Galilee, teaching in their synagogues, and preaching the gospel of the kingdom, and healing all manner of sickness and all manner of disease among the

people. ^{24} And his fame went throughout all Syria: and they brought unto him all sick people that were taken with divers diseases and torments, and those which were possessed with devils, and those which were lunatick, and those that had the palsy; and he healed them. ^{25} And there followed him great multitudes of people from Galilee, and *from* Decapolis, and *from* Jerusalem, and *from* Judaea, and *from* beyond Jordan."

The Lord's healing ministry was a foretaste of the healing that He would bring to the nation when He returns to reign. Jeremiah describes that healing ministry in Jeremiah 30:7-17. It is important to note that the Lord healed all people and not just those that believed. In Mark 6:5 & 6 we see the Lord healing people in spite of their unbelief. This should put to rest the claim that healing depends upon the belief in the one being healed as we see being made among the so-called healers in the world today. We note also in this passage that there is a distinction between those that were lunatic and those that were possessed of devils. (See this also in Acts 5:15 & 16).

Chapter 4 Study Guide Questions

1. Why (in Verse 1) was Jesus led of the Spirit into the wilderness to be tempted of the devil?

2. In how many ways was Jesus tempted? Identify them and compare them with the temptation of Eve in Genesis 3.

3. Why do you think the devil used scripture to tempt the Lord? Did he do that with Eve?

4. What did the Lord use to counter the devil's temptation? Do we have that available to us?

5. In Verse 8, the devil offered all of the kingdoms of the world to Jesus in return for the Lord's worship of him. Were the kingdoms of the world Satan's to offer?

6. Who created the physical earth in which those kingdoms reside?

7. The Lord had a plan to reconcile the kingdoms of this world to Himself. What was that plan? What nation was central to that plan?

Chapter 5

MATTHEW 5:1-12

Matthew 5:1 thru to 8:1 is all part of the same sermon setting. We call it the Sermon on the Mount. This is not (as most of professing Christianity calls it) the normal Christian life. This sermon is a verbal picture of what life in the kingdom of heaven would be like. In 5:1 He sees the multitude and goes up into a mountain. His disciples follow Him and He tells them what the Kingdom of Heaven will be like. In 8:1 He comes down form the mountain and His disciples follow Him again.

The preparation of the King

Matthew 5:1-12 "¹ And seeing the multitudes, he went up into a mountain: and when he was set, his disciples came unto him: ² And he opened his mouth, and taught them, saying,
³ Blessed *are* the poor in spirit: for theirs is the kingdom of heaven.
⁴ Blessed *are* they that mourn: for they shall be comforted.
⁵ Blessed *are* the meek: for they shall inherit the earth.
⁶ Blessed *are* they which do hunger and thirst after righteousness: for they shall be filled.
⁷ Blessed *are* the merciful: for they shall obtain mercy.
⁸ Blessed *are* the pure in heart: for they shall see God.
⁹ Blessed *are* the peacemakers: for they shall be called the children of God.
¹⁰ Blessed *are* they which are persecuted for righteousness' sake: for theirs is the kingdom of heaven.
¹¹ Blessed are ye, when *men* shall revile you, and persecute *you*, and shall say all manner of evil against you falsely, for my sake.
¹² Rejoice, and be exceeding glad: for great *is* your reward in heaven: for so persecuted they the prophets which were before you".

The term "blessed" in 5:3-12 means to be happy in spite of being in unpleasant present circumstances because the real blessing is coming when the kingdom is established. Matthew 5: 3-12 comprise what we call the beatitudes. Let's look at each in particular:

- "³ Blessed *are* the poor in spirit: for theirs is the kingdom of heaven."

The poor in spirit are those who humbly admit their spiritual condition and their need. Such are not proud people but meek and humble. Their cause for happiness is that the kingdom of heaven belongs to them. We will see more on this when we get to such passages as Luke 12:32 "Fear not little flock for it is your father's good pleasure to give you the kingdom." "¹⁸ The LORD *is* nigh unto them that are of a broken heart; and saveth such as be of a contrite spirit." (Psalm 34:18) "¹ Thus saith the LORD, The heaven *is* my throne, and the earth *is* my footstool: where *is* the house that ye build unto me? and where *is* the place of my rest? ² For all those *things* hath mine hand made, and all those *things* have been, saith the LORD: but to this *man* will I look, *even* to *him that is* poor and of a contrite spirit, and trembleth at my word." (Isa. 66 1 & 2)

- "Blessed *are* they that mourn: for they shall be comforted. "

The mourning here is for Israel. This is the mourning of those who see the truth but who mourn for the fact the nation as a whole remains in unbelief. There are many passages that speak of mourning in prophecy. Zechariah 12:10-12 describes the mourning of Israel when "...they shall look upon Him whom they have pierces, and shall mourn for Him as one mourneth for his only son." Matthew 24:30 tells us that one day all of the tribes of the earth shall mourn when Christ comes in the clouds of heaven with power and great glory. Revelation 1:7 says "…all kindreds of the earth shall wail because of him…" The mourning of Israel and that of the nations will be different though. Israel will mourn because she had rejected her Messiah. (Isa. 40:2; 51:11).

- "⁵ Blessed *are* the meek: for they shall inherit the earth."

To be meek is the opposite of being puffed up with arrogance and pride. In the world today, meekness is mistaken for weakness. However, meekness is actually power under control. Pride is one of the seven things that the LORD hates in Proverbs 6:17 – in fact it is the first on the list. When the kingdom is set up, it will be given to the meek in Israel. They will comprise what Zephaniah 2:1 addresses in "O nation not desired." Psalm 37:10-11 also addresses the change in leadership of Israel from the proud to the meek "¹⁰ For yet a little while, and the wicked *shall* not *be*: yea, thou shalt diligently consider his place, and it *shall* not *be*. ¹¹ But the meek shall inherit the earth; and shall delight themselves in the abundance of peace."

- "⁶ Blessed *are* they which do hunger and thirst after righteousness: for they shall be filled."

Godly people today cry for righteousness to prevail in the world today but it is not here. It seems at almost every turn unrighteousness prevails. In the kingdom, the inhabitants of the earth will learn righteousness (Isa. 26:9).

- "⁷ Blessed *are* the merciful: for they shall obtain mercy."

Those that go into the kingdom will receive mercy but they will be the ones that showed mercy to others. This is "…Do unto others as you would have them do unto you…" in action (Matt. 7:12).

- "⁸ Blessed *are* the pure in heart: for they shall see God."

The pure in heart are described in Isaiah 34:15. They will see God in the person of Jesus Christ when He reigns on the earth.

- "⁹ Blessed *are* the peacemakers: for they shall be called the children of God."

The peacemakers are those that work to dispel hostilities between people. Those that enter the kingdom will be called the children of God because they manifest this attribute of God.

- "¹⁰ Blessed *are* they which are persecuted for righteousness' sake: for theirs is the kingdom of heaven. "¹¹ Blessed are ye, when *men* shall revile you, and persecute *you*, and shall say all manner of evil against you falsely, for my sake. ¹² Rejoice, and be exceeding glad: for great *is* your reward in heaven: for so persecuted they the prophets which were before you."

Taking a stand for the Lord in a world that rejects Him will always bring resentment. It is true today as it was then (2Tim. 3:12). The mature saint will respond to such persecution by blessing them that persecute them. Paul tells us to do the same today (Rom. 12:14). Great will be their reward <u>in heaven</u>. The reward of the kingdom saints is in heaven (1Peter 1:4) but the Lord will bring it with him to earth when He returns to set up His kingdom (Rev. 22:12).

The Lord begins His ministry to Israel telling them about the blessings that are in store for them in the Kingdom. These blessings are found in the prophecies of the kingdom presented in the Old Testament scriptures. However, at the end of His earthly ministry to Israel, he tells them of corresponding woes that would come upon them because they refused to be that channel of blessing to the world.

Table 2: The Beatitudes and the Woes

The Prophecy	The Beatitudes (Matt. 5:3-12)	The Woes (Matt. 23:13-33)
Psa. 40:17	The Kingdom opened to the poor in spirit -- Verse 3	The kingdom shut up to the poor – Verse 13
Psa. 119:134-136	Comfort for the mourners – Verse 4	Mourners distressed by unjust leaders – Verse 14
Psa. 37:10-11	The meek inherit the earth – Verse 5	The meek oppressed by religious fanatics – Verse 15
Psa. 42:1-2	True righteousness sought by those that love God. – Verse 7	False righteousness sought by religious hypocrites. Verses 16-22
Psa. 41:1	The merciful obtain mercy – Verse 7	Expensive gifts brought but justice, mercy and faith omitted – Verses 23 & 24
Psa. 24: 4 & 5	Purity in heart and the opportunity to see God – Verse 8	Clean of the outside but unclean on the inside -- Verses 25 & 26
Psa. 133: 1	Peace makers will be called the sons of God (Verse 9) i.e. spiritual life.	Hypocrisy and spiritual death.
Psa. 37: 39-40	The persecuted – Verses 10-12	The persecutors – Verses 27 & 28

Matthew 5: 13 "¹³ Ye are the salt of the earth: but if the salt have lost his savour, wherewith shall it be salted? it is thenceforth good for nothing, but to be cast out, and to be trodden under foot of men."

Salt is that which prevents decay and corruption. The remnant is "The salt of the earth…" They were the only hope that the world had for deliverance from corruption. Today since the kingdom program has been interrupted by the dispensation of grace, we (members of the body of Christ) are the ones that keep the world from total decay (2Thess. 2:7). "If the salt has lost its savor…" – i.e. if the remnant do not do their work, the preserving influence is not in place and corruption ensues.

Matthew 5:14-16 "¹⁴ Ye are the light of the world. A city that is set on an hill cannot be hid. ¹⁵ Neither do men light a candle, and put it under a bushel, but on a candlestick; and it giveth light unto all that are in the house. ¹⁶ Let your light so shine before men, that they may see your good works, and glorify your Father which is in heaven. The believer's conduct is to reflect favorably on the Word of God so as to draw men to the Word.

The Believer's conduct is to reflect favorably on the Word of God so as to draw men to the Word. Light is that which dispels the darkness. The remnant was to be the light of the world then. We (members of the body of Christ) are to be that influence in the world today (1Thess 5:5; Eph. 5:8). The real light is Christ (John 8:9, 12). The believer simply reflects that light. It was <u>day</u> for the world when He was in the world (John 9:4&5). Paul refers to this present evil age as the night in Romans 13:12 saying "The night is far spent, the day is at hand: let us put on the armour of light." Believers today live on earth in this present, dark age but God regards them as children of light" (Eph. 5:8, 11, 13, 14). The darkness of this world is a spiritual darkness imposed by Satan (2Cor. 4:4). Believers are not in that darkness "For God, who commanded light to shine out of darkness, hath shined in our hearts, to give the light of the knowledge of the glory of God in the face of Jesus Christ." (2Cor. 4:6). Believers today have been made "meet [equipped by the gospel] to be partakers of the inheritance of the saints in light. Who hath delivered us from the power of darkness, and hath translated us into the kingdom of his dear Son:.." (Col.1:12 & 13). In 1Thessalonians 5:4-5 Paul tells us "But ye, brethren, ar not in darkness that that day should overtake us as a thief. Ye are all the children of the light, and the children of the day: we are not of the night, nor of darkness."

Getting back to the Lord's address to Israel, He tells them that one day "…the righteous shall shine forth as the sun in the kingdom of their Father…" (Matt. 13:43). Isaiah prophesied of this saying "[1] Arise, shine; for thy light is come, and the glory of the LORD is risen upon thee. [2] For, behold, the darkness shall cover the earth, and gross darkness the people: but the LORD shall arise upon thee, and his glory shall be seen upon thee. [3] And the Gentiles shall come to thy light, and kings to the brightness of thy rising. [4] Lift up thine eyes round about, and see: all they gather themselves together, they come to thee: thy sons shall come from far, and thy daughters shall be nursed at *thy* side. [5] Then thou shalt see, and flow together, and thine heart shall fear, and be enlarged; because the abundance of the sea shall be converted unto thee, the forces of the Gentiles shall come unto thee." (Isa. 60:1-5). Again in Isaiah 60:20 & 21 he says "[20] Thy sun shall no more go down; neither shall thy moon withdraw itself: for the LORD shall be thine everlasting light, and the days of thy mourning shall be ended. [21] Thy people also *shall be* all righteous: they shall inherit the land for ever, the branch of my planting, the work of my hands, that I may be glorified." This will be fulfilled in the kingdom as the remnant shine together with the glory of Christ. We see it in Revelation 21:23-24 "[23] And the city had no need of the sun, neither of the moon, to shine in it: for the glory of God did lighten it, and the Lamb *is* the light thereof. [24] And the nations of them which are saved shall walk in the light of it: and the kings of the earth do bring their glory and honour into it."

The Old Testament scriptures close with these words: "[1] For, behold, the day cometh, that shall burn as an oven; and all the proud, yea, and all that do wickedly, shall be stubble: and the day that cometh shall burn them up, saith the LORD of hosts, that it shall leave them neither root nor branch. [2] But unto you that fear my name shall the Sun of righteousness arise with healing in his wings; and ye shall go forth, and grow up as calves of the stall. [3] And ye shall tread down the wicked; for they shall be ashes under the soles of your feet in the day that I shall do *this*, saith the LORD of hosts." (Mal 4:1-3). The Lord will be the Light to the remnant but He will be a consuming fire to the unbelievers.

> **Matthew 5: 17-23** "[17] Think not that I am come to destroy the law, or the prophets: I am not come to destroy, but to fulfil. [18] For verily I say unto you, Till heaven and earth pass, one jot or one tittle shall in no wise pass from the law, till all be fulfilled. [19] Whosoever therefore shall break one of these least commandments, and shall teach men so, he shall be called the least in the kingdom of heaven: but whosoever shall do and teach *them*, the same shall be called great in the kingdom of heaven. [20] For I say unto you, That except your righteousness shall exceed *the righteousness* of the scribes and Pharisees, ye shall in no case enter into the kingdom of heaven.

The word "fulfill" in Verse 17 is a different Greek word than the word fulfill in Verse 18. The word in Verse 17 (playroma) is the same word translated fulfill in Colossians 1:25 where Paul tells us that the ministry that he received from Christ was to "fulfill the word of God." The Greek word "playroma" (fulfill in Verse 17 has the idea of fully filling something. Paul's ministry was to fully fill the Word of God (the Bible) by adding to it something that was still missing but that had to be added to make the Word complete. That something that was still missing in the Word to make it complete was the dispensation of the grace of God that was revealed by the Lord through Paul. Here in Verse 17, the Lord is telling His disciples that He did not come to destroy the law but to fulfill it in the sense that he is going to press the righteous standard of the Law to the fullest extent (i.e. to fully fill the Law).

An Israelite who knew Old Testament prophecy might think that when the New Covenant comes to the nation that the Old Covenant will be done away with. What the New Covenant will do is not take the Old Covenant away but will administer it in a different way. He says in Jeremiah 31:33- 34 "…I will put my law in their inward parts, and write it in their hearts and will be their God, and they shall be my people. And they shall teach no more every man his neighbour, and every man his brother, saying know the LORD: for they shall all know me, from the least of them unto the greatest of them…" What we are seeing in Chapters 5 & 6 is the Lord speaking of this heart motivation to keep the righteous standard of the Law out of a pure heart. The Decalogue of Leviticus 20 was only a rough outline of the righteous conduct that God was looking for from His people. The Law dealt with external observance of that standard. What Christ is interested in is what is in the heart. As He said "Blessed are the pure of heart for they shall see God."

For us today, Paul tells us the Law was a school master to bring us unto Christ (Gal. 3:19 – 24). He tells us that the law is not of faith (Gal. 3:19). He tells us further that our righteousness is ". .not of the law, but that which is through the faith of Christ, the righteousness which is of God by faith:.."(Phil. 3:9). It is the work of Christ on Calvary that gives us members of the body of Christ the positional (imputed) righteousness when we respond in faith to trust Him as Savior. Our righteousness today is "Even the righteousness of God which is by faith of Jesus Christ unto all and upon all them that believe: for there is no difference: For all have sinned, and come short of the glory of God;…" (Rom. 3:22, 23). Not only do we have imputed righteousness by faith but there is a practical righteousness that we appropriate by faith as well. That is what grace produces. It is a righteousness that the law demanded of people but could not produce because the law depended upon the strength of the flesh to keep it. The passage in Romans 8:4 tells us that the righteousness of the law might be fulfilled in us who walk not after the flesh (i.e. trying to keep the law as in Romans Chapter 7) but after the spirit (walking after the doctrine of Romans Chapter 6). With this imputed righteousness and its practical outworking in mind, consider Romans 9:30 "(3) What shall we say then? That the Gentiles, which followed not after righteousness, have attained to righteousness, even the righteousness which is of faith. [31] But Israel, which followed after the law of righteousness, hath not attained to the law of righteousness."

Here Matthew 5:17 and in the verses that follow we find the fulfilling to mean the pressing of the Law to it's fullest in order that the law can accomplish what it was given by God to do -- to lead people to Christ (Gal. 3:24). The fulfillment is not a reference to the cross. It is not until some time later that the Lord "…began …to show…that he most suffer… and be killed, and be raised again the third day" The ultimate fulfillment of the law will be done in the kingdom which He was then preaching as being "at hand." (Matt. 16:21). The fulfilling of the law in the kingdom can be understood by considering some Old Testament passages that prophesy of how the law will be kept in the kingdom. Consider the following:
- Burnt offerings, and meat offerings, and drink offerings of the law will still be offered in the kingdom (Ezek. 45:17).
- Israelites will still be keeping the seven feasts of Jehovah (Zach 14:6).
- Worship will still be according to the Law in the Kingdom (Isa. 66:22-23).
- All nations will keep the feast of tabernacles in the Kingdom (Zach. 14:16-17).
- Messiah "…shall purify the sons of Levi; …that they may offer unto the LORD an offering in righteousness." (Malachi 3:3)

In Verse 18, the Lord tells them "Till heaven and earth pass, one jot or one tittle shall in no wise pass from the law, till all be fulfilled." There the word for "fulfilled" means "to come to pass." A jot is the smallest letter of the Greek alphabet (the iota) and the tittle is a part of a letter of the Greek alphabet. Every prophecy of the Old Testament will come to pass to the finest details (i.e. every jot and tittle).

In verse 19 "...whosoever shall do and teach *them*, the same shall be called great in the kingdom of heaven..." tells us that the law will be taught in the Kingdom. Not only will the ceremonies of the law be kept in the kingdom but the Ten Commandments will be taught.

> **Isaiah 2: 1-5** "[1] The word that Isaiah the son of Amoz saw concerning Judah and Jerusalem. [2] And it shall come to pass in the last days, *that* the mountain of the LORD'S house shall be established in the top of the mountains, and shall be exalted above the hills; and all nations shall flow unto it. [3] And many people shall go and say, Come ye, and let us go up to the mountain of the LORD, to the house of the God of Jacob; and he will teach us of his ways, and we will walk in his paths: for out of Zion shall go forth the law, and the word of the LORD from Jerusalem. [4] And he shall judge among the nations, and shall rebuke many people: and they shall beat their swords into plowshares, and their spears into pruninghooks: nation shall not lift up sword against nation, neither shall they learn war any more. [5] O house of Jacob, come ye, and let us walk in the light of the LORD."

> **Isaiah 42:21** "[21] The LORD is well pleased for his righteousness' sake; he will magnify the law, and make *it* honourable."

This will happen not through the Old Covenant but through the New Covenant and the Palestinian Covenant.

> The New Covenant "[26] A new heart also will I give you, and a new spirit will I put within you: and I will take away the stony heart out of your flesh, and I will give you an heart of flesh. [27] And I will put my spirit within you, and cause you to walk in my statutes, and ye shall keep my judgments, and do *them*." (Ezek. 36:26)

> The Palestinian Covenant is presented in Deuteronomy 30:1-6. Note particularly Verse 6 "[6] And the LORD thy God will circumcise thine heart, and the heart of thy seed, to love the LORD thy God with all thine heart, and with all thy soul, that thou mayest live."

Note Verse 20 "For I say unto you, That except your righteousness shall exceed *the righteousness* of the scribes and Pharisees, ye shall in no case enter into the kingdom of heaven." This is still the law principle of being blessed if one measures up to the standard of the law. Israel was under law and will be until the New Covenant is implemented at which time the Old Covenant is incorporated into the New. .

- Israel was under law when they entered the land (Josh 8:34).
- The nation would be expelled from the land for their failure under the law (Deut 29:5). We see from the Old Testament scriptures that they did fail and they were expelled. But God made another Covenant with Israel through Moses whereby they would repossess the land and the LORD would circumcise their heart (Deut 30:6). That covenant is called the Palestinian Covenant and is presented in Deut. 30.
- When that work (under the Palestinian Covenant) of the LORD is completed, the nation would return and obey the voice of the LORD, and do his commandments (Deut 30:8). However, there is a condition involved: "...if thou turn unto the LORD thy God with all thine heart, and with all thy soul." (Deut 30:10).
- Compare Deuteronomy 30:10-14 with Romans 10:6-11.

Table 3: Deuteronomy 30 and Romans 10 Compared

Deuteronomy 30:10-14 (KJV)	Romans 10:6-11 (KJV)
[10] If thou shalt hearken unto the voice of the LORD thy God, to keep his commandments and his statutes which are written in this book of the law, *and* if thou turn unto the LORD thy God with all thine heart, and with all thy soul. [11] For this commandment which I command thee this day, it *is* not hidden from thee, neither *is* it far off. [12] It *is* not in heaven, that thou shouldest say, Who shall go up for us to heaven, and bring it unto us, that we may hear it, and do it? [13] Neither *is* it beyond the sea, that thou shouldest say, Who shall go over the sea for us, and bring it unto us, that we may hear it, and do it? [14] But the word *is* very nigh unto thee, in thy mouth, and in thy heart, that thou mayest do it.	[6] But the righteousness which is of faith speaketh on this wise, Say not in thine heart, Who shall ascend into heaven? (that is, to bring Christ down *from above*:) [7] Or, Who shall descend into the deep? (that is, to bring up Christ again from the dead.) [8] But what saith it? The word is nigh thee, *even* in thy mouth, and in thy heart: that is, the word of faith, which we preach; [9] That if thou shalt confess with thy mouth the Lord Jesus, and shalt believe in thine heart that God hath raised him from the dead, thou shalt be saved. [10] For with the heart man believeth unto righteousness; and with the mouth confession is made unto salvation. [11] For the scripture saith, Whosoever believeth on him shall not be ashamed.

- Deuteronomy 30: 9-12 describes the faith that the Israelite under law must have in order to be regarded by God as righteous. It was the righteousness of faith. The Israelite in Romans 10: 9 & 10 finds the fulfillment of that in the Lord Jesus. The "Just man" under the law was a man whose faith compelled him to keep the law from the heart. When he failed, he none the less knew of (and appealed to) the mercy seat where he could find atonement for his sin. It was a heart attitude toward the covenants that God made with the nation that motivated him. For such a one, it was not an exercise of the flesh to gain God's approval but a motivation of the heart to see God's name praised among the nations. It would be only the inward motivation of the heart that would move people to produce the righteousness described in Matthew 5:20 – 48.

For the believer today, that kind of practical righteousness is produced in the believer by walking after the Spirit (Rom. 8:4). We today have resources that the believing remnant of Israel did not have. We have:

- The work of the Holy Spirit baptizing us into Christ (Rom. 6:3-4; Gal. 3:26; 1Cor. 12:4; Col 2:12)
- The indwelling Holy Spirit to teach us His word (Rom. 8:11)
- A spiritual circumcision (Col 2:10-12; 2Cor. 4:16) that separates the soul and spirit (the inward man that is renewed day be day) from the outward man (the physical body) that perishes.
- A regenerated nature (Titus 3:5)
- The sealing of the Holy Spirit to give us security in Christ. (Eph. 1:13)
- Additionally, we are washed, sanctified, and justified (1Cor. 6:11) in the name of our Lord and by the Spirit of our God.

In Verses 21 thru 48 of Matthew Chapter 15 the Lord is pressing the law to the fullest. The culmination of the passage is in verse 48 in which the Lord tells them "Be ye therefore perfect, even as your Father which is in heaven is perfect." Now obviously, no one is going to measure up if this perfection is sinless perfection. No one but the Lord Himself has ever measured up to that standard. We will look at this more later. For now though let's look at how the Lord fully fills the Law:

Table 4: The Law Pressed to its Fullest Intent

Matt.5	Ye have heard it said	Matt.5	But I say unto you
21	Thou shalt not kill	22	Don't even be angry
27	Thou shalt not commit adultery	28	Don't even look at a woman to lust after her
31	Divorce allowed	32	Don't divorce except for fornication
33	Do not foreswear	34	Swear not at all
38	An eye for an eye	39	Turn the other cheek
43	Love your neighbor and hate your enemy	44	Love your enemies
		48	Be Perfect

Matthew 5:21-26 "[21] Ye have heard that it was said by them of old time, Thou shalt not kill; and whosoever shall kill shall be in danger of the judgment: [22] But I say unto you, That whosoever is angry with his brother without a cause shall be in danger of the judgment: and whosoever shall say to his brother, Raca, shall be in danger of the council: but whosoever shall say, Thou fool, shall be in danger of hell fire. [23] Therefore if thou bring thy gift to the altar, and there rememberest that thy brother hath ought against thee; [24] Leave there thy gift before the altar, and go thy way; first be reconciled to thy brother, and then come and offer thy gift. [25] Agree with thine adversary quickly, whiles thou art in the way with him; lest at any time the adversary deliver thee to the judge, and the judge deliver thee to the officer, and thou be cast into prison. [26] Verily I say unto thee, Thou shalt by no means come out thence, till thou hast paid the uttermost farthing.

Anger is a natural emotion. Here the admonition is to refrain from being anger without a cause. There are times when anger is justified. However, there must be a just cause for it and a limit to it – let not the sun go down on your anger (Eph. 4:26). The Lord Himself was angry when the cause was just (John 2:15; Mark 3:5).

Matthew 5:27-30 "[27] Ye have heard that it was said by them of old time, Thou shalt not commit adultery: [28] But I say unto you, That whosoever looketh on a woman to lust after her hath committed adultery with her already in his heart. [29] And if thy right eye offend thee, pluck it out, and cast *it* from thee: for it is profitable for thee that one of thy members should perish, and not *that* thy whole body should be cast into hell. [30] And if thy right hand offend thee, cut it off, and cast *it* from thee: for it is profitable for thee that one of thy members should perish, and not *that* thy whole body should be cast into hell.

The word translated "hell" here in Verse 30 is "Gehenna." These verses speak of "thy whole body being cast into hell." There is only one time and one place where this can happen – in the Millennium. The word Gehenna refers to a fire that the Lord will kindle in His anger (Deut 32:22) when He returns to earth. There will be capital punishment during the millennium. Isaiah 66:24 speaks of it: "[23] And it shall come to pass, *that* from one new moon to another, and from one sabbath to another, shall all flesh come to worship before me, saith the LORD. [24] And they shall go forth, and look upon the carcasses of the men that have transgressed against me: for their worm shall not die, neither shall their fire be quenched; and they shall be an abhorring unto all flesh."

This is part of the wrath to come that John warned about in Matthew 3:7. This is the baptism by fire that he speaks of in that passage. While the believers of the nation are going to be baptized by the Holy Ghost, the unbelievers are baptized by fire. In Matthew 25:41 the unbelieving Gentiles at the judgment of the nations will also have to "depart into everlasting fire, prepared for the devil and his angels…"(Matt.. 25:41). The basis upon which the Gentiles will be judged at this judgment will be how they had treated the believing remnant of Israel during the tribulation. Here the Lord is advising the believing remnant to pull out all stops to be sure to get into the kingdom (Matt. 18:8). Comparing the term "enter into life" in Mark 9:43-45 with "enter into the kingdom of God" in Mark 9:47 we understand that to enter into the kingdom will be to enter into life for these people. For those interested in further study on the doctrine of Gehenna, the following passages might prove helpful: 2Kings 16:3; 2Chromicles. 28:1-3; 2Chr. 33:1; Leviticus 18:2, 1Kings 11: 5, 7, 33; Joshua 15:3; and 2Kings 23:10 all allude to it.

> **Matthew 5:31-32** "[31] It hath been said, Whosoever shall put away his wife, let him give her a writing of divorcement: [32] But I say unto you, That whosoever shall put away his wife, saving for the cause of fornication, causeth her to commit adultery: and whosoever shall marry her that is divorced committeth adultery.

In Matthew 5:31-32 the Lord addresses the matter of divorce. He states that fornication is the only legitimate cause for divorce. If a man divorce his wife for any other reason, he ". .causeth her that is divorced to commit adultery; and whosoever shall marry her that is divorced committeth adultery." In Mark 10:5 He states "for the hardness of your heart he [Moses] wrote you this precept But from the beginning of creation God made them male and female. For this cause shall a man leave his father and mother, and cleave to his wife; And they twain shall be one flesh: so then they are no more twain but one flesh. What therefore God hath joined together, let not man put asunder." (See also Mark 10:11 & 12; Luke 16:18; Rom. 7:3). Israelites under the law were not to marry anyone but another Israelite. Ezra had to address the matter of intermarriage with Gentiles (Ezra 10:11-19) in the firmest way without compromise. This is a requirement of the Law of Moses (Deut. 7:2 & 3). Because every Israelite was under a covenant relationship with God, there would be no issue of someone under that covenant being married to someone that was not. Today in the dispensation of grace, no one has a relationship to God based on covenants. Rather, God establishes an eternal relationship with individuals based on grace through faith in the redeeming work of Christ regardless of race. However, since eternal life is offered freely to all and is accepted on an individual basis by personal faith, it is possible today for a believer (one who is in the family of God) to find himself or herself married to an unbeliever (one who is not). Therefore Paul, the apostle through whom the instruction for life in the Body of Christ is given, addresses that possibility. He does so in 1Corinthians 7:12-16. God's basic instruction on marriage today is that believers are to marry only believers (1Cor 7:39) and then to regard that as a life long relationship. (1Cor 7:10 & 11; Rom. 7:4).

As an interesting side study on marriage in Israel, study Isaiah 62:1-5 and compare it with Hosea 2:14-20. These passages address Israel's relationship with God.

> **Matthew 5:33-37** "[33] Again, ye have heard that it hath been said by them of old time, Thou shalt not forswear thyself, but shalt perform unto the Lord thine oaths: [34] But I say unto you, Swear not at all; neither by heaven; for it is God's throne: [35] Nor by the earth; for it is his footstool: neither by Jerusalem; for it is the city of the great King. [36] Neither shalt thou swear by thy head, because thou canst not make one hair white or black. [37] But let your communication be, Yea, yea; Nay, nay: for whatsoever is more than these cometh of evil.

On the matter of swearing, the Lord says "do not swear at all." To swear is to call God to witness on what one says. To forswear is to promise with God as a witness that one will perform some thing in the future. Here the Lord is telling Israel not to swear at all because of running the risk of failing to perform the thing and thus to bring God as forth a witness to a false pledge. There are a number of Old Testament passages that address swearing:

- Exodus 20: 7 "Thou shalt not take the name of the Lord thy God in vain."

- Leviticus 19:12 "[12] And ye shall not swear by my name falsely, neither shalt thou profane the name of thy God: I *am* the LORD."
- Deuteronomy 23:23 "[22] But if thou shalt forbear to vow, it shall be no sin in thee. [23] That which is gone out of thy lips thou shalt keep and perform; *even* a freewill offering, according as thou hast vowed unto the LORD thy God, which thou hast promised with thy mouth."
- Zephaniah 3:13 "[13] The remnant of Israel shall not do iniquity, nor speak lies; neither shall a deceitful tongue be found in their mouth: for they shall feed and lie down, and none shall make *them* afraid."

The Lord would have His people be of such personal integrity that if one said he would do a thing that there would be not doubt by any who knew him that he would fail to perform it.

Matthew 5:38-42 "[38] Ye have heard that it hath been said, An eye for an eye, and a tooth for a tooth: [39] But I say unto you, That ye resist not evil: but whosoever shall smite thee on thy right cheek, turn to him the other also. [40] And if any man will sue thee at the law, and take away thy coat, let him have *thy* cloke also. [41] And whosoever shall compel thee to go a mile, go with him twain. [42] Give to him that asketh thee, and from him that would borrow of thee turn not thou away.

The term "An eye for an eye and a tooth for a tooth" describes the justice of the law system. But the Lord would have His kingdom saints hold the welfare of their abusers as being more important than retribution that is legitimately allowed and required by the law.
- If he hits you on the right cheek, give him the other also.
- If he sues you and takes your coat, let him have your cloak with it.
- If he enslaves you for a mile, go another with him.
- Give to him that asketh thee.
- Loan to him that would borrow from you.

These are difficult passages for us to understand today. After all, who could measure up to such a standard? The key to understanding these passages is Matthew 6:33 "But seek ye first the kingdom of God, and his righteousness; and all these things shall be added unto you." The "these things" in that passage are the things of Chapter 5 and 6 that are given up for the kingdom of heaven's sake.

The Old Testament passages that address the "eye for an eye" justice include:

Exodus 21:24 "[23] And if *any* mischief follow, then thou shalt give life for life, [24] Eye for eye, tooth for tooth, hand for hand, foot for foot, [25] Burning for burning, wound for wound, stripe for stripe. [26] And if a man smite the eye of his servant, or the eye of his maid, that it perish; he shall let him go free for his eye's sake. [27] And if he smite out his manservant's tooth, or his maidservant's tooth; he shall let him go free for his tooth's sake."

Deuteronomy 19:21 "[17] Then both the men, between whom the controversy *is*, shall stand before the LORD, before the priests and the judges, which shall be in those days; [18] And the judges shall make diligent inquisition: and, behold, *if* the witness *be* a false witness, *and* hath testified falsely against his brother;…"

This is not for vengeance but for justice. Loss of a member is to be responded with the value of the member.

Matthew 5:43-47 "[43] Ye have heard that it hath been said, Thou shalt love thy neighbour, and hate thine enemy. [44] But I say unto you, Love your enemies, bless them that curse you, do good to them that hate you, and pray for them which despitefully use you, and persecute you; [45] That ye may be the children of your Father which is in heaven: for he maketh his sun to rise on the evil and on the good, and sendeth rain on the just and on the unjust. [46] For if ye love them which love you, what reward have ye? do not even the publicans the same? [47] And if ye salute your brethren only, what do ye more *than others*? do not even the publicans so?

The Lord would have His saints love not just those that love them but to love those that appose them and stand against them. We find a similar admonition in Paul's epistles in Romans 12:14. The Lord is interested in the lost as He is in the believer. He is not willing that any should perish but that all should come to repentance (2 Peter 3:9).

Matthew 5:48 "[48] Be ye therefore perfect, even as your Father which is in heaven is perfect.

This is not talking about sinless perfection but about maturity. It is not possible for man as he is to be perfect in the sense of being sinless. Job 9:20 "[20] If I justify myself, mine own mouth shall condemn me: *if I say*, I *am* perfect, it shall also prove me perverse. [21] *Though* I *were* perfect, *yet* would I not know my soul: I would despise my life."

The Lord told Abraham "…Walk before me and be thou perfect." (Gen. 17:1). God admonishes His people to have His character in them. He tells Israel: "…I am the Lord thy God; ye shall therefore sanctify yourselves, and ye shall be holy; for I am holy…" (Lev. 11:44).

The problem is that the law could never motivate believers to manifest such character. Grace however, can and does provide such motivation (Rom. 8:4). Paul calls such motivation "…The mystery of godliness" (1Tim 3:16). The Hebrew people who heard these words were not able to be "perfect" in the sense of coming to maturity until they "moved on" from where they were in Matthew, Mark, Luke, and John to the doctrine of the Book of Hebrews. When the New Covenant takes effect for Israel (Ezek. 38:27), then they will be caused to walk in the statutes of the law and will be able to perform the law perfectly. Believers today can go on to perfection by being instructed out of the completed Word of God (2Tim. 3:17) rightly divided (1Cor. 2:6; 2Tim 2:15).

Psalm 15 and the Sermon on the Mount

	Psalm 15 **The Ideal Citizen of Zion**		**Mat 5:1 to 7:29** **The Ideal Citizen of the Kingdom of Heaven**
Psalm 15:1	"LORD, who shall abide in thy tabernacle?" …. "Who shall dwell in thy holy hill?"	Matt. 5:1-12	"Blessed are the poor in spirit for theirs is the kingdom of heaven…" Blessed are the pure in heart for they shall see God."
Psalm 15:2	"He that walketh uprightly…."	Matt. 5:13-16	"Ye are the salt of the earth…" Ye are the light of the world…" "Let your light shine"
	"….And worketh righteousness…"	Matt. 5:17-20	"Except your righteousness shall exceed the righteousness of the scribes and Pharisees, ye shall in no case enter into the kingdom of heaven."
Psalm 15:4 Psalm 15:5	"….And speaketh the truth in his heart…" "He that sweareth to his own hurt" "…and changeth not" "He that putteth not out his money to usury…" "…Nor doeth evil to his neighbor…"	Matt. 5:21-6:34	The issue is the heart motivation and not the outward observance

Ye have heard	But I say	(Heart Attitude)
5:21	5:22	Heart hatred
5:27	5:28	Heart adultery
5:31	5:32	"
5:33	5:34-37	Heart sincerity
5:38	5:39-42	Heart concern for others
5:43	5:44-48	Genuine love in the heart
6:1-4		A generous heart
6:5-15		Heart fellowship with God
6:16-24		Service from the Heart
6:25-34		A heart that rests in God

Psalm 15:3	"He that backbiteth not with his tongue…"	Matt. 7:1-5 Matt. 5:43-48	Why beholdeth the mote that is in thy brother's eye."
Psallm 15:4	"In whose eyes a vile person is condemned" "…But he honoureth them that fear the LORD."	Matt. 7:15-23	Beware false prophets – you will know them by their fruits
Psalm 15:5	"…He that doeth these things shall never be moved."	Matt. 7:24-27	The wise man built his house upon the rock.

Chapter 5 Study Guide Questions:

1. What does it mean to be blessed in the context of the beatitudes?

2. How do the beatitudes of Verses 3 through 12 compare to the woes of Matthew 23:13 to 33?

3. In what sense are believers the salt of the earth? In what sense are believers light?

4. In Verses 13 through 20, in what sense is the Lord fulfilling the Law?

5. Are we under the Law today? Was Israel? Will Israel be under the Law in the Kingdom?

6. There are three covenants that relate to the Law: the Mosaic, the Palestinian, and the New. How does the Law relate to each?

7. Jeremiah 31:33 & 34 implies a relationship of the Old Covenant of the Law with the New Covenant that God will make with Israel. How will the Law relate with the New Covenant?

8. Is Verse 20 talking about imputed righteousness or righteousness in practice? How is practical righteousness produced in believers today?

9. In Verses 21 through 47 "Ye have heard … but I say…" is describing what we might call "kingdom law." How does that compare with the Law of Moses?

10. The Lord says in Verse 48 "Be ye perfect…" – what kind of perfection is this?

Chapter 6

MATTHEW 6:1-34

THE SERMON ON THE MOUNT CONTINUES

Matthew 6:1-4 "*¹ Take heed that ye do not your alms before men, to be seen of them: otherwise ye have no reward of your Father which is in heaven. ² Therefore when thou doest thine alms, do not sound a trumpet before thee, as the hypocrites do in the synagogues and in the streets, that they may have glory of men. Verily I say unto you, They have their reward. ³ But when thou doest alms, let not thy left hand know what thy right hand doeth: ⁴ That thine alms may be in secret: and thy Father which seeth in secret himself shall reward thee openly.*

Here the Lord addresses the matter of giving. It is the heart motivation that is important. The Lord continues instruction to the little flock to set their sight on the highest standard there is: "be thou perfect as your Father in heaven is perfect." The purpose for this standard is that Israel was to be "the light of the world." (5:14) and "the salt of the earth" (5:13).They were to be God's witnesses in the world to represent Him as the means of reaching the nations. Israel will not be able to fully live up to that standard until the New Covenant takes effect (Jer. 31:31-34; Ezek. 16:26-27). Peter considered Israel's inability to live up to that standard when he said "Now therefore why tempt ye God, to put a yoke upon the neck of the disciples which neither our fathers nor we were able to bear?" (Acts 15:10) Yet under the New Covenant Israel will be able to bear that yoke. Giving was to be done from the heart and not for show. It has been said that, as regarding the motives people's actions in giving that there are three categories of motivaiton:

1. As a show for people to see.
2. To satisfy an emotional need.
3. To bring glory and honor to God.

The first motive is clearly to impress people. Under this motivation, people would not do the same thing in private as they would in public. If you could do anything you wanted and no one would know what you did, then what you would do under these circumstances define the real you.

The second motivation (i.e. to satisfy an emotional need) is more honorable but is still not the motivation that God seeks. Much of good parenting results in children who need to do the right thing because it satisfies an emotional need to please mom and dad. Much of upright moral conduct in the world (in believer or unbeliever) is the result of a need to regard oneself as a man of integrity that we might feel good about ourselves.

The third motivation is the one that God seeks in His saints. This is the motivation of the believer today who walks after the Spirit (Rom. 8:4) because he/she is constrained by the love of Christ (2Cor 5:14).

Matthew 6:5-13 "*⁵ And when thou prayest, thou shalt not be as the hypocrites are: for they love to pray standing in the synagogues and in the corners of the streets, that they may be seen of men. Verily I say unto you, They have their reward. ⁶ But thou, when thou prayest, enter into thy closet, and when thou hast shut thy door, pray to thy Father which is in secret; and thy Father which seeth in secret shall reward thee openly. ⁷ But when ye pray, use not vain repetitions, as the heathen do: for they think that they shall be heard for their much speaking. ⁸ Be not ye therefore like unto them: for your Father knoweth what things ye have need of, before ye ask him. ⁹ After this manner therefore pray ye: Our Father which art in heaven, Hallowed be thy name. ¹⁰ Thy kingdom come. Thy will be done in earth, as it is in heaven. ¹¹ Give us this day our daily bread. ¹² And forgive us our debts, as we forgive our debtors. ¹³ And lead us not into temptation, but deliver us from evil: For thine is the kingdom, and the power, and the glory, for ever. Amen.*"

Matthew 6:9-14 is what is commonly called the Lord's Prayer. It should more properly be called the disciples prayer because He is telling His disciples "after this manner pray." It is a pattern of what the general content of their prayers should be. It was not intended to be a rote prayer (though people use it as such today) because He tells them "use not vain repetition". The general content of their prayer was to include:

- That the Father's name be hallowed in the whole world. This was to be Israel's purpose in the world – to honor God's name in the world. (1Sam 12:22; 1Kings 8:42; Psa. 23:3; 79:9 106:8; Isa. 48:11; Jer. 14: 21; Exek.20: 9, 22).

- The prayer was to be made to Israel's Father (Exodus 4:22-23)

- Israel's Father was in heaven at the time. He once was in Israel's temple and dwelled between the cherubim (2Kings 9:15; Psalm 80:2; Isa. 37:16; et. al.) He was once the Lord of all the earth (Josh. 3:11`). When Israel was taken captive because of their sin, he became the God of heaven (Dan. 2:19) who would one day set up a kingdom on the earth again (Dan. 2:44).

- They were to pray for that kingdom to come.

- When that kingdom comes, God's will is going to be done in the earth as it is in the third heaven (2Cor 12:2) where God's throne is.

- He instructs them to pray for their daily bread. We today in America pray more for discipline not to eat so much daily bread. In the tribulation period though, they will not be able to buy or sell without taking the mark of the beast (Rev. 13:17; cf. Lam. 5:7-10). But the Lord will feed Israel in that time of trouble (Matt. 6:25) as he fed Israel in the wilderness (Rev. 12:14).

- Lead us not into temptation – Israel is to pray for deliverance from the temptation of the antichrist (Rev. 3:10).

- For thine is the kingdom – 1Chr. 29:10-11. The kingdom is the Lord's as is the power and the glory.

Matthew 6:14-15 "[14] For if ye forgive men their trespasses, your heavenly Father will also forgive you: [15] But if ye forgive not men their trespasses, neither will your Father forgive your trespasses."

Israel's sins would be forgiven according to how they forgive others (Matt. 18: 21-35). We today are to forgive because we have been forgiven (Eph. 4:23).

Matthew 6:16-18 "[16] Moreover when ye fast, be not, as the hypocrites, of a sad countenance: for they disfigure their faces, that they may appear unto men to fast. Verily I say unto you, They have their reward. [17] But thou, when thou fastest, anoint thine head, and wash thy face; [18] That thou appear not unto men to fast, but unto thy Father which is in secret: and thy Father, which seeth in secret, shall reward thee openly."

This is one of many passages which talk about rewards for faithful service. Here the reward is for fasting quietly without letting it be apparent that one is fasting.

Matthew 6:19-34 "[19] Lay not up for yourselves treasures upon earth, where moth and rust doth corrupt, and where thieves break through and steal: [20] But lay up for yourselves treasures in heaven, where neither moth nor rust doth corrupt, and where thieves do not break through nor steal: [21] For where your treasure is, there will your heart be also. [22] The light of the body is the eye: if therefore thine eye be single, thy whole body shall be full of light. [23] But if thine eye be evil, thy whole body shall be full of darkness. If therefore the light that is in thee be darkness, how great *is* that darkness! [24] No man can serve two masters: for either he will hate the one, and love the other; or else he will hold to the one, and despise the other. Ye cannot serve God and mammon. [25] Therefore I say unto you, Take no thought for your life, what ye shall eat, or what ye shall drink; nor yet for your body, what ye shall put on. Is not the life more than meat, and the body than raiment? [26] Behold the fowls of the air: for they sow not, neither do they reap, nor gather into barns; yet your heavenly Father feedeth them. Are ye not much better than they? [27] Which of you by taking thought can add one cubit unto his stature? [28] And why take ye thought for raiment? Consider the lilies of the field, how they grow; they toil not, neither do they spin: [29] And yet I say unto you, That even Solomon in all his glory was not arrayed like one of these. [30] Wherefore, if God so clothe the grass of the field, which to day is, and to morrow is cast into the oven, *shall he* not much more *clothe* you, O ye of little faith? [31] Therefore take no thought, saying, What shall we eat? or, What shall we drink? or, Wherewithal shall we be clothed? [32] (For after all these things do the Gentiles seek:) for your heavenly Father knoweth that ye have need of all these things. [33] But seek ye first the kingdom of God, and his righteousness; and all these things shall be added unto you. [34] Take therefore no thought for the morrow: for the morrow shall take thought for the things of itself. Sufficient unto the day *is* the evil thereof."

Verses 19-21 "Lay up treasures in heaven." Israelites were laying up treasures in heaven for their faithfulness. However, their eternal home would be on the earth. In Revelation 22:12 we see that the Lord would bring those rewards (treasures) with Him when He comes to set up His kingdom. Where your treasure is that is what you value. It will be in the kingdom that the kingdom saints will enjoy the fruits of their labors. We today will be enjoying our rewards in heaven because that will be where the resurrection bodies of the members of the church, the body of Christ will be (2Cor. 5:1).

Verse 22-23 What you focus on is what will dominate you. If you focus on the things of the Lord, your whole body will manifest it and all will take notice. If you focus on the things of the darkness of this world, that too will be evident to all as well.

Verse 24 You can not be focused on the dollar and on the Lord at the same time.

Verses 25-34 "Take no thought [i.e. no anxious thought] for your life. Seek ye first the kingdom of God and his righteousness and all these things will be added to you." (Verse. 33). What things will be added to you? Food (Verses 25 & 26), Property (Verse. 27), Raiment (Verses 28-30), All your needs met (Verses 31-32), etc. All of your (i.e. Israel's) needs will be met (Verses 31-32) in the kingdom of heaven. In the kingdom of heaven, God will provide for His citizens but today as we who live here on earth during the present dispensation of grace, the order is "If any will not work, neither shall he eat." (2Thess. 3:10)

Chapter 6 Study Guide Questions:

1. Verses 1 through 9 says basically "Don't do right to put on a show." What should be the believer's motivation for doing right?

2. Verse 14 says that if an Israelite did not forgive men, their Heavenly Father would not forgive them. Does this apply to us today? Is there a Pauline passage that tells us something different?

3. Should believers today pattern their prayers after the pattern of Matthew 6:9 to 13?

4. Verses 19 to 34 lay out a very lax approach to financial planning for providing for oneself. Is this a good system for us today to follow? Why not?

MATTHEW 7:1-29

THE CITIZENS OF THE KINGDOM

Matthew 7:1-5 "¹ Judge not, that ye be not judged. ² For with what judgment ye judge, ye shall be judged: and with what measure ye mete, it shall be measured to you again. ³ And why beholdest thou the mote that is in thy brother's eye, but considerest not the beam that is in thine own eye? ⁴ Or how wilt thou say to thy brother, Let me pull out the mote out of thine eye; and, behold, a beam *is* in thine own eye? ⁵ Thou hypocrite, first cast out the beam out of thine own eye; and then shalt thou see clearly to cast out the mote out of thy brother's eye."

The Bible says a lot about judging others. The thought here is – don't be quick to judge that which you cannot see. You cannot see and therefore cannot know a man's heart. There are times and circumstances in which we are to judge others (e.g. 1Cor. 5:11) and times not to. In 1Corinthians 5:11 the actions of sin are to be judged because it is an outward manifestation of the heart. Therefore, believers who are fornicators, covetous people, idolaters, drunkards, and extortionist are to be noted and the local fellowship is to not welcome them into fellowship while they are involved in these activates.

Here in Matthew 7:1 the Lord is instructing Israel not to judge. Let's consider the context in which we find this admonition. The context is forgiving (Matt. 6:14) and laying up treasures in heaven (Matt. 6:17). The parallel passage in Luke 6:37-38 might help us understand this passage. "³⁷ Judge not, and ye shall not be judged: condemn not, and ye shall not be condemned: forgive, and ye shall be forgiven: ³⁸ Give, and it shall be given unto you; good measure, pressed down, and shaken together, and running over, shall men give into your bosom. For with the same measure that ye mete withal it shall be measured to you again." Here again the judging is in connection with forgiving others and giving to others."

In the Old Testament, Israel as a nation would be blessed with wealth when they kept the Law (Deut. 28:28; 29:9; Josh. 1:7; 1Kings 2:3; etc.). To be poor then was an indication that they were being judged by God. However, in the coming tribulation (which was then coming soon if it had not been for the interruption of the dispensation of grace) it will be those who are living godly who will be poor. They will not be able to buy or sell without taking the mark of the beast (Rev. 13:7). It is important to first be a doer of the law before one can be a judge and then such judging is to be done out of a heart of love that is compelled to genuinely help a brother. James says on the subject "¹¹ Speak not evil one of another, brethren. He that speaketh evil of *his* brother, and judgeth his brother, speaketh evil of the law, and judgeth the law: but if thou judge the law, thou art not a doer of the law, but a judge. ¹² There is one lawgiver, who is able to save and to destroy: who art thou that judgest another?" (James 4:11&12)

On the matter of judging, Paul says "³ But with me it is a very small thing that I should be judged of you, or of man's judgment: yea, I judge not mine own self. ⁴ For I know nothing by myself; yet am I not hereby justified: but he that judgeth me is the Lord. ⁵ Therefore judge nothing before the time, until the Lord come, who both will bring to light the hidden things of darkness, and will make manifest the counsels of the hearts: and then shall every man have praise of God." (1Cor. 4:3-5)

Matthew 7:6-10 "⁶ Give not that which is holy unto the dogs, neither cast ye your pearls before swine, lest they trample them under their feet, and turn again and rend you. ⁷ Ask, and it shall be given you; seek, and ye shall find; knock, and it shall be opened unto you: [8] For every one that asketh receiveth; and he that seeketh findeth; and to him that knocketh it shall be opened. [9] Or what man is there of you, whom if his son ask bread, will he give him a stone? [10] Or if he ask a fish, will he give him a serpent?

This and the verses to follow are talking about false prophets and unbelieving teachers of the law who lack discernment of the truth. The pearls and "that which is holy…" here are the truths of the glory of the kingdom. The dogs and the swine in this narrative are to be understood to be the unbelieving scribes and Pharisees.

A pertinent question here is: What is the antecedent of the pronoun "it" in Verse 7 "Ask, and it shall be given you"? This goes back to Matthew 6:19 – 34 where the Lord is talking about provision for life in the kingdom.

Matthew 7:11-12 "[11] If ye then, being evil, know how to give good gifts unto your children, how much more shall your Father which is in heaven give good things to them that ask him? [12] Therefore all things whatsoever ye would that men should do to you, do ye even so to them: for this is the law and the prophets.

The members of the believing remnant are to ask for what they need and it shall be given to them. For the remnant, the fifth course of judgment of Leviticus 26 is past. Verse 12 is talking about mutual care and assistance toward each other. The Lord is preparing them for the mutual concern and common ownership of property that we will see in Acts 2:34.

Matthew 7:13-14 "[13] Enter ye in at the strait gate: for wide *is* the gate, and broad *is* the way, that leadeth to destruction, and many there be which go in thereat: [14] Because strait *is* the gate, and narrow *is* the way, which leadeth unto life, and few there be that find it."

Then, as today, though the way to eternal life is available to all, there are few that actually go through that narrow gate to enter into eternal life.

Matthew 7:15-20 "[15] Beware of false prophets, which come to you in sheep's clothing, but inwardly they are ravening wolves. [16] Ye shall know them by their fruits. Do men gather grapes of thorns, or figs of thistles? [17] Even so every good tree bringeth forth good fruit; but a corrupt tree bringeth forth evil fruit. [18] A good tree cannot bring forth evil fruit, neither *can* a corrupt tree bring forth good fruit. [19] Every tree that bringeth not forth good fruit is hewn down, and cast into the fire. [20] Wherefore by their fruits ye shall know them."

The false prophets look like sheep but are wolves that come in to devour. The key by which they can be identified is by their fruits. Here again we see fruit bearing as a requirement to enter the kingdom. In Matthew 10:16 & 17 the Lord says to the disciples "[16] Behold, I send you forth as sheep in the midst of wolves: be ye therefore wise as serpents, and harmless as doves. [17] But beware of men: for they will deliver you up to the councils, and they will scourge you in their synagogues…" Their defense was to be alert, be wary, and be innocent. In Matthew 24:11 the Lord tells them "Many false prophets shall rise, and shall deceive many."

Matthew 7:21-23 "[21] Not every one that saith unto me, Lord, Lord, shall enter into the kingdom of heaven; but he that doeth the will of my Father which is in heaven. [22] Many will say to me in that day, Lord, Lord, have we not prophesied in thy name? and in thy name have cast out devils? And in thy name done many wonderful works? [23] And then will I profess unto them, I never knew you: depart from me, ye that work iniquity."

Do not be deceived by miracles. The false prophets in this passage can perform miracles which they use to deceive people. Matthew 24:24 "And, many false Christs and false prophets shall arise and shall shew great signs and wonders; insomuch that if it were possible, they shall deceive the very elect." There will be tremendous demonic activity during the tribulation period. The following passages from the book of the Revelation exemplify those last days' phenomena:

- "[11] And I beheld another beast coming up out of the earth; and he had two horns like a lamb, and he spake as a dragon. [12] And he exerciseth all the power of the first beast before him, and causeth the earth and them which dwell therein to worship the first beast, whose deadly wound was healed. [13] And he doeth great wonders, so that he maketh fire come down from heaven on the earth in the sight of men, [14] And deceiveth them that dwell on the earth by _the means of_ those miracles which he had power to do in the sight of the beast; saying to them that dwell on the earth, that they should make an image to the beast, which had the wound by a sword, and did live." (Rev. 13:11-14) The work of the false prophet is to point all worship to the antichrist.

- "[13] And I saw three unclean spirits like frogs _come_ out of the mouth of the dragon, and out of the mouth of the beast, and out of the mouth of the false prophet. [14] For they are the spirits of devils, working miracles, _which_ go forth unto the kings of the earth and of the whole world, to gather them to the battle of that great day of God Almighty. " (Rev. 16:13-16) Here we see the unholy trinity.

The satanic purpose for the signs and wonders is seen from passages as Deuteronomy 13:1-4 "[1] If there arise among you a prophet, or a dreamer of dreams, and giveth thee a sign or a wonder, [2] And the sign or the wonder come to pass, whereof he spake unto thee, saying, Let us go after other gods, which thou hast not known, and let us serve them; [3] Thou shalt not hearken unto the words of that prophet, or that dreamer of dreams: for the LORD your God proveth you, to know whether ye love the LORD your God with all your heart and with all your soul. [4] Ye shall walk after the LORD your God, and fear him, and keep his commandments, and obey his voice, and ye shall serve him, and cleave unto him."

> **Mathew 7:24-27** "[24] Therefore whosoever heareth these sayings of mine, and doeth them, I will liken him unto a wise man, which built his house upon a rock: [25] And the rain descended, and the floods came, and the winds blew, and beat upon that house; and it fell not: for it was founded upon a rock. [26] And every one that heareth these sayings of mine, and doeth them not, shall be likened unto a foolish man, which built his house upon the sand: [27] And the rain descended, and the floods came, and the winds blew, and beat upon that house; and it fell: and great was the fall of it.

The wise man hears the Word. Then he believes the Word. Then he does the Word. Just knowing the truth does not produce godliness in a person's life – not then and not now. However, applying the truth of the Word of God produces stability in a believer's life.

> **Matthew 7:28-29** "[28] And it came to pass, when Jesus had ended these sayings, the people were astonished at his doctrine: [29] For he taught them as _one_ having authority, and not as the scribes."

He had the authority of the Word of God because He is the eternal living Word (John 1:1-4). The only authority that anyone has in spiritual matters today is the authority that comes from the written Word of God.

Chapter 7 Study Guide Questions:

1. Matthew 7:1 says "Judge not, that ye be not judged." How do we take this in consideration of 1Corinthians 4:3-5 and 1Corinthians 5:11-13?

2. What are the pearls in verse 6 that they were not to cast before the swine? Who are the swine?

3. According to verses 15 to 20, how were they to recognize the wolves?

4. In verses 21 to 23 there will be people doing wonderful works in the Lord's name but were not believers. How would these be recognized for what they are?

5. What authority did Jesus have that attracted people to Him?

Chapter 8

MATTHEW 8:1-27

THE CREDENTIALS OF THE KING

An Overview of Chapters 8 and 9

In Mathew Chapters 8 & 9 the Lord performs certain specific miracles that demonstrate His qualification and credentials by which He can claim to be the Messiah. These are performed in a certain specific order for the purpose of showing that He can and will one day do for man what man needs in order to have eternal life and to bring about the removal of the curse of Genesis Chapter 3. He demonstrates:

1. His power as Messiah over human diseases (Verses 2-16)
   "   "   "   over the natural world (Verses 24-26)
   "   "   "   over the spirit world (Verses 28-32).
2. His ability to destroy the works of the devil (Verse 34). However, men prefer to live with the diseases and demons rather than to enjoy the blessings of Messiah's kingdom.
3. Israel's need:
   • His ability to remove the defilement of sin from Israel (represented by the leprosy). (Verses. 2-8)
   • His ability to enable Israel to be the blessing to the Gentiles that Abraham's seed was to be. (Verses 5-13)
   • His ability to give Israel strength (Verses 14 and 15)
   • His ability to bring the curse of Genesis 3:17 under the control of man. (Verses 23-27)
   • His ability to deliver man from the grip of the Devil (Verses 28-34).

Chapters 8 & 9 present the credentials of Jesus Christ as the Rightful King

Matthew 8:1-4 "¹ When he was come down from the mountain, great multitudes followed him. ² And, behold, there came a leper and worshipped him, saying, Lord, if thou wilt, thou canst make me clean. ³ And Jesus put forth *his* hand, and touched him, saying, I will; be thou clean. And immediately his leprosy was cleansed. ⁴ And Jesus saith unto him, See thou tell no man; but go thy way, shew thyself to the priest, and offer the gift that Moses commanded, for a testimony unto them.

Leprosy is a type for sin in Bible typology. Just as leprosy defiles a person's body, so does sin defile the soul. It defiles a person under the law to touch a leper (Lev. 13:46). The Lord touched him but was not defiled because He was separate from sinners and thus could not be defiled (Heb. 7:26). Israel's main need was to be cleansed from sin – the same need we had before we were justified by His grace.. There are some interesting notes that we can take from this passage that we can apply to our lives regarding sin's defilement:

• The leper recognized his defiled condition.
• The leper knew that Christ could cleanse him.
• The Lord, though He was undefiled and could not be defiled, touched the defiled leper. He was ultimately made to be sin for us that we might be made the righteousness of God in Him.(2Cor. 5:21)
• Only God can cleanse a leper.(Lev. 14:3)
• The leper was to tell no one but was to show himself to the priest. This is real interesting because the priest should have known from this that God was in the midst of Israel.

Matthew 8: 5-13 "⁵ And when Jesus was entered into Capernaum, there came unto him a centurion, beseeching him, ⁶ And saying, Lord, my servant lieth at home sick of the palsy, grievously tormented. ⁷ And Jesus saith unto him, I will come and heal him. ⁸ The centurion answered and said, Lord, I am not worthy that thou shouldest come under my roof: but speak the word only, and my servant shall be healed. ⁹ For I am a man under authority, having soldiers under me: and I say to this *man*, Go, and he goeth; and to another, Come, and he cometh; and to my servant, Do this, and he doeth *it*. ¹⁰ When Jesus heard *it*, he marveled, and said to them that followed, Verily I say unto you, I have not found so great faith, no, not in Israel. ¹¹ And I say unto you, That many shall come from the east and west, and shall sit down with Abraham, and Isaac, and Jacob, in the kingdom of heaven. ¹² But the children of the kingdom shall be cast out into outer darkness: there shall be weeping and gnashing of teeth. ¹³ And Jesus said unto the centurion, Go thy way; and as thou hast believed, *so* be it done unto thee. And his servant was healed in the selfsame hour.

The healing of the Gentile Centurion's servant is significant here in that Israel was to be a blessing to the Gentiles (Gen. 12:2; 22:17 & 18). The Gentiles were ready to receive the blessing that would come to them through the nation but Israel was still in unbelief. The salvation of the Gentiles would come through Israel but only as the Gentiles would do as this Gentile did – recognize his unworthy state. This Gentile man had a clear understanding of authority and knew that Israel's' Messiah was the ultimate final authority. How amazing! When the kingdom will be established, there will be many Gentiles who will sit down with Abraham, Isaac, and Jacob while many of the Israelite will be cast out into a place called outer darkness.

Matthew 8:14-15 "¹⁴ And when Jesus was come into Peter's house, he saw his wife's mother laid, and sick of a fever. ¹⁵ And he touched her hand, and the fever left her: and she arose, and ministered unto them."

Here Peter's mother in law was sick with a fever. This is a type of Israel being without strength to serve God. Christ is the one that strengthens Israel for service.

Matthew 8:16-17 "¹⁶ When the even was come, they brought unto him many that were possessed with devils: and he cast out the spirits with *his* word, and healed all that were sick: ¹⁷ That it might be fulfilled which was spoken by Esaias the prophet, saying, Himself took our infirmities, and bare *our* sicknesses."

Israel was in bondage to devils. We observe that demonic activity was rampant during the gospel era. We will see more on this in verses 28-34 below.

Matthew 8:18-20 "¹⁸ Now when Jesus saw great multitudes about him, he gave commandment to depart unto the other side. ¹⁹ And a certain scribe came, and said unto him, Master, I will follow thee whithersoever thou goest. ²⁰ And Jesus saith unto him, The foxes have holes, and the birds of the air *have* nests; but the Son of man hath not where to lay *his* head.

Jesus understands that the great multitude is following Him because of the miracles. This certain scribe desired to follow him. He is telling him that to follow Him would be difficult because He had no certain dwelling place.

Matthew 8:21-22 "²¹ And another of his disciples said unto him, Lord, suffer me first to go and bury my father. ²² But Jesus said unto him, Follow me; and let the dead bury their dead.

The Lord was the true life. All who were not with Him were dead even when they were still physically alive. There are unbelievers who can minister to the rest of the unbelievers. The believer must focus on the real needs of men – the spiritual needs.

Matthew 8:23-27 "²³ And when he was entered into a ship, his disciples followed him. ²⁴ And, behold, there arose a great tempest in the sea, insomuch that the ship was covered with the waves: but he was asleep. ²⁵ And his disciples came to *him*, and awoke him, saying, Lord, save us: we perish. ²⁶ And he saith unto them, Why are ye fearful, O ye of little faith? Then he arose, and rebuked the winds and the sea; and there was a great calm. ²⁷ But the men marveled, saying, What manner of man is this, that even the winds and the sea obey him!

Nature is under the curse of sin (Gen. 3:17). The message conveyed by this passage is that Christ is the one who can undo the curse and bring nature under man's control. This will happen in the kingdom when not only the forces of nature but the animal creation (Isa. 11:6; 65:25) and the vegetable creation (Isa. 35:1) will be under man's control through Christ.

Matthew 8:28-34 "²⁸ And when he was come to the other side into the country of the Gergesenes, there met him two possessed with devils, coming out of the tombs, exceeding fierce, so that no man might pass by that way. ²⁹ And, behold, they cried out, saying, What have we to do with thee, Jesus, thou Son of God? Art thou come hither to torment us before the time? ³⁰ And there was a good way off from them an herd of many swine feeding. ³¹ So the devils besought him, saying, If thou cast us out, suffer us to go away into the herd of swine. ³² And he said unto them, Go. And when they were come out, they went into the herd of swine: and, behold, the whole herd of swine ran violently down a steep place into the sea, and perished in the waters. ³³ And they that kept them fled, and went their ways into the city, and told every thing, and what was befallen to the possessed of the devils. ³⁴ And, behold, the whole city came out to meet Jesus: and when they saw him, they besought *him* that he would depart out of their coasts.

There was much demonic activity in Israel at that time. Mark Chapter 5 has a parallel passage to this account that says volumes about what was going on spiritually in Israel at the time. Let's read the passage and then make some observations:

Mark 5:1-20 "¹ And they came over unto the other side of the sea, into the country of the Gadarenes. ² And when he was come out of the ship, immediately there met him out of the tombs a man with an unclean spirit, ³ Who had *his* dwelling among the tombs; and no man could bind him, no, not with chains: ⁴ Because that he had been often bound with fetters and chains, and the chains had been plucked asunder by him, and the fetters broken in pieces: neither could any *man* tame him. ⁵ And always, night and day, he was in the mountains, and in the tombs, crying, and cutting himself with stones. ⁶ But when he saw Jesus afar off, he ran and worshipped him, ⁷ And cried with a loud voice, and said, What have I to do with thee, Jesus, *thou* Son of the most high God? I adjure thee by God, that thou torment me not. ⁸ For he said unto him, Come out of the man, *thou* unclean spirit. ⁹ And he asked him, What *is* thy name? And he answered, saying, My name *is* Legion: for we are many. ¹⁰ And he besought him much that he would not send them away out of the country. ¹¹ Now there was there nigh unto the mountains a great herd of swine feeding. ¹² And all the devils besought him, saying, Send us into the swine, that we may enter into them. ¹³ And forthwith Jesus gave them leave. And the unclean spirits went out, and entered into the swine: and the herd ran violently down a steep place into the sea, (they were about two thousand;) and were choked in the sea. ¹⁴ And they that fed the swine fled, and told *it* in the city, and in the country. And they went out to see what it was that was done. ¹⁵ And they come to Jesus, and see him that was possessed with the devil, and had the legion, sitting, and clothed, and in his right mind: and they were afraid. ¹⁶ And they that saw *it* told them how it befell to him that was possessed with the devil, and *also* concerning the swine. ¹⁷

And they began to pray him to depart out of their coasts. [18] And when he was come into the ship, he that had been possessed with the devil prayed him that he might be with him. [19] Howbeit Jesus suffered him not, but saith unto him, Go home to thy friends, and tell them how great things the Lord hath done for thee, and hath had compassion on thee. [20] And he departed, and began to publish in Decapolis how great things Jesus had done for him: and all *men* did marvel."

Observe about this passage in Mark 5:1-20 that:
- The man was possessed by <u>an</u> (as in singular) unclean spirit.
- The spirit's name was "Legion" for there were many spirits in the man (Vs 9).
- The spirit drove the man to live among the tombs and to cut himself.
- The spirit gave him great strength.
- The spirit made him so wild that no man could tame him.
- The spirit recognized Jesus as the "Son of the most high." The spirits knew who He is.
- The unclean spirit asked the Lord that He not send him out of the country. This is the most significant part of the event. The spirit knew that his job was to occupy the land of Israel. Satan wanted his hordes in the land because he knew that the conflict between him and Christ was at hand.
- The unclean spirits besought Him to allow them to enter the herd of swine and the Lord allowed it.
- Here it gets real interesting. There were at least 2 thousand swine in the herd. We presume then that there was at least one unclean spirit per swine so there were at least 2,000 unclean spirits in that one man. When the demons entered into the herd of swine, these "unclean animals" could not handle the presence of the unclean spirits and chose to drown themselves rather than live with these unclean spirits in them. This is the testimony to the spiritual state of the unregenerate heart of man. The man could live with 2000 plus unclean spirits in him but the swine would not live with one (or a few) unclean spirits apiece.
- The account gets even more interesting as the swine keepers got to town to tell the town's people what happened.
- When the town's people saw and heard from the swine keepers what had happened in the casting out of the unclean spirits from the man and the drowning of the swine, they ask Jesus to leave town. What a testimony of the blindness of the unbelief of the nation at that time. Here is the one who could deliver them from the bondage to Satan and they choose to live with the devils rather than be delivered.

How thought provoking this is. Here the creator just got kicked out of town. The one who could have set them free from demonic activity is asked to leave. Israel is said to be "the lawful captive" in Isaiah 49:24 -25 "[24] Shall the prey be taken from the mighty, or the lawful captive delivered? [25] But thus saith the LORD, Even the captives of the mighty shall be taken away, and the prey of the terrible shall be delivered: for I will contend with him that contendeth with thee, and I will save thy children."

Israel was the lawful captive of the devil because they failed to keep the law and thus endured the curses of the law and the five courses of chastisement of Leviticus 26. God told Israel that after they failed and became the lawful captive, that He would free them from their captivity (Deut. 30:1-3). We see this deliverance from captivity in Solomon's prayer for Israel in 2Chronicals 6: 37-42. The LORD tells Jeremiah regarding Israel how he will deliver Israel from her captivity one day in Jeremiah 29:14 and again in Zephaniah 3:20.

Chapter 8 Study Guide Questions:

1. Why would the Lord not want the leper in 8:1 to 4 to tell anyone of being cleansed? Why was he to go and tell the priest?

2. Who will be those people in verse 11 that will sit down with Abraham, Isaac, and Jacob in the Kingdom? Who are the children in verse 12? Why would the children of the kingdom be cast out?

3. The Gentile centurion in verses 5 to 13 was a man of some importance. What does his humble attitude say about the readiness of the Gentiles to receive the blessing from Abraham's seed (Gen. 12:2; 22:17) and Israel's receptiveness?

4. Does the healing of Peter's wife's mother and those saved from demonic possession have any bearing on Israel's plight as a nation relative to the Lord's supply?

5. The account of the two possessed of devils in verses 28 to 34 warrant much thought:

    a. What should be made of the devils' address to Christ in verse 29?
    b. Should there be swine raised in Israel?
    c. What do we understand of the fact that the swine would rather die than live with demonic possession while these men could live with it.
    d. Why would the men of that country ask the Lord to leave when they saw what transpired?
    e. Why did the demons request that they not be expelled from the country?

MATTHEW 9:1-37

JESUS RETURNS TO CAPERNAUM

In Chapter 8 the Lord was asked to leave the country of the Gergesenes. In Chapter 9 He returns to His own city of Capernaum (Matt. 4:12-15) in Galilee. In Chapter 4 we saw Him leave Jerusalem and go to the land of Zabulon. The people of Zabulon were regarded as being of low estate by the Jews of Jerusalem and were not regarded as being a part of the nation. These are the people that Paul refers to in Romans 10:19 & 20 "I will provoke you to jealousy by them that are no people, and by a foolish nation ..." Peter refers to these people saying that them "which in times past were not a people..." (1Peter 2:9-10). The Lord calls out His little flock from that group of people and He will eventually tell them that the kingdom will be taken from the leaders of Israel and given to that group of people. (Matt. 21:43). This little flock will be the branches that will bear fruit (Matt. 3:10; 7:17-19; 13:8, 23; etc.). It is from them that He calls out the new government of the nation that will replace the then existing government. The twelve apostles will sit on twelve thrones judging the twelve tribes of Israel (Matt. 19:28). The faithful of the little flock will have authority over cities on earth in the kingdom (Luke 19:12-27). He tells them "...fear not little flock for it is your Father's good pleasure to give you the kingdom." (Luke 12:32). All of the apostles except Judas were from Galilee.

> **Matthew 9:1-8** "¹ And he entered into a ship, and passed over, and came into his own city. ² And, behold, they brought to him a man sick of the palsy, lying on a bed: and Jesus seeing their faith said unto the sick of the palsy; Son, be of good cheer; thy sins be forgiven thee. ³ And, behold, certain of the scribes said within themselves, This *man* blasphemeth. ⁴ And Jesus knowing their thoughts said, Wherefore think ye evil in your hearts? ⁵ For whether is easier, to say, *Thy* sins be forgiven thee, or to say, Arise, and walk? ⁶ But that ye may know that the Son of man hath power on earth to forgive sins, (then saith he to the sick of the palsy,) Arise, take up thy bed, and go unto thine house. ⁷ And he arose, and departed to his house. ⁸ But when the multitudes saw *it*, they marveled, and glorified God, which had given such power unto men.

The Lord makes a profound point here in a humorous way. When he returned He is met by a group of people who bring him a man sick of the palsy. In Verse 2, He sees their faith. In this He manifests the Spirit of the LORD that would be in the Messiah (Isa. 11:1-3). He is able to look at not just what appears on the outside but what he sees is in the heart. He could perceive the thoughts of the inward man. We see this or a similar incident in Luke 5:18-26. He performed these miracles in front of these simple people of faith but would not do so for the unbelieving scribes and Pharisees in Matthew 12:38. The order of events is important here:

- He sees their faith (including the man sick of the palsy).
- He tells the man "Thy sins are forgiven thee."
- The scribes say within themselves "This man blasphemeth." No one can forgive sins but God (Psa. 32:5; Isa 43:25). Note particularly Isaiah 43:25 "²⁵ I, *even* I, *am* he that blotteth out thy transgressions for mine own sake, and will not remember thy sins."
- He reads their minds (Verses 3&4) – something that only God can do.
- He asks them a question to get them to think "For whether is easier, to say, *Thy* sins be forgiven thee; or to say, Arise, and walk?" (Verse 5) Obviously, it is easy to say thy sins are forgiven thee but to say "Arise and take up thy bed and go to thy house" one has to be able to deliver on the words spoken.

- The Lord then proves (Verse 6) that He is God in the flesh by healing the man by simply speaking the word. Here He is demonstrating that He is the living Word (John 1:1-4, 14) who framed the worlds by the word of God (Heb. 11:3). One day all the dead will rise at his word (John 5:25).
- The man gets up and obediently goes home (Verse 7).
- The multitude are standing there left to marvel and wonder in amazement. They glorify God for the power that He gave to man but they have totally missed the point (Verse 8).

The point that they miss is that this is the Word made flesh. This is God in the flesh. Jesus Christ is 100% fully God and 100% fully man and is the only avenue of approach by which any man can come to God. To simply believe because of one seeing a miracle is not the faith that God is looking for. God is looking for faith that is produced by the Word of God. In John 2:23-25 "²³ Now when he was in Jerusalem at the passover, in the feast *day*, many believed in his name, when they saw the miracles which he did. ²⁴ But Jesus did not commit himself unto them, because he knew all *men*, ²⁵ And needed not that any should testify of man: for he knew what was in man." He knew what is in man. Man is very flesh oriented. In John 6: 26 the multitude followed Him not so much for that they saw the miracles but that they had their bellies full from the fish that were miraculously produced. He then tells them "⁵¹ I am the living bread which came down from heaven: if any man eat of this bread, he shall live forever: and the bread that I will give is my flesh, which I will give for the life of the world." (John 6:51).

The Call of Matthew

> **Matthew 9:9-13** "⁹ And as Jesus passed forth from thence, he saw a man, named Matthew, sitting at the receipt of custom: and he saith unto him, Follow me. And he arose, and followed him. ¹⁰ And it came to pass, as Jesus sat at meat in the house, behold, many publicans and sinners came and sat down with him and his disciples. ¹¹ And when the Pharisees saw *it*, they said unto his disciples, Why eateth your Master with publicans and sinners? ¹² But when Jesus heard *that*, he said unto them, They that be whole need not a physician, but they that are sick. ¹³ But go ye and learn what *that* meaneth, I will have mercy, and not sacrifice: for I am not come to call the righteous, but sinners to repentance.

In Verse 9 we see the call of Matthew (called Levi in Luke 5:29). Mark 2:14-17 gives a more expanded account of the call of Matthew. We are not told so directly but it appears that he was an observer of the events with the man with the palsy. Matthew was a tax collector. He worked for the Roman government to asses taxes from his fellow countrymen and was thus resented by the Jews. Matthew follows Jesus and hosts a party to which he invites some of his worldly friends. The Lord sits down with these publicans and sinners and eats with them. The Pharisees see it and criticize Him for it. He then makes a reference to a passage in Hosea "⁶ For I desired mercy, and not sacrifice; and the knowledge of God more than burnt offerings." (Hosea 6:6). He did not come to call the righteous but sinners to repentance. He is actually being somewhat facetious in this for there is none righteous. The Pharisees needed to repent as did the publicans and sinners. What was happening there was that the Pharisees were letting their pride get in the way of them coming to Christ for salvation.

In 1Corinthians 5:11 Paul tells us "¹¹ But now I have written unto you not to keep company, if any man that is called a brother be a fornicator, or covetous, or an idolater, or a railer, or a drunkard, or an extortioner; with such an one no not to eat." We ask "why the difference?" Why did the Lord eat with sinners and we are separate from them in this passage. The difference is that the Lord is calling sinners to repentance while 1Corinthians 5:11 is talking about believers who should be acting differently.

> **Matthew 9:14-17** " ¹⁴ Then came to him the disciples of John, saying, Why do we and the Pharisees fast oft, but thy disciples fast not? ¹⁵ And Jesus said unto them, Can the children of the

bridechamber mourn, as long as the bridegroom is with them? But the days will come, when the bridegroom shall be taken from them, and then shall they fast. [16] No man putteth a piece of new cloth unto an old garment, for that which is put in to fill it up taketh from the garment, and the rent is made worse. [17] Neither do men put new wine into old bottles: else the bottles break, and the wine runneth out, and the bottles perish: but they put new wine into new bottles, and both are preserved.

Here we see Jesus as the bridegroom. Who then is the bride?
- John the Baptizer is not a part of the bride (John 3:29).
- The twelve are not part of the bride (Luke 12:36).
- He church which is Christ's Body is not the bride but is a part of the bridegroom being members of Christ (1Cor. 6:15; Eph 2:15).
- The Bride is the New Jerusalem (Rev. 21:9-10).

Consider the progression regarding Israel in her relationship with the Lord.
- God was married to Israel (Jer. 31:32).
- God divorced Israel (Hosea 1:9).
- God will one day be again married to Israel (Hosea 2:23)
- Israel will then be married to the land (Isa. 62:1-5).

Verse 17 talks about not putting new wine in old bottles. The point that the Lord is making is that the kingdom will be set up based on the New Covenant that has different operating principles than the Old Covenant. Just as old bottles (wine skins) could not stretch to accommodate new wine, so the Old Covenant could not accommodate the principles of the New Covenant.

> **Matthew 9:18-26** "[18] While he spake these things unto them, behold, there came a certain ruler, and worshipped him, saying, My daughter is even now dead: but come and lay thy hand upon her, and she shall live. [19] And Jesus arose, and followed him, and *so did* his disciples. [20] And, behold, a woman, which was diseased with an issue of blood twelve years, came behind *him*, and touched the hem of his garment: [21] For she said within herself, If I may but touch his garment, I shall be whole. [22] But Jesus turned him about, and when he saw her, he said, Daughter, be of good comfort; thy faith hath made thee whole. And the woman was made whole from that hour. [23] And when Jesus came into the ruler's house, and saw the minstrels and the people making a noise, [24] He said unto them, Give place: for the maid is not dead, but sleepeth. And they laughed him to scorn. [25] But when the people were put forth, he went in, and took her by the hand, and the maid arose. [26] And the fame hereof went abroad into all that land.

In these passages we find two women who are each referred to as daughters both of whom are healed and/or raised. The first is the daughter of a ruler. In the account in Mark 5:22-43 we see that the man was a ruler of the synagogue and that his name was Jairus. This account is also found in Luke 8:41-56. The first is a woman in the crowd who the Lord addressed as "daughter." This woman had an issue of blood for 12 years. This address ("Daughter") is significant in that the Lord is making a point of His position as Messiah of Israel. Isaiah 9:6 says that the Messiah will be called "the everlasting Father." Both of these women represent the nation as a whole in its relationship to Jesus Christ as Messiah. The nation as a whole was spiritually dead. The Lord is on His way to raise Israel and to heal Israel. However, on His way to raise the girl (i.e. the nation) another woman who had hemorrhaged for 12 years understands that she would be healed by touching his garments. The number 12 makes us think of Israel being presented here in type. The woman represents the twelve apostles and the little flock whom the Lord saves on the way to saving the nations as a whole. On the way to saving the nation as whole, He finds the little flock that are not dead but are sick (spiritually). They are made whole by their contact with Christ. Her disease is the loss of blood. The blood represents the life of the individual (Deut. 9:4; 12:23; Lev. 17:14). The remnant, when the Lord found them was loosing their spiritual life. We see that it was her faith that made her whole. So too it was the little flock's faith that saved them.

When the Lord gets to the ruler's house, he tells the crowd "...the maid is not dead but sleepeth." Comparing this passage in Matthew 9:24 with the parallel passage in John 11:11-15 we understand that the maid truly was physically dead. The Bible refers to physical death as sleep because people who are dead are temporarily unable to function in the physical world. After the Lord raises His saints into resurrection life, they will again be able to function in a physical environment. Today, and especially prior to 1947, people regard Israel as being dead. But the Lord says that Israel is asleep and will be until the Lord comes to raise her. One day the Lord will raise Israel from the dead (raising her both physically and spiritually). The apostle Paul says "...If the casting away of them be the reconciling of the world, what shall the receiving of them be, but life from the dead?" (Rom. 11:15). But today "...blindness in part is happened to Israel until the fullness of the Gentiles be come in." (Rom. 11:25) And then "All Israel shall be saved: as it is written, There shall come out of Sion the Deliverer and shall turn away ungodliness from Jacob." (Rom. 11:26).

In the account in Mark Chapter 5, the Lord tells those that observed the raising of Jairus' daughter that no man should know it (Mark 5:43). However, in Mark 5:19 when He cast out the demon from the man, the Lord tells him to go home to his friends and to tell them how great things the Lord had done for him. Why the difference? The difference was that the case of the casting out of the demon was addressing the spiritual need of Israel while the raising of the dead was the physical need. The Lord wants Israel to focus on the spiritual needs first.

> **Matthew 9:27-31** "²⁷ And when Jesus departed thence, two blind men followed him, crying, and saying, *Thou* Son of David, have mercy on us. ²⁸ And when he was come into the house, the blind men came to him: and Jesus saith unto them, Believe ye that I am able to do this? They said unto him, Yea, Lord. ²⁹ Then touched he their eyes, saying, According to your faith be it unto you. ³⁰ And their eyes were opened; and Jesus straitly charged them, saying, See *that* no man know *it.* ³¹ But they, when they were departed, spread abroad his fame in all that country.

Two blind men follow the Lord as He leaves Jairus' house. These two blind men receive their sight. He heals them "according to their faith." Not the quantity of their faith but the object of it. This is a type of Israel in spiritual blindness. Israel was to be a kingdom of priests to reach the Gentiles with the gospel. However, before Israel could do that they needed spiritual vision.

> **Matthew 9:32-34** "³² As they went out, behold, they brought to him a dumb man possessed with a devil. ³³ And when the devil was cast out, the dumb spake: and the multitudes marvelled, saying, It was never so seen in Israel. ³⁴ But the Pharisees said, He casteth out devils through the prince of the devils.

In Matthew 9:30, two blind men receive their vision. Not only did Israel need spiritual vision if they were to accomplish what God had called them to do in the world but she also needed to find her voice to be God's witnesses in the world. Israel was to be a light to the Gentiles (Isa. 42:6). Here we see the Lord cast a devil out of a man that was dumb. As soon as the devil was cast out, the man spoke. Obviously the devil was keeping the man from speaking. God was calling the believing remnant of Israel to be his witnesses to Jerusalem, Judea, Samaria, and then to the entire world (Acts 1:8; 2:32; 3:35; 5:32; 10:38, 41). In the Millennium, Satan will be bound for 1,000 years. Israel will then be speaking forth the gospel of the kingdom to the entire world.

In verse 34 we come to a significant event in the Gospel of Matthew. The leaders of the nation start to attack the Lord by telling people that He casts out devils by the prince of devils. In Matthew 12:4-34 we will see that this blaspheming of the Lord by the leaders of Israel will eventually lead to the nation committing the unpardonable sin.

> **Matthew 9:35-37** "[35] And Jesus went about all the cities and villages, teaching in their synagogues, and preaching the gospel of the kingdom, and healing every sickness and every disease among the people. [36] But when he saw the multitudes, he was moved with compassion on them, because they fainted, and were scattered abroad, as sheep having no shepherd. [37] Then saith he unto his disciples, The harvest truly *is* plenteous, but the labourers *are* few; [38] Pray ye therefore the Lord of the harvest, that he will send forth labourers into his harvest.

The Lord continues His ministry to Israel to demonstrate that He is Israel's Messiah and that he can and will provide for the nation what the nation needs to be the means whereby God establishes His kingdom in the earth. However, we will see as Matthew goes on in his gospel account that the Lord will start to confine his ministry to the believing remnant and to the twelve apostles in particular. In Verses 37 & 38 we see the Lord lamenting the lack of true leadership in Israel and the lack of laborers to labor in the harvest of souls. He will now focus His attention on the new leaders of Israel.

Chapter 9 Study Guide Questions:

1. How did the people of Jerusalem view the people of Galilee? Why is it significant that the Lord returned to Galilee?

2. The Lord seems to be provoking the scribes in Verse 2 by telling the man sick of the palsy his sins are now forgiven. What point is the Lord making?

3. In Verses 18 to 26 we find two women both referred to as daughters. One is healed and the other is raised from the dead. How might these women be seen as representative of Israel in the nation's relationship to Messiah?

4. Why would the Lord instruct the blind men who He healed in Verses 27 to 31 to tell no man while in Mark 5:19 when He cast out a demon from a man He instructed him to tell his friend what great things the Lord had done?

5. In Verse 32 to 34 the Lord casts out a demon that made a man dumb. What need in Israel is this passage identifying that the Lord came to meet?

6. In Verse 34 we see the Pharisees start attacking the Lord. What is the nature of their attack?

Chapter 10

MATTHEW 10:1-42

THE KING'S REPRESENTATIVES

Matthew 10:1 "¹ And when he had called unto *him* his twelve disciples, he gave them power *against* unclean spirits, to cast them out, and to heal all manner of sickness and all manner of disease."

Here in Chapter 10, the Lord starts to give power and authority to His apostles.

Matthew 10:2-4 "² Now the names of the twelve apostles are these; The first, Simon, who is called Peter, and Andrew his brother; James *the son* of Zebedee, and John his brother; ³ Philip, and Bartholomew; Thomas, and Matthew the publican; James *the son* of Alphaeus, and Lebbaeus, whose surname was Thaddaeus; ⁴ Simon the Canaanite, and Judas Iscariot, who also betrayed him.

Matthew lists the twelve apostles (including Judas who is here as empowered as are the rest). We see these listed in Mark 3:14-9 and Luke 6: 13-16. In Luke, we see that He chose these twelve apostles out from a larger group of disciples (Luke 6:1). In Luke 12:32 He refers to this group of disciples from which He chose the twelve as the "Little Flock." They comprise the believing remnant of Israel at that time. This believing remnant will grow later in the Book of Acts to many thousands (Acts 4:4; 21:20).

It should be noted that this is not the first time that God had chosen twelve men out from the nation to be leaders in the nation:
- In Numbers 1:1-16, The Lord chose out a leader from each of the twelve tribes to be the leader of that tribe.
- In 1Chronicles 27:1-15 the Lord chose out twelve men to lead Israel in successive courses month by month. Each leader for each month had under him 24,000 who worked with him in administering the affairs of state under King David.
- In 1Chronicles 27:16-23 each of the tribes had a leader over them.
- In Isaiah 1:26 we see that God had promised to restore the judges as at the first. In Isaiah 32:1 we see that in the promised kingdom "A king shall reign in righteousness, and princes shall rule in judgment."
- In Matthew 19:27– 28 we will see that the twelve apostles will sit on twelve thrones judging the twelve tribes of Israel in the kingdom.

Matthew 10:5-8 "⁵ These twelve Jesus sent forth, and commanded them, saying, Go not into the way of the Gentiles, and into *any* city of the Samaritans enter ye not: ⁶ But go rather to the lost sheep of the house of Israel. ⁷ And as ye go, preach, saying, The kingdom of heaven is at hand. ⁸ Heal the sick, cleanse the lepers, raise the dead, cast out devils: freely ye have received, freely give.

This passage picks up on the concern that the Lord has for laborers for the harvest in the house of Israel. He is interested in expanding His force of laborers in a systematic way.
- The Father sent the Son only to the house of Israel. That effort results in the calling out of the little flock.
- The Lord sent the little flock out to preach the gospel of the kingdom to Israel. That effort resulted in the calling out of the remnant.

- The Remnant would then be sent to reach the world beginning with Jerusalem, then Judea, then Samaria and then the uttermost parts of the earth – i.e. the Gentiles. (Acts 1:8).

As they go about their assignment, they were to keep their message very simple – The kingdom of Heaven is at hand. He commissions them to exercise the supernatural powers that He gives them in Verse 1. The miracles that they were given to perform were what the writer of Hebrews calls: "The powers of the world to come" (Heb. 6:5). These signs were to confirm the message that the kingdom is indeed at hand.

Matthew 10:9-10 "⁹Provide neither gold, nor silver, nor brass in your purses, ¹⁰Nor scrip for *your* journey, neither two coats, neither shoes, nor yet staves: for the workman is worthy of his meat.

This passage is still addressing the need for laborers in the harvest. The workman is worthy of His meat. The Lord is going to provide for the wages and the livelihood of the workmen. They were to provide for themselves:

- No money in their purses.
- No itinerary for their journey.
- No change of clothes.
- No shoes.
- Nothing for self defense.

As we compare this passage with Luke 22:35-38, we see that things will change later. They will later be asked to provide both a purse and a sword. That however, will be after He left them via the cross. Their supernatural power and their provision would be temporarily withdrawn but they would be again restored later when the Holy Ghost would minister the gospel of the kingdom through them.

Matthew 10: 11-15 "¹¹And into whatsoever city or town ye shall enter, enquire who in it is worthy; and there abide till ye go thence. ¹²And when ye come into an house, salute it. ¹³And if the house be worthy, let your peace come upon it: but if it be not worthy, let your peace return to you. ¹⁴And whosoever shall not receive you, nor hear your words, when ye depart out of that house or city, shake off the dust of your feet. ¹⁵Verily I say unto you, It shall be more tolerable for the land of Sodom and Gomorrha in the day of judgment, than for that city.

Several questions come to mind with regard to Verse 11. First - to whom do they enquire? Secondly, what is the basis of worthiness? To understand this we need to remember the time frame and the context. In Israel during this time, it was necessary to believe and to then demonstrate faith by action (James 2:22). This is what John 12:42 is referring to regarding the priests who believed on Jesus but would not confess him lest they be put out of the synagogue. Belief in the heart plus confession with the mouth was needed for an Israelite under the proclamation of the gospel of the kingdom. It appears that Romans 10: 9 & 10 alludes to that as well. Therefore an inquiry of anyone in the city should direct the disciples to a house where the occupants believed on Jesus. Today however, justification is by faith alone apart from works. Therefore, simply heart belief will justify a person today (Eph. 2: 8 & 9).

Verse 13 is tied to the Abrahamic Covenant in which God would bless them that bless Israel and curse them that curse Israel. The real Israel is the little flock.
We learn from verse 15 that punishment for unbelief is going to be proportional according to works. See also: Matt. 11:22-24; Luke 12:47-48; Rom. 2:6; Rev. 20: 12-13.

Verse 13 is tied to the Abrahamic Covenant in which God would bless them that bless Israel and curse them that curse Israel. The real Israel is the little flock. We learn from verse 15 that punishment for unbelief is going to be proportional according to works. See His words of criticism for Capernaum in Matthew 11:22-24 in spite of witnessing His mighty works. See also Luke 12:47-48 on how the degree of knowledge a servant had of the Lord's will is going to affect the degree of the punishment for failing to do the Master's will.

This draws our thoughts to Romans 2:5-6 about "…the righteous judgment of God who will render to every man according to his deeds." It draws our thoughts also to the basis of judgment at the great white throne in Revelation 20:12-13 where all the lost are judged according to their works:

"¹² And I saw the dead, small and great, stand before God; and the books were opened: and another book was opened, which is *the book* of life: and the dead were judged out of those things which were written in the books, according to their works. ¹³ And the sea gave up the dead which were in it; and death and hell delivered up the dead which were in them: and they were judged every man according to their works."
Revelation 20:12-13

Matthew 10:16-"¹⁶ Behold, I send you forth as sheep in the midst of wolves: be ye therefore wise as serpents, and harmless as doves.

From Verse 16 thru the end of the chapter the Lord is telling them what they will endure during the tribulation period. Were it not for the fact that the program was interrupted by the dispensation of grace, the twelve and the little flock would have gone through these trying circumstances. In Verses 16 thru 20 He is sending them to a world that rejects Him. Therefore, they will have to be:

- Wise to understand the wickedness of men.
- Harmless to be effective in reaching people
- The wolves are the false prophets (Matt. 7:15; 24:11, 24), the false teachers, and the false religious system (Acts 20:29).

Matthew 10:17-18 "¹⁷ But beware of men: for they will deliver you up to the councils, and they will scourge you in their synagogues; ¹⁸ And ye shall be brought before governors and kings for my sake, for a testimony against them and the Gentiles.

The men to beware of are unregenerate men. They operate on the basis of a heart rejection of the Lord (Psalm 2:2 & 3). These are religious councils that speak against the true faith. This has happened many times in the last 2000 years. Verse 18 speaks of governments. Until the kingdom is set up, there will be no government that is truly a godly government in which the LORD and His Christ is truly welcome. The real danger comes though when the professing church is in league with the government (Acts 12: 1-3).

Matthew 10:19-20 "¹⁹ But when they deliver you up, take no thought how or what ye shall speak: for it shall be given you in that same hour what ye shall speak. ²⁰ For it is not ye that speak, but the Spirit of your Father which speaketh in you.

The Holy Spirit would be giving the believers of Israel the words to say. God had done this a number of times in Israel in the past:
- He gave Moses the words to say (Exodus 4:12)
- He gave Jeremiah the words to say (Jer. 7)
- He gave Samuel the word to say (2Sam 23:2)

However, what the Lord has to say to the world today He said through the pen of the apostle Paul (2Tim 4:16-18). In order to know what to say today, we must study the Bible rightly divided. God gave us our script in 2Corinthians 5:19-21 as ambassadors for Christ.

Matthew 10:21 "²¹ And the brother shall deliver up the brother to death, and the father the child: and the children shall rise up against *their* parents, and cause them to be put to death.

Though the spiritual warfare that goes on today is great (Eph……. 6:12), it will be particularly intense during the tribulation period when the stakes will be much higher (Rev. 12:12). Then it will be all out warfare between Christ and the antichrist.

> **Matthew 10:22-23** "²² And ye shall be hated of all *men* for my name's sake: but he that endureth to the end shall be saved. ²³ But when they persecute you in this city, flee ye into another: for verily I say unto you, Ye shall not have gone over the cities of Israel, till the Son of man be come.

Verse 22 speaks of the tribulation period while Verse 23 speaks of the Lord's return to reign. In the tribulation period, the believer will have to endure the persecution to the end (whether to the end of the tribulation period or the end of his life) to be saved. Hebrews 6:1-4 addresses this requirement for salvation. The temptation to capitulate will be great but so will be the reward for faithfulness (Luke 19:17 & 18; Rev. 2: 26 & 27). See also Matthew 24:13-15 on enduring to the end.

Verse 23 needs some special study: "Ye shall not have gone over the cities of Israel, till the Son of man be come." There is a particle in the Greek that is difficult to translate into English. It is translated here and in Matthew 16:28 "till." (See also Matthew 23:39 and 24:34) The condition here is that had the prophetic program continued, they would not have gone over all of the cities of Israel before Christ would return. This going over the cities is a reference to Acts 1:8 where the Lord commissions the twelve to represent Him to Israel once they receive the empowering of the Holy Ghost.

The term "the end" as used in Bible references to end time events needs to be explained. The term is a reference to the end of the Gentile dominion over Israel and the world. We see the term used in Daniel 7:26; 8:17-19; 11:35; 12:4, 8, 9, 13 and Hebrews 3:6, 14). It is a reference to the tribulation period when the Gentiles will make a last ditch effort to keep Christ and Israel from reigning on earth.

Let's pause here to talk about the various commissions that the Lord gives to the believing remnant of Israel. The commission given here in Matthew 10:1–23 is the first of a series of commissions given to the twelve. This is the broadest of the commissions given to them in that it starts here with the disciples (now appointed as apostles) and continues until the end of the tribulation period.

The Commissions:

1. Matthew 16:16–19 gives to Peter the keys to the kingdom of heaven and with it authority to act in the Lord's absence.
2. Matthew 19:28–30 commissions the twelve to sit on twelve thrones on which they will judge the twelve tribes of Israel in the kingdom.
3. Matthew 28:19 & 20 commissions the twelve to:
   Go into all the world and teach all nations to observe all things the Lord commanded them. This included the keeping of the Law of Moses (Matt. 23:1-4). This commission included water baptism.
4. Mark 16:15–18 also commissions the twelve to:
   Go into all the world and preach the gospel to every creature. In this commission water baptism was required for salvation along with belief. Supernatural signs would be the evidence of belief. The signs include casting out devils, healing the sick, speaking with new tongues, and being unaffected by serpents or deadly poison.
5. John 20:22 imparts the Holy Ghost and equips them to remit sins and retain sins.
6. Acts 1:6-8 empowers the twelve with the Holy Ghost to be witnesses of Christ in Jerusalem, then Judea, then Samaria, and then the uttermost parts of the earth.

These commissions all pertain to Israel and the promised Kingdom of Heaven. There is another commission that is given to us today through the apostle of the Gentiles (Paul). The commission to us is given in 2Corinthians 5:19-21. In that commission, we are ambassadors for Christ in which role we plead with lost men to be reconciled to God by faith in the work that Jesus Christ accomplished on Calvary where He was made to be sin for us so that we might be made the righteousness of God in Him.

> **Matthew 10:24-27** "²⁴ The disciple is not above *his* master, nor the servant above his lord. ²⁵ It is enough for the disciple that he be as his master, and the servant as his lord. If they have called the master of the house Beelzebub, how much more *shall they call* them of his household? ²⁶ Fear them not therefore: for there is nothing covered, that shall not be revealed; and hid, that shall not be known. ²⁷ What I tell you in darkness, *that* speak ye in light: and what ye hear in the ear, *that* preach ye upon the housetops.

Deuteronomy 29:29 says "²⁹ The secret *things belong* unto the LORD our God: but those *things which are* revealed *belong* unto us and to our children for ever, that *we* may do all the words of this law." Everything that the LORD does, He reveals through his servants the prophets (Amos 3:7). The Lord was mistreated and the disciples can expect the same treatment. However, one day the real motives of the hearts will be revealed. At that time, the victor will be the one who stood for truth.

> **Matthew 10:28-31** "²⁸ And fear not them which kill the body, but are not able to kill the soul: but rather fear him which is able to destroy both soul and body in hell. ²⁹ Are not two sparrows sold for a farthing? and one of them shall not fall on the ground without your Father. ³⁰ But the very hairs of your head are all numbered. ³¹ Fear ye not therefore, ye are of more value than many sparrows. ³² Whosoever therefore shall confess me before men, him will I confess also before my Father which is in heaven. ³³ But whosoever shall deny me before men, him will I also deny before my Father which is in heaven.

The word translated "hell" in verse 28 is gehenna. See the notes on Matthew 5:22-30 for information on this gehenna fire.

Here we find the distinction made between the soul and the body. Only the Word of God can accurately identify the soul verses the body. In fact only the Word of God can distinguish between the soul and the spirit (Heb. 4:12). The spirit, soul and body are the three separate entities that comprise the human frame (1Thess. 5:23). We each are an individual soul who has a spirit (to give us a God consciousness) and a body (to enable us to function in the physical world). 1Corinthians 6:20 tells us that we each have a spirit as well (to give us a God consciousness). The soul of every man is in the hands of God (Job 12:10, Ezek. 18:4). When the body experiences pain, the soul mourns (Job 14: 22). The soul acts through the body (Lev. 5:2; 7:18; 22:6).

Today, in the dispensation of grace, there is a spiritual circumcision (Col. 2:11) that separates the body (the outward man) from the soul and the spirit (the inward man – 2Cor 4:16). The sin nature dwells in the body (Rom 7:17-20). Therefore, what the sin nature does in the believer today will not be imputed to the believer's spiritual account (Rom 4:8) because of the spiritual circumcision that the Holy Spirit does in the believer today (Col. 2:10-12). However, all of that is unique to the operation of God in the dispensation of grace. Here in Matthew's gospel, we are dealing with a nation (Israel) that was under the Law of Moses. Israel under the Law had a physical circumcision but not the spiritual one.

Verse 33 "…whosoever shall deny me before men, him will I also deny before my Father…" is on the performance based acceptance system of the Law and not the absolute security basis of the believer today (cf. 2Tim. 2:9&10). The true believer in Israel's program will endure suffering for Christ. In the tribulation period, enduring to the end will be required for salvation (see notes on 10:22). Some will say "but Peter himself denied Christ in Matthew 26:24. However, that was not in the tribulation period. We today need to be willing to suffer for Christ as well. The thrust of 2Timothy 2:9-10 is that if we deny Him our suffering today, He will deny us the privilege of reigning with Him but He will not deny us life (2Tim. 2:9 & 10).

We need to remember the truth of Verses 30 & 31 as well as Israel will need to. God takes note of every sparrow that dies and has numbered (not just counted) the hairs of your head. He sure knows what is happening to you and cares more for you than many sparrows.

> **Matthew 10:34-39** "³⁴ Think not that I am come to send peace on earth: I came not to send peace, but a sword. ³⁵ For I am come to set a man at variance against his father, and the daughter against her mother, and the daughter in law against her mother in law. ³⁶ And a man's foes *shall be* they of his own household. ³⁷ He that loveth father or mother more than me is not worthy of me: and he that loveth son or daughter more than me is not worthy of me. ³⁸ And he that taketh not his cross, and followeth after me, is not worthy of me. ³⁹ He that findeth his life shall lose it: and he that loseth his life for my sake shall find it.

God is a divider of men. When a person today enters God's family, he or she enters into a new family circle wherein only are believers. It might not be that one's family of origin follows him into the family of God. This passage is not saying that a man should not love his father or mother or son or daughter. It is saying that a man should not love them above the love that he has for the Lord. If a man were to loose his life by being totally absorbed with Christ, he will gain everything else but if he seek to hang unto all of the other things of life without Christ, he will loose everything.

> **Matthew 10:40-42** "⁴⁰ He that receiveth you receiveth me, and he that receiveth me receiveth him that sent me. ⁴¹ He that receiveth a prophet in the name of a prophet shall receive a prophet's reward; and he that receiveth a righteous man in the name of a righteous man shall receive a righteous man's reward. ⁴² And whosoever shall give to drink unto one of these little ones a cup of cold *water* only in the name of a disciple, verily I say unto you, he shall in no wise lose his reward.

The man who humbly receives a true minister of Christ receives Christ and the Father who sent Him. The one who receives a prophet receives the blessing of being a prophet (cf. John 14:16-20; 17:17-27). The one who receives a righteous man receives the blessing of being a righteous man. The term "receive" here has to do with identification with Christ. We today call that fellowship.

Chapter 10 Study Guide Questions:

1. Describe the Commission the Lord gives in Verses 5 to 15. Where were they to go? Who were they to go to? What were they to take? What power did they have?

2. Compare this with the other commissions given to Israel (e.g. Matt. 28:19 & 20; Mark 16:16–19). What abilities or charges does each give to the apostles?

3. Verses 22 & 23 speak about enduring to the end in order to be saved. Should we preach this today?

4. What is verse 28 talking about regarding both the body and soul being destroyed in hell? When (at what time period in Bible history) will this be applicable? Can one's body be destroyed in hell today?

5. Verses 4 and 5 speak of personal conflicts even within families. How do we relate this with verses like Romans 12:18 "Live peaceably with all men..."?

Chapter 11

MATTHEW 11:1-30

The King is Rejected

Chapters 11 & 12 give the historical account of the first rejection of Christ by Israel as their King

Matthew 11:1-30 (KJV)

Mathew 11:1 "¹ And it came to pass, when Jesus had made an end of commanding his twelve disciples, he departed thence to teach and to preach in their cities."

A review of chapter 10 is in order here before we go on into chapter 11. In Chapter 10 we saw the Lord commission the twelve with the first of the commissions given to them. He commissions them to act against unclean spirits (10:1) and to heal all manner of diseases. Their names are given 10:2-4. Their commission was clear and precise:

Don't go to the Gentiles. (verse 6)

Don't go to the Samaritans

Go to the lost sheep of the house of Israel.

> Their message was simple "The kingdom of Heaven is at hand."
>
> Heal the sick (v. 8).
>
> Cleanse the lepers.
>
> Raise the dead.
>
> Cast out devils.
>
> Don't take any money (v. 9).
>
> Don't take a map.
>
> Don't take a change of clothes (v. 10).
>
> Don't arm yourselves.
>
> Seek out those who love the message (vv. 11-14).
>
> You will be as sheep in the mist of wolves (vv. 15-27).
>
> Don't worry you will be in the Father's hands (vv. 28–33).
>
> You will be in for an all out effort (vv. 34-39).
>
> Your focus must be the message:
>
> > Those that love the message will receive you.
> >
> > Those that receive you receive me.
> >
> > Those that receive me receive the Father.

Here in 11:1 He sends them out and goes out Himself to teach and to preach.

Matthew 11:2-6 "² Now when John had heard in the prison the works of Christ, he sent two of his disciples, ³ And said unto him, Art thou he that should come, or do we look for another? ⁴ Jesus answered and said unto them, Go and shew John again those things which ye do hear and see: ⁵ The blind receive their sight, and the lame walk, the lepers are cleansed, and the deaf hear, the dead are raised up, and the poor have the gospel preached to them. ⁶ And blessed is *he*, whosoever shall not be offended in me.

John is confused by what he hears. Why isn't the kingdom being established? Why is he in jail? He was put in jail in Matthew 4:12 & 13 and he will be until he is beheaded in (Matt. 14:10). John was wondering "What is going on?" John knew that Jesus is the Messiah (John 1:29–34). He expected that the kingdom would be rapidly established (Isa. 28:16). John is growing impatient. However, the Lord is teaching him a lesson that he and His disciples and the rest of the tribulation saints will have to learn – i.e. patience (Heb. 10:36). John did here what all of us should do when we are confused – go to the Word. John heard of the works that the Lord was doing. The Lord points to the works to dispel John's confusion because the works were the fulfillment of the Old Testament prophecies of Him. We saw Him point to the works that He was doing several times before (John 5:36 and 10:25). We will see Him do it again in John 14:11. John, as a student of the Bible could then look at the works of Jesus as the fulfillment of the prophecies such as:

> Isaiah 29:18 "[18] And in that day shall the deaf hear the words of the book, and the eyes of the blind shall see out of obscurity, and out of darkness."

> Isaiah 35:3-6 "[3] Strengthen ye the weak hands, and confirm the feeble knees. [4] Say to them *that are* of a fearful heart, Be strong, fear not: behold, your God will come *with* vengeance, *even* God *with* a recompence; he will come and save you. [5] Then the eyes of the blind shall be opened, and the ears of the deaf shall be unstopped. [6] Then shall the lame *man* leap as an hart, and the tongue of the dumb sing: for in the wilderness shall waters break out, and streams in the desert."

> Isaiah 42:6&7 "[6] I the LORD have called thee in righteousness, and will hold thine hand, and will keep thee, and give thee for a covenant of the people, for a light of the Gentiles; [7] To open the blind eyes, to bring out the prisoners from the prison, *and* them that sit in darkness out of the prison house."

> Isaiah 61:1 & 2 "[1] The Spirit of the Lord GOD *is* upon me; because the LORD hath anointed me to preach good tidings unto the meek; he hath sent me to bind up the brokenhearted, to proclaim liberty to the captives, and the opening of the prison to *them that are* bound; [2] To proclaim the acceptable year of the LORD, and the day of vengeance of our God; to comfort all that mourn…"

John could simply now believe and be patient – the Kingdom will come.

John and Elijah

> **Matthew 11:7-15** "[7] And as they departed, Jesus began to say unto the multitudes concerning John, What went ye out into the wilderness to see? A reed shaken with the wind? [8] But what went ye out for to see? A man clothed in soft raiment? behold, they that wear soft *clothing* are in kings' houses. [9] But what went ye out for to see? A prophet? yea, I say unto you, and more than a prophet. [10] For this is *he*, of whom it is written, Behold, I send my messenger before thy face, which shall prepare thy way before thee. [11] Verily I say unto you, Among them that are born of women there hath not risen a greater than John the Baptist: notwithstanding he that is least in the kingdom of heaven is greater than he. [12] And from the days of John the Baptist until now the kingdom of heaven suffereth violence, and the violent take it by force. [13] For all the prophets and the law prophesied until John. [14] And if ye will receive *it*, this is Elias, which was for to come. [15] He that hath ears to hear, let him hear."

Matthew 11:7-15 is an important passage to understand for its dispensational significance. This passage is the Lord's testimony to the faithfulness of John which He here gives to the multitude. In Verse 10 the Lord quotes Malachi 3:1 to tie John's ministry to the coming of the Messiah and the kingdom. John was a prophet and more than a prophet. John was the greatest of the prophets because he introduces the King and the Kingdom. But the least in the Kingdom would be greater than he (speaking of the glory of the kingdom). Verse 12 is to be understood that ever since John announced the kingdom, those who were in rulership in Israel (i.e. the violent in this verse – cf Luke 16:16) were jealous of their power and would take the kingdom from Christ by force to keep it to themselves. We will see more on this violence in the parable of the nobleman in Matthew 21:33-38. Verse 13 is to be understood that all of the work of the prophets pointed to that crisis point in time when John proclaimed the kingdom as being at hand. Verse 14 is to be understood as "And if ["until" cf.10:23] ye [Israel] will receive it [the kingdom of heaven referred to in Verse 12], this is Elias [Elijah (Mal. 4:5)] which was for to come." The point of Verse 14 is that "if" Israel would have repented and trusted Jesus Christ as Messiah, John would have filled the role of Elijah and Jesus would filled the role of the prophet like unto Moses and the kingdom would have been established. This was necessary in order for a genuine offer of the kingdom to be made.

It is important to note that God knew that Israel would reject the kingdom. However, He would have Israel without excuse. Therefore, he sends John the Baptist in the Spirit and power of Elijah. Remember what the angel tells Zacharias (John's father) regarding John "And he [John] shall go before him [the Lord] in the spirit and power of Elias, to turn the hearts of the fathers to the children, and the disobedient to the wisdom of the just; to make ready a people prepared for the Lord." This is exactly what Elijah was to do when he comes (Mal. 4:6). Also, Israel was to look for a prophet like unto Moses (Deut. 18:15). The Lord was that prophet (Acts 3:22-26; 7:37). Interestingly, we will see both Moses and Elijah appear with the Lord on the Mount of the Transfiguration in Matthew 17: 3-4.We find these two men in the Revelation as the two witnesses (Rev. 11:3 & 4) who turn out to be the two olive trees referred to in Zachariah 4:1-14. Comparing Malachi 3:1 with Mark 1:2-3 we can see that John is the promised messenger who was to prepare the way of the Lord (John 1:15-17).

Wisdom in Justified of her Children

Matthew 11:16-19 "16 But whereunto shall I liken this generation? It is like unto children sitting in the markets, and calling unto their fellows, 17 And saying, We have piped unto you, and ye have not danced; we have mourned unto you, and ye have not lamented. 18 For John came neither eating nor drinking, and they say, He hath a devil. 19 The Son of man came eating and drinking, and they say, Behold a man gluttonous, and a winebibber, a friend of publicans and sinners. But wisdom is justified of her children.

This is frustration on the part of Jesus and His disciples in the similitude of children calling to their playmates in the marketplace bidding them to participate but to no avail. They speak of joy of the Lord but there is no response. They speak of the mourning of the state of the nation but there is no lament or sympathy. John the Baptist came as an austere man who did not eat fine food nor drink wine and they did not listen to him but said he was possessed. The Lord came as a friendly man (a friend of sinners) to appeal to the lost as those who pipe.

The term: "Wisdom is justified of her children..." in Verse 19 needs some explanation. God uses many techniques to communicate Bible truth. The wise man understands that he must at times be "all things to all men..." (1Cor. 9:22) The Lord uses many different means to reach people. There are diversities of operations but one Spirit working through all (1Cor. 12:6). Some are "sons of thunder" (Mark 3:17) in their personalities while others are "sons of consolation: (Acts 4:36) but they both have their places in the ministry of reaching others with the gospel. The real issue is not the messenger but rather it is the wisdom from God communicated by the message. God's children acquire wisdom from the message and not from the messenger.

The Recalcitrant Generation

Matthew 11:20-24 "20 Then began he to upbraid the cities wherein most of his mighty works were done, because they repented not: 21 Woe unto thee, Chorazin! Woe unto thee, Bethsaida! For if the mighty works, which were done in you, had been done in Tyre and Sidon, they would have repented long ago in sackcloth and ashes. 22 But I say unto you, It shall be more tolerable for Tyre and Sidon at the day of judgment, than for you. [23] And thou, Capernaum, which art exalted unto heaven, shalt be brought down to hell: for if the mighty works, which have been done in thee, had been done in Sodom, it would have remained until this day. [24] But I say unto you, That it shall be more tolerable for the land of Sodom in the day of judgment, than for thee."

This is interesting – the Lord knows what would have been in Sodom, Tyre, and Sidon had the works done at the hands of the Lord and His disciples been done in that wicked city. Yet Chorazin and Bethsaida were rejecting Christ. Capernaum was exalted to heaven by the Lord's presence but will be brought down to hell. The Lord lived in Capernaum instead of Nazareth because his own family did not believe in Him (John 7:5). His friends taught that He had gone insane (Mark 3:21). His friends did not believe that He was God and could forgive sins (Luke 7:44-50).

Matthew 11:25-27 "[25] At that time Jesus answered and said, I thank thee, O Father, Lord of heaven and earth, because thou hast hid these things from the wise and prudent, and hast revealed them unto babes. [26] Even so, Father: for so it seemed good in thy sight. [27] All things are delivered unto me of my Father: and no man knoweth the Son, but the Father; neither knoweth any man the Father, save the Son, and *he* to whomsoever the Son will reveal *him*.

The only way to know the Father is through the Son. Peter was informed of the Son by the Father (Matt. 16:17). Knowledge of God comes from the triune God being at work in a person's life (1Cor. 1:18-21). He says that all things are delivered unto Him of the Father but He was experiencing rejection by all but a few babes.

Matthew 11:28-30 "[28] Come unto me, all *ye* that labour and are heavy laden, and I will give you rest. [29] Take my yoke upon you, and learn of me; for I am meek and lowly in heart: and ye shall find rest unto your souls. [30] For my yoke *is* easy, and my burden is light."

Jesus has given up on the nation at large and is focused on those that labor and are heavy laden for the nation. He speaks loving and comforting words to them because He knows that they will experience the same rejection that He experienced. The faithful believer can have perfect peace and rest in his heart in spite of seeming failure. That is a lesson that we who take a stand for the truth of the Word rightly divided today must learn and keep in memory.

This is a major crisis point for the nation. Isaiah 49: 1-12 (see below) is prophetic of this situation in Israel that we see developing and coming to the forefront here in Matthew Chapter 11. "Thou *art* my servant, O Israel, in whom I will be glorified." This is in Isaiah 49:3. This passage is calling Israel God's servant in whom the Lord will be glorified. However, as we read Verse 2 "he hath made my mouth like a sharp sword…" we understand that it is also talking about Jesus. In Revelation 19:15 it is said of Jesus "And out of his mouth goeth a sharp sword, that with it he should smite the nations." Then as we read Verse 4 "I have laboured in vain, I have spent my strength for nought, and in vain: *yet* surely my judgment *is* with the LORD, and my work with my God…" our thoughts go to the discouragement that our Lord must have felt here in Matthew Chapter 11. Yet, though the Lord was rejected and it appeared that he had labored in vain, His confidence was in the Father. "Though Israel be not gathered, yet shall I be glorious in the eyes of the LORD, and my God shall be my strength." (Isa. 49:5) Israel was not gathered as a result of the Lord's earthly ministry to the nation but one day the nation will be gathered. That will be joy as Paul cites in Romans 11:12 "Now if the fall of them *be* the riches of the world, and the diminishing of them the riches of the Gentiles; how much more their fulness?"

Isaiah 49:8 is referenced in 2Corinthians 6:2 "(For he saith, I have heard thee in a time accepted, and in the day of salvation have I succoured thee: behold, now *is* the accepted time; behold, now *is* the day of salvation.)" It is as though the apostle in 2Corinthians 6:2-10 takes us to this time of frustration in our

Lord's ministry to encourage us in times of adversity to look past the short term failures to the ultimate success of total victory that was finally the Lord's as a result of Calvary.

Isaiah 49:1-12

[1] Listen, O isles, unto me; and hearken, ye people, from far; The LORD hath called me from the womb; from the bowels of my mother hath he made mention of my name. [2] And he hath made my mouth like a sharp sword; in the shadow of his hand hath he hid me, and made me a polished shaft; in his quiver hath he hid me; [3] And said unto me, Thou *art* my servant, O Israel, in whom I will be glorified.

[4] Then I said, I have laboured in vain, I have spent my strength for nought, and in vain: *yet* surely my judgment *is* with the LORD, and my work with my God. [5] And now, saith the LORD that formed me from the womb *to be* his servant, to bring Jacob again to him, Though Israel be not gathered, yet shall I be glorious in the eyes of the LORD, and my God shall be my strength. [6] And he said, It is a light thing that thou shouldest be my servant to raise up the tribes of Jacob, and to restore the preserved of Israel: I will also give thee for a light to the Gentiles, that thou mayest be my salvation unto the end of the earth. [7] Thus saith the LORD, the Redeemer of Israel, *and* his Holy One, to him whom man despiseth, to him whom the nation abhorreth, to a servant of rulers, Kings shall see and arise, princes also shall worship, because of the LORD that is faithful, *and* the Holy One of Israel, and he shall choose thee. [8] Thus saith the LORD, In an acceptable time have I heard thee, and in a day of salvation have I helped thee: and I will preserve thee, and give thee for a covenant of the people, to establish the earth, to cause to inherit the desolate heritages; [9] That thou mayest say to the prisoners, Go forth; to them that *are* in darkness, Shew yourselves. They shall feed in the ways, and their pastures *shall be* in all high places. [10] They shall not hunger nor thirst; neither shall the heat nor sun smite them: for he that hath mercy on them shall lead them, even by the springs of water shall he guide them. [11] And I will make all my mountains a way, and my highways shall be exalted. [12] Behold, these shall come from far: and, lo, these from the north and from the west; and these from the land of Sinim." (Isaiah 49: 4- 12)

This passage in Isaiah is prophetic of what the Lord experienced in His earthly ministry to Israel. Isaiah Chapter 49 begins the prophecy of the Messiah as the suffering Savior. The suffering intensifies as the book of Isaiah progresses to Chapter 53 where we see the full prophecy of the suffering. Note on Verse 12 – Sinim is what we call China today.

Chapter 11 Study Guide Questions:

1. Why is John the Baptist confused and bewildered in Verses 2 to 6?

2. What should we conclude from Verses 7 through 14? Is John actually Elias?

3. Explain the phrase "wisdom is justified of her children" in Verse 19.

4. How do you see the Lord's focus of the attention changing in Chapter 11? Do we see a shift in what He puts His attention on from here on in Matthew's Gospel?

MATTHEW 12:1-50

THE SON IS BLASPHEMED

In Chapter 11, we see the Lord realizing that the nation at large will reject Him. He then (in Chapter 12) proceeds to demonstrate that he is the creator of the Sabbath, (12:1-14), the Redeemer (12:22-37), and the Savior of men (12:38-50). He shows that he is greater than the temple (Verse 6), greater than Jonah (Verse 41), and greater than Solomon (Verse 47). These all relate to His three fold office to Israel as Prophet (i.e. greater than Jonah), Priest (i.e. greater that the temple), and King (i.e. greater than Solomon).

Matthew 12:1-8 "[1] At that time Jesus went on the sabbath day through the corn; and his disciples were an hungred, and began to pluck the ears of corn, and to eat. [2] But when the Pharisees saw *it*, they said unto him, Behold, thy disciples do that which is not lawful to do upon the sabbath day. [3] But he said unto them, Have ye not read what David did, when he was an hungred, and they that were with him; [4] How he entered into the house of God, and did eat the shewbread, which was not lawful for him to eat, neither for them which were with him, but only for the priests? [5] Or have ye not read in the law, how that on the sabbath days the priests in the temple profane the sabbath, and are blameless? [6] But I say unto you, That in this place is *one* greater than the temple. [7] But if ye had known what *this* meaneth, I will have mercy, and not sacrifice, ye would not have condemned the guiltless. [8] For the Son of man is Lord even of the sabbath day.

It was a lawful thing to pluck ears (kernels of corn or wheat of one's neighbor as long as you didn't take it with a sickle -- Deut 23:35). It would have been a violation of the law to grind the wheat and bake it on the Sabbath. The Pharisees went beyond the law with their traditions and could not in their minds separate the Law from their traditions. In Matthew 15:2 they ask: why do thy disciples transgress the tradition of the elders? For they wash not their hands when they eat bread." The Lord's response in Verse 3 is another question, "why do ye also transgress the commandment of God by your traditions?"

In Verse 6 He is staking His claim as the Messiah in that He is greater than the temple. The temple where the priests do their service is given for the worship of God but here in their presence was God in the flesh. The Sabbath is a token of the Mosaic covenant between God and men. As God, He is not bound by the Sabbath but is Lord of the Sabbath even though as Man He did not violate the Sabbath.

It should be noted that the only Sabbath that the Lord has ever observed was in Genesis when he rested on the seventh day of creation week after He made the earth a suitable habitation for man. Man's sin has broken the Sabbath of rest for God. Ever since then, God has been at work repairing that broken rest. "My Father worketh hitherto and I work" (John 5:17). A Sabbath can only be truly celebrated when there is nothing to be done. Our Lord while on earth had no rest. The Sabbath of the law was not given to God but to man. He is the Lord of the Sabbath; the one who owns the Sabbath (Matt. 12:8). That is because the Sabbath was made for man (Mark 2:27). The fact that Christ worked on the Sabbath (Luke 6:8) is proof that He is God much as was His power to forgive sins (Mark 2:5-11; Luke 5:20-21). It should be noted that Christ was in the grave working redemption while man was celebrating the Sabbath. The Sabbath was never changed (Matt. 28:1). The Sabbath belonged to the law and to Israel. The church which is Christ's body is free from the law and the Sabbath being as free as Christ Himself (Col. 2:10). We do not keep the day that our Lord spent in the tomb. Rather, Christians traditionally gather on the first day of the week (1Cor. 16:2;

Acts 20:7) while the Sabbath continued to be the meeting day for Israel (Acts 13:14; 44). Paul attended meetings on the Sabbath (Acts 17:2) but told believers to remain free from Sabbath keeping (Col. 2:16).

Note from Matthew 28:1-6 that it was on "end of the Sabbath" that our Lord arose from the grave (cf. Luke 24:1; John 20:1, 19, 26). So we ask "Did God change the Sabbath from the seventh day to the first day of the week?" No! There is no statement to this anywhere in scripture. We find a tradition of the first day meeting (1Cor. 16:2; Acts 20:7) but no command for we are free from the law (Col. 2:14-16) today in the dispensation of grace. Fellowship is indispensable in a believer's life and it is good to have a day devoted to fellowship. We gather for the purpose of mutual appreciation of faith and Christian practice rather than mere duty and obligation. The Sabbath was given to Israel and Israel will one day have her Sabbath (Heb. 4:9 cf. 3:11). We living today in the Dispensation of Grace can have rest for our souls as we assume our position of being seated with Christ far above principalities and powers (Eph. 4:10). However, though we look forward to rest at the rapture (2Thess. 1:7), we have no rest in our spirit as we labor to reach others in this present evil world (Gal. 1:4; 2Cor. 2:13; 2:5). The Sabbath was not given as a command until Sinai (Neh. 9:13). We see it given in Exodus 20:11 as a "sign" between God and Israel. It was the sign of the Mosaic covenant.

Verse 7 is a quote from Hosea 6:6 "But I desired mercy, and not sacrifice; and the knowledge of God more than burnt offerings." The Pharisees were so concerned with the letter of the law and with the traditions that they added to it that they had forgotten that God is a God of mercy and that he provides for His people. Had they remembered that they would not have jumped to the conclusion that they did. The scribes and Pharisees have added their traditions to the law and were not going to give up on their traditions. When the Lord exposes their hardness of heart, they decide to destroy Him rather than to repent and be converted.

> **Matthew 12:9-13** "⁹ And when he was departed thence, he went into their synagogue: ¹⁰ And, behold, there was a man which had *his* hand withered. And they asked him, saying, Is it lawful to heal on the sabbath days? that they might accuse him. ¹¹ And he said unto them, What man shall there be among you, that shall have one sheep, and if it fall into a pit on the sabbath day, will he not lay hold on it, and lift *it* out? ¹² How much then is a man better than a sheep? Wherefore it is lawful to do well on the sabbath days. ¹³ Then saith he to the man, Stretch forth thine hand. And he stretched *it* forth; and it was restored whole, like as the other."

The Scribes and Pharisees have decided in their hearts to reject the Lord Jesus Christ as Messiah. They have to find some way to justify their decision. Therefore, they need to find some way to accuse Him of wrong doing. Though the Lord had every right to pluck corn, He none the less takes them to 1Samuel 21:1-6 where David ate the shew bread. David was a type of Christ as a prophet and a king. Christ is a prophet, a priest and a king. Moses too was a type of Christ as he was both a prophet and a king (Deut. 18:15; 33:5). The scribes should have known that Christ would be a prophet, a priest, and a king. Since the priest can work on the Sabbath without violating it, He could too.

Here in Verses 9-14 He heals a man on the Sabbath to further press the point that He is Lord even of the Sabbath. The Sabbath was given to Israel as a sign (Ezekiel.20:20) by which they were to remember that they as a nation were God's unique possession and that God would one day give them rest (Exodus 31:12-18). Neither the Covenant nor the Sabbath was given to the Gentiles.

> **Matthew 12:14** ¹⁴ Then the Pharisees went out, and held a council against him, how they might destroy him.

Here is the turning point in Matthew's Gospel. From here to the end of the book the Lord changes His Modus Operandi. He is no longer presenting the offer of the Kingdom to Israel but is preparing the little flock to carry on in offering the kingdom to Israel during His absence from them.

> **Matthew 12:15-21** "¹⁵But when Jesus knew *it*, he withdrew himself from thence: and great multitudes followed him, and he healed them all; ¹⁶And charged them that they should not make him known: ¹⁷That it might be fulfilled which was spoken by Esaias the prophet, saying, ¹⁸Behold my servant, whom I have chosen; my beloved, in whom my soul is well pleased: I will put my spirit upon him, and he shall shew judgment to the Gentiles. ¹⁹He shall not strive, nor cry; neither shall any man hear his voice in the streets. ²⁰A bruised reed shall he not break, and smoking flax shall he not quench, till he send forth judgment unto victory. ²¹And in his name shall the Gentiles trust.

The reference to the bruised reed and the smoking flax is hard for people to understand. It is a reference to Isaiah 42:1-4. The bruised reed is a type of unbelief while the burning flax is a type of the offensiveness of Israel's rebellion. When He returns the second time to Israel He will deal with both. However, for now he makes a resolve to heal all who come to Him. However, as he does, He charges those healed to not make Him known. He is preparing to go to the cross and to be able to say "Father forgive them for they know not what they do."

> **Matthew 12:22-37** "²²Then was brought unto him one possessed with a devil, blind, and dumb: and he healed him, insomuch that the blind and dumb both spake and saw. ²³And all the people were amazed, and said, Is not this the son of David? ²⁴But when the Pharisees heard *it*, they said, This *fellow* doth not cast out devils, but by Beelzebub the prince of the devils ²⁵And Jesus knew their thoughts, and said unto them, Every kingdom divided against itself is brought to desolation; and every city or house divided against itself shall not stand: ²⁶And if Satan cast out Satan, he is divided against himself; how shall then his kingdom stand? ²⁷And if I by Beelzebub cast out devils, by whom do your children cast *them* out? therefore they shall be your judges. ²⁸But if I cast out devils by the Spirit of God, then the kingdom of God is come unto you. ²⁹Or else how can one enter into a strong man's house, and spoil his goods, except he first bind the strong man? and then he will spoil his house. ³⁰He that is not with me is against me; and he that gathereth not with me scattereth abroad. ³¹Wherefore I say unto you, All manner of sin and blasphemy shall be forgiven unto men: but the blasphemy *against* the *Holy* Ghost shall not be forgiven unto men. ³²And whosoever speaketh a word against the Son of man, it shall be forgiven him: but whosoever speaketh against the Holy Ghost, it shall not be forgiven him, neither in this world, neither in the *world* to come. ³³Either make the tree good, and his fruit good; or else make the tree corrupt, and his fruit corrupt: for the tree is known by *his* fruit. ³⁴O generation of vipers, how can ye, being evil, speak good things? for out of the abundance of the heart the mouth speaketh. ³⁵A good man out of the good treasure of the heart bringeth forth good things: and an evil man out of the evil treasure bringeth forth evil things. ³⁶But I say unto you, That every idle word that men shall speak, they shall give account thereof in the day of judgment. ³⁷For by thy words thou shalt be justified, and by thy words thou shalt be condemned.

Verses 22 to 28 are a very significant passage of scripture to understand if one is to see the dispensational changes that take place in the New Testament scriptures. This passage introduces the "Unpardonable Sin." In Verses 22-28, a man possessed of a devil which caused blindness and dumbness was brought to Him and He heals the man by casting out the devil. People start to realize that this is what the Messiah would be doing and begin to ask if Jesus is the promised Son of David – their Messiah.

In Verse 24 the Pharisees attribute His work of casting out devils to Beelzebub the prince of devils. They are blaspheming Jesus Christ the Son of God by attributing His work to Satan.

In Verses 25-26 the Lord is pointing out that Satan has a kingdom that he is maintaining. Someone is making an assault on that kingdom. Obviously that someone would not be Beelzebub. In Verse 27 The Lord asks them "By whom do your children cast them out?" This is a reference to the little flock that had followed Him and had been casting out devils (Luke 10:17). In Verses 28 and 29, Christ is casting out devils by the Spirit of God who is making an attack on the kingdom of Satan. The strong man in Verse 29 is Satan and the strong man's house is Israel. Christ came to spoil the strong man's house. However, He must first bind the strong man (Beelzebub) to do so.

Verse 30 makes the important point of the passage. Christ will spoil Satan. Those that are with Him will participate in His victory. Those that are not with Him will be with the adversary and will be scattered in defeat. Isaiah 50:5-10 describes the conflict that occurred on the cross in which Christ wins the victory over Satan.

Verse 31 defines the unpardonable sin for us. They blasphemed the Son by attributing the work that He did to the devil. They were also blaspheming the Holy Spirit by attributing the work that the Holy Spirit did through the Son to the devil. What was said against the Son would be forgiven. However, what is said against the Holy Spirit will not be forgiven – not then nor in the world to come (which will be at Pentecost in the Book of Acts).

The stoning of Stephen is what is in view here. The blasphemy against the Holy Spirit would not be forgiven: "…but whosoever speaketh against the Holy Ghost, it shall not be forgiven him, neither in this world, neither in the *world* to come." It would not be forgiven in this world (that being the gospel era in which the Lord ministered to Israel during His earthly ministry) nor in the world to come (that being Pentecost and the tribulation which was to follow). Stephan was "…a man full of faith and of the Holy Ghost…" (Acts 6:5). He tells Israel "…ye do always resist the Holy Ghost…" (Acts 7:51 cf. Neh. 9:30; Prov. 29:1).

The culpability of the scribes and Pharisees is seen in John 9:32-41 "[39] And Jesus said, For judgment I am come into this world, that they which see not might see; and that they which see might be made blind. [40]And *some* of the Pharisees which were with him heard these words, and said unto him, Are we blind also? [41]Jesus said unto them, If ye were blind, ye should have no sin: but now ye say, We see; therefore your sin remaineth." In this matter of culpability, 1Timothy 1:13 must be considered with regard to Paul who had also committed the unpardonable sin of blaspheming the Holy Ghost in that he did not believe the testimony of the remnant of Israel as the Holy Ghost ministered through them. He blasphemed the Holy Spirit but was forgiven. This serves as proof that a new dispensation began with the saving of Saul of Tarsus. In order to save Saul of Tarsus (and us) God put a new dispensation between the world represented by the earthly ministry of Christ and the world to come (that being Pentecost and the coming tribulation period).

Verses 33-37 "Every idle word that a man shall speak, they shall give account thereof in the day of judgment. For by thy words thou shalt be justified, and by they words shalt thou be condemned." Israel had to confess Christ to be justified. "If thou shalt confess with thy mouth the Lord Jesus, and shalt believe in thine heart that God hath raised him from the dead, thou shalt be saved." (Rom 10:9 & 10 cf. John 12:42 & 43).

Israel is condemning herself by these words against Christ. But an interesting thing happens here in Israel's situation at this point in time. We read in John 12:40 (cf. Isa. 6:9 & 10 & Matt. 13:14) "He hath blinded their eyes, and hardened their heart: that they should not see with their eyes, nor understand with their heart, and be converted, and I should heal them." God imposed a judicial blindness on the nation so that the Lord could say from the cross "Father forgive them for they know not what they do:" (Luke 23:34) and Peter could tell them "I wot that through ignorance ye did it, as did your rulers. But those things, which God before shewed by the mouth of all his prophets; that Christ should suffer, he hath so fulfilled." (Acts 3:17 & 18).

The Sign of the Prophet Jonah

> **Matthew 12:38-40** "[38] Then certain of the scribes and of the Pharisees answered, saying, Master, we would see a sign from thee. [39] But he answered and said unto them, An evil and adulterous generation seeketh after a sign; and there shall no sign be given to it, but the sign of the prophet Jonas: [40] For as Jonas was three days and three nights in the whale's belly; so shall the Son of man be three days and three nights in the heart of the earth.

Verses 39 and 40 speak of the sign of the prophet Jonah. Jonah died and rose three days later. The next sign that Israel will be getting will be the resurrection of Jesus Christ three days after His death and burial. However, they will not believe it. If one will not believe the Word of God, no sign will suffice (Luke 16:31). The sign of the prophet Jonah was that he was three days and three nights in the whale's belly. The following is proof that Christ did not die on a Friday:

- Christ died before the Sabbath (Matt. 27:62; 28:1; John 19:31)
- Christ rose on the third day (1Cor. 15:3)
- He rose on the first day of the week (Luke 24:1 & 2)
- He told them that He would rise from the dead in three days (John 2:19).
- They understood what He meant (Matt. 27:62-64)
- Three days is significant in scripture as a time of proving.
  - (2Chronicles 10:5-12)
  - (Ester 4:16-5:1)
  - (1Samuel 30: 11-13)
- John 19:31 refers to the Sabbath as the high Sabbath (That means it was one of the seven feasts of the Lord -- in this case the Passover). The order of events for the Passover was:
  - They select a lamb on the tenth day of the month (Exodus 12)
  - They watch it three days (That would be the 11th, 12th, and 13th) In Chapter 12 we will see him examined by the Herodians, the Sadducees, and the Pharisees.
  - They kill the lamb on the 14th
  - They roast the lamb and eat it on the 15th.
- The Feast of Unleavened bread followed on the 15th thru the 21st of the month. (the first and last days of the feast were holy convocations)
- Christ entered Jerusalem on the 10th to be the real Passover lamb.

> **Matthew 12:41** "[41] The men of Nineveh shall rise in judgment with this generation, and shall condemn it: because they repented at the preaching of Jonas; and, behold, a greater than Jonas *is* here."

We understand several things from this verse:
1. The men of Nineveh were saved by repenting and turning from their sins at the preaching of Jonah
2. The generation that the Lord was addressing here will perish for not believing Christ.

> **Matthew 12:42** "[42] The queen of the south shall rise up in the judgment with this generation, and shall condemn it: for she came from the uttermost parts of the earth to hear the wisdom of Solomon; and, behold, a greater than Solomon *is* here."

We understand from this:
1. The queen (Of Sheba) was saved by what she learned from Solomon about God's dealing with man.

2. While God sent Jonah to Nineveh, the queen of the south came of her own accord to learn wisdom from Solomon.
3. Israel had the blessing of God sending His Son to them but they shunned His wisdom.

Matthew 12:43-45 "⁴³ When the unclean spirit is gone out of a man, he walketh through dry places, seeking rest, and findeth none. ⁴⁴ Then he saith, I will return into my house from whence I came out; and when he is come, he findeth *it* empty, swept, and garnished. ⁴⁵ Then goeth he, and taketh with himself seven other spirits more wicked than himself, and they enter in and dwell there: and the last *state* of that man is worse than the first. Even so shall it be also unto this wicked generation."

The man with the unclean spirit in this passage represents Israel at the time of the captivity in Babylon. Israel was under the influence of demonic possession when they were steeped in the idolatry that led to the 70 years of captivity. The captivity resulted in them giving up on their idolatry. The demons that left Israel came back to the nation again and brought reinforcements. However, this time the demons were not interested on getting Israel back into idolatry but rather on getting the nation to reject her Messiah. The last state of the nation (Verse 45) is a reference to the state in which the nation was in during the Lord's earthy ministry to Israel. It is also a reference to the state of the nation during the ministry of the Holy Spirit to the nation in the early part of the Book of Acts,

Matthew 12:46-50 "⁴⁶ While he yet talked to the people, behold, *his* mother and his brethren stood without, desiring to speak with him. ⁴⁷ Then one said unto him, Behold, thy mother and thy brethren stand without, desiring to speak with thee. ⁴⁸ But he answered and said unto him that told him, Who is my mother? and who are my brethren? ⁴⁹ And he stretched forth his hand toward his disciples, and said, Behold my mother and my brethren! ⁵⁰ For whosoever shall do the will of my Father which is in heaven, the same is my brother, and sister, and mother."

Just as today, when we get saved, we find that we have a new set of brothers and sisters. In verses 49 & 50, the Lord is setting the nation at large aside and is focusing on the believing remnant in the nation. The kingdom is being taken away from the leaders of the nation and is being given to the "Little Flock of believers." (Matt. 21:43; Luke 12:31)

Chapter 12 Study Guide Questions:

1. Did the Lord and His disciples violate the Law by plucking grain on the Sabbath?

2. Did the Lord violate the Sabbath by healing in Verses 9 through 13?

3. What change in direction does the Lord make in His ministry in Verses 15 – 20?

4. What exactly is the unpardonable sin in Verses 22 through 28?

5. Why was blaspheming the Lord pardonable but blaspheming the Holy Ghost was not?

6. Did Israel blaspheme the Spirit? When did the nation do that?

7. In Verses 28 and 29:

   a. What is the strong man's house?
   b. Who is the strong man?
   c. Who came to spoil the strong man's house?
   d. What must He do in order to spoil that house?

8. How could Paul have gotten saved having committed the unpardonable sin?

9. Who does the man with the unclean Spirit in Verses 43 to 45 represent? What eventually happened to that man in the parable?

MATTHEW 13:1-58

The Mysteries of the Kingdom of Heaven

The Lord makes a major shift in His ministry to Israel here in Matthew Chapter 13. From here on in Matthew's gospel, He ministers to Israel speaking in parables. In Verse 34 we are informed by Matthew that "…without a parable spoke he not unto them…" There are seven parables here in Chapter 13. They are:

1. The Parable of the Sower (Verse 3)
2. The Parable of the tares among the wheat (Verse 24)
3. The Parable of the mustard seed (Verse 31)
4. The Parable of the leavened meal (Verse 33)
5. The Parable of the treasure hid in a field (Verse 44)
6. The Parable of the pearl of great price. (Verse 45)
7. The Parable of the dragnet (Verse 47)

The Parable of the Sower

Matthew 13:1-8 "[1] The same day went Jesus out of the house, and sat by the sea side. [2] And great multitudes were gathered together unto him, so that he went into a ship, and sat; and the whole multitude stood on the shore. [3] And he spake many things unto them in parables, saying, Behold, a sower went forth to sow; [4] And when he sowed, some *seeds* fell by the way side, and the fowls came and devoured them up: [5] Some fell upon stony places, where they had not much earth: and forthwith they sprung up, because they had no deepness of earth: [6] And when the sun was up, they were scorched; and because they had no root, they withered away. [7] And some fell among thorns; and the thorns sprung up, and choked them: [8] But other fell into good ground, and brought forth fruit, some an hundredfold, some sixtyfold, some thirtyfold."

This parable is explained below by the Lord. We will study it in some detail there. First however, He explains why he is speaking to them in parables.

Matthew 13:9 "[9] Who hath ears to hear, let him hear."

This expression is used often by the Lord. This is actually a sort of warning. The one who hears the message is responsible to obey and will be ultimately judged on whether or not he did obey the message that he heard.

Matthew 13:10-17 "[10] And the disciples came, and said unto him, Why speakest thou unto them in parables? [11] He answered and said unto them, Because it is given unto you to know the mysteries of the kingdom of heaven, but to them it is not given. [12] For whosoever hath, to him shall be given, and he shall have more abundance: but whosoever hath not, from him shall be taken away even that he hath. [13] Therefore speak I to them in parables: because they seeing see not; and hearing they hear not, neither do they understand. [14] And in them is fulfilled the prophecy of Esaias, which saith, By hearing ye shall hear, and shall not understand; and seeing ye shall see, and shall not perceive: [15] For this people's heart is waxed gross, and *their* ears are dull of hearing, and their eyes they have closed; lest at any time they should see with *their* eyes, and hear with *their* ears, and should understand with *their* heart, and should be converted, and I should heal them. [16] But blessed *are* your eyes, for they see: and your ears, for they hear. [17] For verily I say unto you, That many prophets and righteous *men* have desired to see *those things* which ye see, and have not seen *them*; and to hear *those things* which ye hear, and have not heard *them*.

The parables are all about the mysteries of the kingdom of heaven (Verses 10 & 11). There are seven mysteries presented in the seven parables in Chapter 13; all which relate to the fact that the kingdom of heaven is going to be presented, preached, and proclaimed to Israel without the king being present. The Lord will instruct His disciples on these mysteries through the remainder of the Book of Matthew. To understand the parables, we need to remember:

- They all pertain to Israel.
- They all relate to the Kingdom of Heaven being established on the earth.
- None of them relate to or are about us living in the Dispensation of the Grace of God.
- They have an interpretation found elsewhere in the Scriptures (i.e. they can be interpreted by comparing scripture with scripture).
- Every detail is there for a reason.
- The seven parables of Matthew 13 relate to the seven churches of the Revelation and the seven stars (See the *Study on the Book of the Revelation* by the same author).
- The understanding of the first parable (given in Verses 18 – 23) gives the key to understanding the other parables (Mark 4:13).

The disciples question is certainly a logical one - "Why is the Lord all of a sudden starting to speak in parables when before this He was speaking plainly to them in simple to understand terms?" From here on in His earthly ministry he is operating with the cross in view. He wants to be able to say from the cross "Father, forgive them for they know not what they do." (Luke 23:34). He is going to be telling them about the mysteries of the kingdom of heaven but it is only the believing remnant that is going to understand. Those in Israel outside of the remnant have closed their eyes so they would not see and have stopped their ears so they could not hear or understand. We see people do that today. In Verse 12, a gift unused is lost but, if it is used, it grows and develops. The gift in view here is spiritual vision. In Verses 13 thru 15 seeing they see not, hearing they hear not, and their mental faculties have they not used to grasp the truth. They deliberately chose to not see, to not hear, and thus to not understand and therefore not believe. Therefore, the Lord speaks in parables so that, though they see, they will not understand; and though they hear, they will not perceive. Verse 14 is a reference to Isaiah 6:9-10 where we see the Lord telling Isaiah of Israel's obstinacy "[9] And he said, Go, and tell this people, Hear ye indeed, but understand not; and see ye indeed, but perceive not. [10] Make the heart of this people fat, and make their ears heavy, and shut their eyes; lest they see with their eyes, and hear with their ears, and understand with their heart, and convert, and be healed."

Note also the Lord's words to Ezekiel in 12:1-2 "[1] The word of the LORD also came unto me, saying, [2] Son of man, thou dwellest in the midst of a rebellious house, which have eyes to see, and see not; they have ears to hear, and hear not: for they *are* a rebellious house."

Consider John 12:37– 42 in light of this:

"[37] But though he had done so many miracles before them, yet they believed not on him: [38] That the saying of Esaias the prophet might be fulfilled, which he spake, Lord, who hath believed our report? and to whom hath the arm of the Lord been revealed? [39] Therefore they could not believe, because that Esaias said again, [40] He hath blinded their eyes, and hardened their heart; that they should not see with *their* eyes, nor understand with *their* heart, and be converted, and I should heal them. [41] These things said Esaias, when he saw his glory, and spake of him [42] Nevertheless among the chief rulers also many believed on him; but because of the Pharisees they did not confess *him*, lest they should be put out of the synagogue: [43] For they loved the praise of men more than the praise of God."

The Reason for the Judicial, Temporary Blindness

Romans 10:9 & 10 is a significant passage in light of John 12:42-43. In Israel, it was important to not only believe but to confess Christ publically. About half way through the Lord's earthly ministry to Israel, He imposed a judicial blindness on the nation at large. That blindness was imposed to keep them from grasping what he is telling the believing remnant. The reason for this is understood when we realize that the Lord did not want Israel as a nation culpable for the crucifixion. After the cross, the blindness was removed so that the nation could have an opportunity to repent and to trust Jesus Christ as her Messiah and many did (Acts 2:47). However, the nation at large, in spite of having the blindness removed after the cross, still did not trust Him (Acts 28:25-28) . As a result, yet another type of blindness happened to Israel as Romans Chapter 11 explains (Rom. 11:7-13, 25) that blindness which is actually a dispensationally significant blindness.

Romans 11:5-15 (KJV)

"[5] Even so then at this present time also there is a remnant according to the election of grace. [6] And if by grace, then *is it* no more of works: otherwise grace is no more grace. But if *it be* of works, then is it no more grace: otherwise work is no more work. [7] What then? Israel hath not obtained that which he seeketh for; but the election hath obtained it, and the rest were blinded [8] (According as it is written, God hath given them the spirit of slumber, eyes that they should not see, and ears that they should not hear;) unto this day. [9] And David saith, Let their table be made a snare, and a trap, and a stumblingblock, and a recompence unto them: [10] Let their eyes be darkened, that they may not see, and bow down their back alway. [11] I say then, Have they stumbled that they should fall? God forbid: but *rather* through their fall salvation *is come* unto the Gentiles, for to provoke them to jealousy. [12] Now if the fall of them *be* the riches of the world, and the diminishing of them the riches of the Gentiles; how much more their fulness? [13] For I speak to you Gentiles, inasmuch as I am the apostle of the Gentiles, I magnify mine office: [14] If by any means I may provoke to emulation *them which are* my flesh, and might save some of them. [15] For if the casting away of them *be* the reconciling of the world, what *shall* the receiving *of them be*, but life from the dead?"

The "election of grace" in Romans 11:5 marks the distinction between a member of the "little flock" (Luke 12:32) and the Body of Christ -- the elect of the mystery program. Under the Kingdom program, the performing of the works of the Law and the submission to water baptism where required manifestations of faith (Matthew 19:21; Mark 10:21; Luke 12:33; Acts 2:44; 4:32). Under the dispensation of the grace of God, there is a remnant of believers that is being saved by the pure unmerited grace of God (Ephesians 2:8-9) without works.

Romans 11:6 (quoted above) is as clear a statement the Holy Spirit could make to the effect that works and grace are two mutually exclusive concepts as a means of justification today in the dispensation of grace. There is absolutely no mix of the two in Paul's epistles. Justification today in the dispensation of the grace of God is purely on the basis of grace through the means of faith (Romans 4:3-5). Under the Kingdom program, works were a factor in justification (James 2:21-22) as James says "Ye see then how that by works a man is justified, and not by faith only." (James 2:24) Paul on the other hand (writing to a different group – the Body of Christ) writes "…We conclude that a man is justified by faith without the deeds of the Law" (Rom 3:28) and "…To him that worketh not, but believeth on him that justifieth the ungodly, his faith is counted for righteousness." (Rom. 4:5).

We might ask here "What was it that Israel was seeking?" The answer is in Romans 10:3, 6-10; and 9:31-32). Israel followed after the law of righteousness but did not attain to it because they did not follow after it by faith. Instead they, being ignorant of God's righteousness and going about to establish their own righteousness hath not attained to the righteousness of God. What Israel was seeking but did not attain to was righteousness. The elect however, in this passage receive righteousness by faith. Faith was the missing ingredient for Israel as a nation during the Acts period.

"The rest" (in Romans 11:7) who were blinded here are the unbelievers of Israel at the time when Israel was set aside as a nation. It isn't that they were blind when the gospel of the kingdom was offered to them. That would have given them an excuse. Rather, they were blinded in a sense by God because they refused to see the truth. Let's consider the sequence of events leading up to this blindness:

First we note that our Lord during His earthly ministry to Israel began by speaking plainly to Israel. However, in Mathew 12 something started to change. Israel's leaders blasphemed Christ by saying that He casts out devils by Beelzebub the prince of devils. The Lord responds by introducing the unpardonable sin (Matt. 12:28-32).

Then, in Matthew 13, He begins to speak in Parables so that only the disciples can understand what he is saying. He explained His motives saying: "Because it is given unto you to know the mysteries of the kingdom of heaven, but to them it is not given. [12] For whosoever hath, to him shall be given, and he shall have more abundance: but whosoever hath not, from him shall be taken away even that he hath. [13] Therefore speak I to them in parables: because they seeing see not; and hearing they hear not, neither do they understand. [14] And in them is fulfilled the prophecy of Esaias, which saith, By hearing ye shall hear, and shall not understand; and seeing ye shall see, and shall not perceive: [15] For this people's heart is waxed gross, and their ears are dull of hearing, and their eyes they have closed; lest at any time they should see with their eyes, and hear with their ears, and should understand with their heart, and should be converted, and I should heal them." (Matt. 13:11-15) Because they refused to see, He blinds their eyes so that they couldn't see. He did this so that He could genuinely say on the cross "Father forgive them for they know not what they do." However, the blindness lasted only until after His death, burial and resurrection.

Israel as a nation finally committed the unpardonable sin when they refused to believe the gospel as the Holy Ghost ministered to the nation through the believing remnant in early Acts. They reject the witness of the Holy Spirit as He ministered to Israel through the twelve. This act of rejection was in effect to blaspheme the Holy Spirit. It was at the stoning of Stephen that the nation was set aside and the dispensation of grace began.

Paul cites Isaiah 29:9-10 to explain the nature of the blindness and the reason for it (Romans 11:8). Going to Isaiah 29, we can see what the nature of the blindness really is:

> Isaiah 29:9-11 "Stay yourselves, and wonder; cry ye out, and cry: they are drunken, but not with wine; they stagger, but not with strong drink. For the LORD hath poured out upon you the spirit of deep sleep, and hath closed your eyes: the prophets...the seers hath he covered and your rulers And the vision of all is become unto you as the words of a book that is sealed, which men deliver to one that is learned, saying, Read this, I pray thee: and he saith, I cannot; for it is sealed: And the book is delivered to him that is not learned, saying, Read this, I pray thee: and he saith, I am not learned" (Isaiah 29:9-12).

From Isaiah 29:11 we see that the blindness is that "... the wisdom of their [Israel's] wise men shall perish, and the understanding of their prudent men shall be hid." We understand from this that God is no longer giving insight to Israel and they therefore no longer have spiritual vision. The result of that spiritual blindness is twofold:

1. Israel's prophets no longer receive instruction from the Holy Spirit (Isaiah 29:11).
2. The people no longer have the discernment to understand what has been written (Isaiah 29:12).

In short, the blindness is the withdrawal of the Holy Spirit from Israel. Israel is then no longer the means whereby God reaches lost men.

Comparing Isaiah 29:9, 13 with 28:1-3 we see the reason for the blindness. Israel became drunk with pride. Israel began to think that she was the object of God's blessing and love rather than the channel of blessing to the nations. Israel could not see that she was as much in need of spiritual redemption as the nations were.

The Parable of the Sower Explained

Matthew 13:18-23 "¹⁸Hear ye therefore the parable of the sower. ¹⁹When any one heareth the word of the kingdom, and understandeth *it* not, then cometh the wicked *one*, and catcheth away that which was sown in his heart. This is he which received seed by the way side. ²⁰But he that received the seed into stony places, the same is he that heareth the word, and anon with joy receiveth it; ²¹Yet hath he not root in himself, but dureth for a while: for when tribulation or persecution ariseth because of the word, by and by he is offended. ²²He also that received seed among the thorns is he that heareth the word; and the care of this world, and the deceitfulness of riches, choke the word, and he becometh unfruitful. ²³But he that received seed into the good ground is he that heareth the word, and understandeth *it*; which also beareth fruit, and bringeth forth, some an hundredfold, some sixty, some thirty."

The Lord Interprets the parable of the Sower (Verses 1-8)

- The sower is the Lord Jesus Christ.
- The seed is the Word which He spoke regarding the Kingdom of heaven (Mark 4:13 & 14).
- The seed falls on four different grounds. Each represents a different heart attitude in the hearers.
    1. The seed that fell on the wayside is devoured by the fowl. (Verse 4) These are Israelites who did not understand their program. The Word of the kingdom meant nothing to them because of their unbelief. The antichrist (the fowl = the wicked one) catches the word of the kingdom away from them.
    2. The seed that fell in the stony places (Verses 5 & 6) is the Israelite who understands the program but does not have the faith to endure to the end (cf. Matt. 24:3-13). This is the 1John 2:19 Jew. There was enough soil (Bible understanding) to germinate the seed but not enough to produce growth.
    3. The seed that fell among the thorns (Verse 7) is the Israelite that had good ground. He receives the Word and understands it. However, along with the Word taking root in his heart, the cares of this world also take root (13:22) He is the man in Matthew 6:24 who is trying to serve two masters. When this man comes to the command to sell his possessions and give the money to the poor, he stops and goes no further (Matt. 19 21-24).
    4. Verse 8 speaks of the remnant (i.e. the little flock of Luke 12:32) which bears the "fruit" of the kingdom (Matt. 21:43). This is the group that James speaks about in James 2:22 & 23 who show their faith by their works and are thereby justified. They receive the promise only after they have done the will of God (Heb. 10:36). Three categories of fruit bearing are listed: some 100 fold, some 60 fold, and some 30 fold. Compare this with passages as Matthew 25: 14-28 on the talents, Luke 19: 13-16 of the pounds, and John 15: 1-10 on fruit bearing. These are the overcomers of Revelation 12:11.

Of these four, only the last group will get into the kingdom. These are the little flock and those of the tribulation period.

The Parable of the Tares Among the Wheat

Matthew 13:24 "²⁴ Another parable put he forth unto them, saying, The kingdom of heaven is likened unto a man which sowed good seed in his field: ²⁵ But while men slept, his enemy came and sowed tares among the wheat, and went his way. ²⁶ But when the blade was sprung up, and brought forth fruit, then appeared the tares also. ²⁷ So the servants of the householder came and said unto him, Sir, didst not thou sow good seed in thy field? From whence then hath it tares? ²⁸ He said unto them, An enemy hath done this. The servants said unto him, Wilt thou then that we go and gather them up? ²⁹ But he said, Nay; lest while ye gather up the tares, ye root up also the wheat with them. ³⁰ Let both grow together until the harvest: and in the time of harvest I will say to the reapers, Gather ye together first the tares, and bind them in bundles to burn them: but gather the wheat into my barn."

The Lord explains this parable (the second parable) in verses 36 to 43 below.

The Parable of the Mustard Seed

Matthew 13:31-32 "³¹ Another parable put he forth unto them, saying, The kingdom of heaven is like to a grain of mustard seed, which a man took, and sowed in his field: ³² Which indeed is the least of all seeds: but when it is grown, it is the greatest among herbs, and becometh a tree, so that the birds of the air come and lodge in the branches thereof."

The third parable on the mustard seed deals with the little flock of believers. They see themselves as being insignificant. Normally a mustard seed grows to be a relatively small thing (a mustard plant). However, this plant grows beyond all expectations to become a tree and not just a tree, but the largest of trees.

- Trees are often used to represent kingdoms in scripture (Dan. 4:10-26; Ezek. 31:1-11; 15:1-10; 17:24, etc.) Israel was chosen because they were the fewest of people (Deut. 7:7). However, God brought them out of Egypt as a nation that grew from 70 people to a nation "as the stars of heaven for multitude." In Deuteroniomy 28:62-64 we see the effect of the Law on Israel if they would not obey it: "...ye shall be left few in number, whereas ye were as the stars of heaven for multitude; because thou wouldest not obey the voice of the LORD thy God...And the LORD shall scatter thee among all people..."
- The birds (winged creatures) when used symbolically in scripture represent the presence of Satan through the antichrist (Rev. 18:2; Jer. 4:25).
- The field is again the world. Israel is planted in the world as the means whereby God will establish His kingdom in the world.

The Parable of the Leavened Meal

Matthew 13:33 "³³ Another parable spake he unto them; The kingdom of heaven is like unto leaven, which a woman took, and hid in three measures of meal, till the whole was leavened."

Leaven represents false doctrine. False doctrine spreads and permeates the whole lump. "Take heed and beware of the leaven of the Pharisees and Sadducees." (Matt. 16:6). In Matt. 16:12 the disciples understand that He is talking about the doctrine of the Pharisees and Sadducees. See also Luke 12:1. The three measures of meal represent the three parts of the Law of Moses which have been corrupted by three different sects of the leaders of Israel.

- Israel's moral law was corrupted by the hypocrisy (Matt. 23:13) and religious formalism (Matt. 22:23) of the Pharisees.

- Israel's ceremonial Law was corrupted by the Sadducees who denied the supernatural.
- Israel's civil Law was corrupted by the striving for political power of the Herodians (Mark 8:16).

The woman represents Israel who put leaven in all three parts of the Law. Note that the meal offering of Leviticus 2:7 was to be unleavened. These three false doctrines will be combined into one false system in the Tribulation period under the leadership of the antichrist and the false prophet. That false religious system (under the antichrist) will be the woman called "Jezebel" and "Mystery Babylon the Great" (Rev. 2:20; 17:5).

> **Matthew 13:34-35** "[34] All these things spake Jesus unto the multitude in parables; and without a parable spake he not unto them: [35] That it might be fulfilled which was spoken by the prophet, saying, I will open my mouth in parables; I will utter things which have been kept secret from the foundation of the world."

This reference to the prophet in Verse 35 is a reference to Psalm 78:2. The mysteries of the kingdom reveal a thing related to the prophetic program about which could not be revealed until the time was right. That piece of information is the fact that the kingdom would not immediately appear when Christ first appeared (Act 1:6). The parables of Matthew 13 reveal information of the coming tribulation period and the fact that the kingdom of heaven will be preached without the King being present with them. The parables would enable the disciples to gain information on how they would have to operate and carry on the ministry of the gospel of the kingdom in His absence.

> **Matthew 13: 36-43** "[36] Then Jesus sent the multitude away, and went into the house: and his disciples came unto him, saying, Declare unto us the parable of the tares of the field. [37] He answered and said unto them, He that soweth the good seed is the Son of man; [38] The field is the world; the good seed are the children of the kingdom; but the tares are the children of the wicked one; [39] The enemy that sowed them is the devil; the harvest is the end of the world; and the reapers are the angels. [40] As therefore the tares are gathered and burned in the fire; so shall it be in the end of this world. [41] The Son of man shall send forth his angels, and they shall gather out of his kingdom all things that offend, and them which do iniquity; [42] And shall cast them into a furnace of fire: there shall be wailing and gnashing of teeth. [43] Then shall the righteous shine forth as the sun in the kingdom of their Father. Who hath ears to hear, let him hear."

This passage interprets the second parable. From this point on in the Lord's ministry, He limits His focus to the disciples and prepares them to preach and proclaim the kingdom of Heaven in His absence. After His death, burial, and resurrection, He broadens the scope of the ministry (through the disciples) to encompass the entire world (Mark 16:15 & 16; Luke 24:47; Matt. 28:20; Acts 1:6-8). In interpreting the parable, the Lord explains:

- The Sower is the Son of Man. This is the title that is given to the Messiah in Daniel 7:13 & 14 and is applied by the Lord to Himself often in Matthew's gospel (and the others as well). We find that title appears again in the Revelation (Rev. 1:13; 14:14).
- The field is the world. The spread of the gospel was to start in Jerusalem, then go to Judea (the two southern tribes), then to Samaria (the ten northern tribes), then to the world (Acts 1:8). However, the gospel of the kingdom never has been preached in all of the world even yet in our day. One day it will be (Matt. 24:14): "And this gospel of the kingdom shall be preached in all the world for a witness unto all nations; and then shall the end come."
- The good seed are the children of the kingdom. Remember that the seed in the first parable was the gospel of the kingdom. Here it is the believing remnant that is being called out by that gospel. Ultimately it will be the believing remnant in the Tribulation period. The nation will be scattered through the entire world at that time. God calls out the 144,000 Jewish evangelists through the ministry of the two witnesses (Rev. 11:2). The two witnesses are the two olive trees

of Revelation 11:3 & Zechariah 4:3-11. The 144,000 will then call the nation back to the land. There is an interesting reference to the "man child" that is caught up to God and to His throne in Revelation 12:5-6. It is commonly thought that the man child is Christ and that the woman in Revelation 12 is Mary. However, the time frame is the Tribulation period not the gospel era or the Book of Acts. The woman that brought forth the man child is led into the wilderness where she has a place prepared of God, that they would feed her there 1260 days (3 ½ years of 360 days each). This is the period of time called the great tribulation. The woman is Israel. The man child would be the 144,000. They (the 144,000) will one day rule all nations with a rod of iron (Rev. 12:5) with Christ (Psalm 2:9; Rev. 2:4) for 1000 years. Isaiah 66:1-10 speaks of the nation bringing forth this man child who will go out to reach the nation scattered over the earth. There will also be Gentiles that respond in faith to the gospel of the kingdom. They are the sheep of Matthew 25:31-46 who fed and protected the remnant of Israel during the Tribulation Period.

- The tares are the false believers. Satan and the antichrist will have a false religious system that will make it difficult to identify the true (2Thess. 2:11; Rev. 2:2, 9) from the false. Only the elect angels will be able to sort them out (Rev. 14: 1-7; Matt. 24:36-42). Psalm 110:2 apparently foresees these tares in the kingdom saying "… rule thou in the midst of thy enemies." Tares apparently occur during the tribulation and in the kingdom.

- The harvest is the end of the world – i.e. the end of the times of the Gentiles (Luke 21:24).

- The reapers are the elect angels (Rev. 14:1-7; Matt. 24:36).

- The tares and the wheat are allowed to grow up together until the harvest. The tares will be those taken in Matthew 24:48-51. The wheat (the believers) will shine in the kingdom (Dan. 12:3).

The Parable of the Hidden Treasure

:

Matthew 13:44-[44] Again, the kingdom of heaven is like unto treasure hid in a field; the which when a man hath found, he hideth, and for joy thereof goeth and selleth all that he hath, and buyeth that field."

- The treasure is the nation of Israel.
- The field is the world; the nations into which Israel is scattered.
- The hiding of the treasure: Today Israel is hidden among the nations. The Israel in Palestine today was created by man. The Israel of God is still hidden. For all that can be seen of Israel today, one can not see the Israel of God. Yet the high priestly ministry of Christ behind the veil (Heb. 6:18) assures Israel that her High Priest (Christ) has entered behind the veil (Heb. 6:7 & 8) to make intersession for Israel. Hebrews 9:26 – 28 "[26] For then must he often have suffered since the foundation of the world: but now once in the end of the world hath he appeared to put away sin by the sacrifice of himself. [27] And as it is appointed unto men once to die, but after this the judgment: [28] So Christ was once offered to bear the sins of many; and unto them that look for him shall he appear the second time without sin unto salvation." See the book *A Study of Hebrews* by the same author.
- He buyeth the field: This speaks of the fact that Christ paid the price of redemption for the whole world in order to establish Israel in the kingdom of heaven as the "days of heaven upon the earth" (Deut. 11:21).

The Pearl of Great Price

Matthew 13:45-46 "[45] Again, the kingdom of heaven is like unto a merchant man, seeking goodly pearls: [46] Who, when he had found one pearl of great price, went and sold all that he had, and bought it."

Let's identify the types:
- The merchant man is Christ.
- Goodly Pearls are believers (1Pet. 2:14).
- One pearl of great price is the Little Flock.
- Sold all that He hath – speaks of Christ death of Calvary.

The Parable of the Drag Net

Matthew 13:47-50 "[47] Again, the kingdom of heaven is like unto a net, that was cast into the sea, and gathered of every kind: [48] Which, when it was full, they drew to shore, and sat down, and gathered the good into vessels, but cast the bad away. [49] So shall it be at the end of the world: the angels shall come forth, and sever the wicked from among the just, [50] And shall cast them into the furnace of fire: there shall be wailing and gnashing of teeth."

To understand the drag net we see the sea as the whole world.
- The sea – type of the nations.
- Everyone will be judged (Matt. 25:32).
- The separation of the sheep from the goats.
- The angels shall sever the <u>wicked</u> from the <u>just</u>.
- The furnace of fire (cf. Matt. 3:10, 11; 25:30-46 see the book *You and Your Creator* by the same author).

Things Old and New

Matthew 13:51-52 "[51] Jesus saith unto them, Have ye understood all these things? They say unto him, Yea, Lord. [52] Then said he unto them, Therefore every scribe *which is* instructed unto the kingdom of heaven is like unto a man *that is* an householder, which bringeth forth out of his treasure *things* new and old."

The Lord is revealing new things and adding to that which was revealed in the Old Testament Scriptures. He asks them if they understand these things. They claim that they do. Yet, we find that they still do not understand the cross (Mat 16:22; Lk. 24:45).

Matthew 13:53-58 "[53] And it came to pass, *that* when Jesus had finished these parables, he departed thence. [54] And when he was come into his own country, he taught them in their synagogue, insomuch that they were astonished, and said, Whence hath this *man* this wisdom, and *these* mighty works? [55] Is not this the carpenter's son? Is not his mother called Mary? And his brethren, James, and Joses, and Simon, and Judas? [56] And his sisters, are they not all with us? Whence then hath this *man* all these things? [57] And they were offended in him. But Jesus said unto them, A prophet is not without honour, save in his own country, and in his own house. [58] And he did not many mighty works there because of their unbelief."

Mary and Joseph had at least 4 sons together and 2 daughters after the Lord was born. These were half brothers and half sisters to the Lord. His own family did not believe Him at this point in His ministry. He did no mighty works there because of their unbelief. He would not (and will not) cater to unbelief. Two of his half brothers (James and Jude) eventually became believers and in fact wrote scripture.

Chapter 13 Study Guide Questions:

1. What shift do we see the Lord making in His teaching methods here in Chapter 13?

2. Here are four classes of people in the parable in Verses 1 through 8. How many of these are people who will go into the Kingdom?

3. What does the expression "Who hath ears to hear let him hear" mean?

4. What are the mysteries of the Kingdom referred to in Verse 11? Are they related to what Paul calls the mystery?

5. In the parable of the good seed and the tares in verses 24 through 30 (and explained in Verses 36 through 43) identify what the tares are, who planted them, when were they planted? What time period in Israel's prophetic future does this parable apply?

6. Identify what the treasure is in Verse 44 and what the field is. What was the price that was paid for the field?

7. How many half-brothers and half-sisters did the Lord have according to Verses 55 to 57?

Matthew Chapter 14

MATTHEW 14:1-36

Matthew 14:1-11 "At that time Herod the tetrarch heard of the fame of Jesus, [2] And said unto his servants, This is John the Baptist; he is risen from the dead; and therefore mighty works do shew forth themselves in him. [3] For Herod had laid hold on John, and bound him, and put *him* in prison for Herodias' sake, his brother Philip's wife. [4] For John said unto him, It is not lawful for thee to have her. [5] And when he would have put him to death, he feared the multitude, because they counted him as a prophet. [6] But when Herod's birthday was kept, the daughter of Herodias danced before them, and pleased Herod. [7] Whereupon he promised with an oath to give her whatsoever she would ask. [8] And she, being before instructed of her mother, said, Give me here John Baptist's head in a charger. [9] And the king was sorry: nevertheless for the oath's sake, and them which sat with him at meat, he commanded *it* to be given *her*. [10] And he sent, and beheaded John in the prison. [11] And his head was brought in a charger, and given to the damsel: and she brought *it* to her mother. [12] And his disciples came, and took up the body, and buried it, and went and told Jesus."

The murder of John the Baptist is the first of three murders that progressively increase Israel's culpability and guilt in their rejection of God's rule over them.

- Here with John, they allow it. Their conscious should have been exercised and they should have objected had they truly desired the truth and the rulership of God over the nation. John is the forerunner of Christ. With this murder, Israel begins her rejection of Jesus of Nazareth as the Messiah.
- With the coming murder of Christ, they actually demand it and become the willing accomplices to it. (John 19:15)
- The third murder will be that of Stephen in Acts Chapter 7. There they will actually commit the murder. In doing so, they attribute the work of the Holy Ghost (who had witnessed through Stephen) to devils. (Acts 2:4; 4:8, 31; 5:3; 6:3, 5; 7:55). That act of blaspheming the Holy Ghost by attributing the work that the Holy Ghost was doing to devils will constitute the blasphemy of the Holy Ghost – which we shall see later in Matthew's gospel is unpardonable.

In these three rejections, Israel completes her rejection of Jesus Christ.

- They reject the Father's plea when they reject John who is sent by the Father to make the Son manifest to Israel.
- They reject the Son in His earthly ministry and seal that rejection by demanding His crucifixion.
- They reject the Holy Ghost's plea by not believing the witness of the little flock to them in the first seven chapters of the Book of Acts.

Feeding the 5,000

Matthew 14:13-21 "[13] When Jesus heard *of it*, he departed thence by ship into a desert place apart: and when the people had heard *thereof*, they followed him on foot out of the cities. [14] And Jesus went forth, and saw a great multitude, and was moved with compassion toward them, and he healed their sick. [15] And when it was evening, his disciples came to him, saying, This is a desert place, and the time is now past; send the multitude away, that they may go into the villages, and buy themselves victuals. [16] But Jesus said unto them, they need not depart; give ye them to eat. [17] And they say unto him, We have here but five loaves, and two fishes. ¹⁸ He said, Bring them hither to me. ¹⁹ And he commanded the multitude to sit down on the grass, and took the five loaves, and the two fishes, and looking up to heaven, he blessed, and brake, and gave the loaves to *his* disciples, and the disciples to the multitude. ²⁰ And they did all eat, and were filled: and they took up of the fragments that remained twelve baskets full. ²¹ And they that had eaten were about five thousand men, beside women and children.

In Verse 13 we see Jesus grieving over the death of John. He goes into a desert place to be alone but the crowd follows Him. Though He is grieving, He none the less ministers to the multitude. The disciples want to send the people away because they do not have the resources to feed the people. The Lord tells the disciples to feed the people (Verse 16). The disciples point out that they have barely enough for themselves (Verse 17). The Lord demonstrates that He will equip them to feed the people. After all of the people were fed, they gather up twelve baskets full. They had more than enough for themselves after they gave up what they had to feed the multitude. There is a spiritual lesson to be learned here. We need not worry about depleting ourselves in ministering to the needs of people who are looking to the Lord for help. The Lord will provide for their needs (spiritual needs today) through you and provide for you in the leftovers. See Psalm 132:13-15 on how the Lord has "…chosen Zion and will abundantly bless her provision: I will satisfy her pour with bread…"

Jesus Walks on the Water

> **Matthew 14: 22-33** "²² And straightway Jesus constrained his disciples to get into a ship, and to go before him unto the other side, while he sent the multitudes away. ²³ And when he had sent the multitudes away, he went up into a mountain apart to pray: and when the evening was come, he was there alone. ²⁴ But the ship was now in the midst of the sea, tossed with waves: for the wind was contrary. ²⁵ And in the fourth watch of the night Jesus went unto them, walking on the sea. ²⁶ And when the disciples saw him walking on the sea, they were troubled, saying, It is a spirit; and they cried out for fear. ²⁷ But straightway Jesus spake unto them, saying, Be of good cheer; it is I; be not afraid. ²⁸ And Peter answered him and said, Lord, if it be thou, bid me come unto thee on the water. ²⁹ And he said, Come. And when Peter was come down out of the ship, he walked on the water, to go to Jesus. ³⁰ But when he saw the wind boisterous, he was afraid; and beginning to sink, he cried, saying, Lord, save me. ³¹ And immediately Jesus stretched forth *his* hand, and caught him, and said unto him, O thou of little faith, wherefore didst thou doubt? ³² And when they were come into the ship, the wind ceased. ³³ Then they that were in the ship came and worshipped him, saying, Of a truth thou art the Son of God.

This passage is rich with types (for those who look at the types in scripture). The Lord is (from Chapter 13 on) preparing His disciples for carrying on their ministry to Israel without Him. They will be alone in a storm of opposition after He leaves them to return to heaven. He is about to give them an important lesson in how to get through the Tribulation that (according to the prophecy of Daniel Chapter 9) was to follow. The Lord goes into a mountain to pray while He sends the disciples in a ship ahead to the other side of the sea. This will be the situation that the believing remnant of Israel will be in during the tribulation – i.e. they will be alone in a storm without His personal presence. The sea in scripture is a type of the masses of humanity. The storm is a type of the turmoil that the remnant will be in during the tribulation. The Lord goes to them during the 4th watch (the end of the day – 6pm to midnight). Israel during the tribulation will be delivered by the coming of the Lord when they are about to give up hope of being delivered. Peter asks that the Lord bid him to come to Him. Peter starts walking on the water for a while but then starts to sink. Peter was doing alright when he had his eyes on the Lord but then took his eyes off the Lord and fixed on the trouble around him in stead of on the one who can deliver him. In the tribulation, the believers will have to keep their eyes on the Lord in order to get through the tribulation and into the kingdom (Matt. 10:22 "…he that endureth to the end shall be saved"). When He comes into the ship, the storm ceases. When

Christ returns to Israel during the Tribulation the turmoil will be over for Israel. Just as the disciples understood who He is by this experience, so it will be for the Tribulation saints. Israel in the Tribulation will be like the bones in Ezekiel Chapter 37:11. Israel will have another wilderness experience much like that of their 40 years of wandering (Rev. 12:6; Hosea 2:14 & 15). The Tribulation saints will know who He is when their Messiah returns and He has wounds in His hands and feet (Zech 13:6).

Jesus Continues His Healing Ministry

> **Matthew 14:34-36** "[34] And when they were gone over, they came into the land of Gennesaret. [35] And when the men of that place had knowledge of him, they sent out into all that country round about, and brought unto him all that were diseased; [36] And besought him that they might only touch the hem of his garment: and as many as touched were made perfectly whole.

The locals heard of the experience of Peter on the sea. This whole experience was a fulfillment of Psalm 107:12-15. "Therefore he brought down their heart with labour; they fell down, and *there was* none to help. Then they cried unto the LORD in their trouble, *and* he saved them out of their distresses. He brought them out of darkness and the shadow of death, and brake their bands in sunder. Oh that *men* would praise the LORD *for* his goodness, and *for* his wonderful works to the children of men!" In the Tribulation, the desired haven will be the Kingdom. Christ will bring Israel through the storm of persecution and opposition and safely into the Kingdom.

Chapter 14 Study Guide Questions:

7. In Verses 1 through 12 we see a murder described in which Israel as a nation was complicit. There are actually three murders that the nation was involved in relative to the gospel of the kingdom. List them and describe how the nation's culpability increases with each.

8. How will the murder of Stephen tie Israel to the unpardonable sin of Matthew 12:31 and 32?

9. What does the feeding of the 5,000 teach the disciples about His provision for Israel?

10. Relate the events of Verses 22 through 33 to the coming tribulation for the remnant of Israel.

Chapter 15

MATTHEW 15:1-38

Matthew 15:1-3 "¹Then came to Jesus scribes and Pharisees, which were of Jerusalem, saying, ²Why do thy disciples transgress the tradition of the elders? for they wash not their hands when they eat bread. ³But he answered and said unto them, Why do ye also transgress the commandment of God by your tradition?"

The Lord tells these men in Mark 7:9 "Full well ye reject the commandments of God, that ye may keep your own tradition." They added to the Word of God. This is expressly forbidden (Deut. 4:1-3). Paul warns believers "beware lest any man spoil you through philosophy and vain deceit, after the traditions of men, after the rudiments of the world, and not after Christ..." (Col. 2:8) Peter also gives the same warning (1Pet. 1:18-19).

Matthew 15:4-6 "⁴For God commanded, saying, Honour thy father and mother: and, He that curseth father or mother, let him die the death. ⁵But ye say, Whosoever shall say to *his* father or *his* mother, *It is* a gift, by whatsoever thou mightest be profited by me; ⁶And honour not his father or his mother, *he shall be free.* Thus have ye made the commandment of God of none effect by your tradition.

Here the Lord illustrates how traditions change the Word of God. The Word says to honor thy father and mother but a tradition was introduced by men that said that if you brought a gift (i.e. made a donation) you were free of that obligation.

Matthew 15:7-9 "⁷*Ye* hypocrites, well did Esaias prophesy of you, saying, ⁸This people draweth nigh unto me with their mouth, and honoureth me with *their* lips; but their heart is far from me ⁹But in vain they do worship me, teaching *for* doctrines the commandments of men.

Because they were teaching for doctrine the traditions of men, people were not able to worship God as He had intended.

Matthew 15:10-11 "¹⁰And he called the multitude, and said unto them, Hear, and understand:¹¹Not that which goeth into the mouth defileth a man; but that which cometh out of the mouth, this defileth a man.

It is what comes out of the heart that defiles a man. The Lord looks on the heart. The Lord is more concerned with why people do what they do than in what they do.

Matthew 15:12-14 "¹²Then came his disciples, and said unto him, Knowest thou that the Pharisees were offended, after they heard this saying? ¹³But he answered and said, Every plant, which my heavenly Father hath not planted, shall be rooted up. ¹⁴Let them alone: they be blind leaders of the blind. And if the blind lead the blind, both shall fall into the ditch.

When the disciples point out to Him that the scribes and Pharisees were offended by His teaching, He tells the disciples to ignore them because they were not the plant of God and were going to be uprooted. Those that follow them will be likewise uprooted.

> **Matthew 15:15-20** "¹⁵ Then answered Peter and said unto him, Declare unto us this parable. ¹⁶ And Jesus said, Are ye also yet without understanding? ¹⁷ Do not ye yet understand, that whatsoever entereth in at the mouth goeth into the belly, and is cast out into the draught? ¹⁸ But those things which proceed out of the mouth come forth from the heart; and they defile the man. ¹⁹ For out of the heart proceed evil thoughts, murders, adulteries, fornications, thefts, false witness, blasphemies: ²⁰ These are *the things* which defile a man: but to eat with unwashen hands defileth not a man."

Peter thinks that the Lord is speaking in a parable in this passage but the Lord tells Him that He is speaking plain truth.

The Woman of Canaan

> **Matthew 15:21-28** "²¹ Then Jesus went thence, and departed into the coasts of Tyre and Sidon. ²² And, behold, a woman of Canaan came out of the same coasts, and cried unto him, saying, Have mercy on me, O Lord, *thou* Son of David; my daughter is grievously vexed with a devil. ²³ But he answered her not a word. And his disciples came and besought him, saying, Send her away; for she crieth after us. ²⁴ But he answered and said, I am not sent but unto the lost sheep of the house of Israel. ²⁵ Then came she and worshipped him, saying, Lord, help me. ²⁶ But he answered and said, It is not meet to take the children's bread, and to cast *it* to dogs. ²⁷ And she said, Truth, Lord: yet the dogs eat of the crumbs which fall from their masters' table. ²⁸ Then Jesus answered and said unto her, O woman, great *is* thy faith: be it unto thee even as thou wilt. And her daughter was made whole from that very hour.

This incident with the woman of Canaan is very interesting. Note her words in verse 22:
1. "Have mercy on me" – She knew where she could get help.
2. "O Lord" – She recognized Him as God.
3. "Thou Son of David" – She knew He was Israel's Messiah. She knew Israel's hope and program and that she as a Gentile could be blessed with just the crumbs that were left over when the Children were fed. Wow!

He ignores her to make an important point to His disciples. The point that He was making was that the Gentiles had to go through them (through the nation of Israel) to get to Him. The children (of Israel) must first be fed (Mark 7:27). She understands Israel's program better than the children of Israel. She acknowledges her position and points out that the family dog gets the crumbs that the children leave behind. She also understands the nature of a righteous man who would take care of the beasts (Prov. 12:10). She was looking only for one of those crumbs. What faith she has! Her request was granted.

The Feeding of the 4,000

> **Matthew 15:29-38** "²⁹ And Jesus departed from thence, and came nigh unto the sea of Galilee; and went up into a mountain, and sat down there. ³⁰ And great multitudes came unto him, having with them *those that were* lame, blind, dumb, maimed, and many others, and cast them down at Jesus' feet; and he healed them: ³¹ Insomuch that the multitude wondered, when they saw the dumb to speak, the maimed to be whole, the lame to walk, and the blind to see: and they glorified the God of Israel. ³² Then Jesus called his disciples *unto him,* and said, I have compassion on the multitude, because they continue with me now three days, and have nothing to eat: and I will not send them away fasting, lest they faint in the way. ³³ And his disciples say unto him, Whence should we have so much bread in the

wilderness, as to fill so great a multitude? [34] And Jesus saith unto them, How many loaves have ye? And they said, Seven, and a few little fishes. [35] And he commanded the multitude to sit down on the ground. [36] And he took the seven loaves and the fishes, and gave thanks, and brake *them*, and gave to his disciples, and the disciples to the multitude. [37] And they did all eat, and were filled: and they took up of the broken *meat* that was left seven baskets full. [38] And they that did eat were four thousand men, beside women and children. [39] And he sent away the multitude, and took ship, and came into the coasts of Magdala.

In Matthew 14:13-20 we saw Him feed the 5,000 men beside the women and children. In light of that, the disciples question in Verse 33 is puzzling. Here He feeds 4,000 with seven loaves and a few fishes. When they were done, they had more than when they started.

Chapter 15 Study Guide Questions:

1. In Verses 4 to 6, what effect did the traditions of the scribes and Pharisees have on the commandments of God?

2. In Verse 13 the Lord is talking about a plant that will be uprooted. What is that plant? Who does it represent?

3. In Verses 21 to 28 it seems the Lord does not care for anyone but Israelites. Is this the case? What point is the Lord making? What is this Gentile woman acknowledging regarding her status in her appeal to the Lord?

4. In Verses 29 to 39, Matthew seems to be repeating a miracle that was recounted in Chapter 14. What is it that He is teaching His disciples through this? What should we make of the disciples question in Verse 33 in light of what they saw in Matthew 14:13 through 20?

Chapter 16

MATTHEW 16:1-28

The Pharisees and Sadducees seek a Sign

Matthew 16:1-4 "¹ The Pharisees also with the Sadducees came, and tempting desired him that he would shew them a sign from heaven. ² He answered and said unto them, When it is evening, ye say, *It will be* fair weather: for the sky is red. ³ And in the morning, *It will be* foul weather to day: for the sky is red and lowring. O *ye* hypocrites, ye can discern the face of the sky; but can ye not *discern* the signs of the times? ⁴ A wicked and adulterous generation seeketh after a sign; and there shall no sign be given unto it, but the sign of the prophet Jonas. And he left them, and departed."

The leaders of Israel ask for a sign from heaven to substantiate His claim to be the Messiah. He had already given them all of the signs that they should have needed. They were now only trying to undermine Him and were only looking for occasion to accuse Him of wrong. He has already given up on this group and tells them that the only sign that they would be given is the sign of the prophet Jonah. That would be the sign of His resurrection after three days and three nights. It is interesting that the wise men from the east (Gentiles) in Matthew 2:1-6 were able to discern the signs of the times but these leaders of Israel refused to consider them.

Matthew 16:5-12 "⁵ And when his disciples were come to the other side, they had forgotten to take bread. ⁶ Then Jesus said unto them, Take heed and beware of the leaven of the Pharisees and of the Sadducees. ⁷ And they reasoned among themselves, saying, *It is* because we have taken no bread. ⁸ *Which* when Jesus perceived, he said unto them, O ye of little faith, why reason ye among yourselves, because ye have brought no bread? ⁹ Do ye not yet understand, neither remember the five loaves of the five thousand, and how many baskets ye took up? ¹⁰ Neither the seven loaves of the four thousand, and how many baskets ye took up? ¹¹ How is it that ye do not understand that I spake *it* not to you concerning bread, that ye should beware of the leaven of the Pharisees and of the Sadducees? ¹² Then understood they how that he bade *them* not beware of the leaven of bread, but of the doctrine of the Pharisees and of the Sadducees."

The disciples forgot to take bread. The Lord tells them to beware of the leaven of the Pharisees and Sadducees. They misunderstand and think that He is speaking of physical bread. Jesus tells (instructs) them telling them to remember the five loaves (Matt. 14) that fed 5,000 and the seven loaves that fed 4,000 (Matt. 15:34) and that there was a more left over than what they started with. The leaven that the Lord is referring to is the doctrine of the Pharisees and Sadducees.

- The leaven of the Pharisees was self righteousness whereby they attempted to make a fair show in the flesh.
- The leaven of the Sadducees was liberalism whereby they presented a human based, man centered view on everything scriptural.
- To this could be added the leaven of the Herodians (We will meet these fellows in Matthew 22:16) who could see the kingdom as only a political entity whereby God would give Israel political power to rule the nations.

PETER'S CONFESSION AND THE BUILDING OF THE MESSIANIC CHURCH

Matthew 16:13-20 "[13] When Jesus came into the coasts of Caesarea Philippi, he asked his disciples, saying, Whom do men say that I the Son of man am? [14] And they said, Some *say that thou art* John the Baptist: some, Elias; and others, Jeremias, or one of the prophets. [15] He saith unto them, But whom say ye that I am? [16] And Simon Peter answered and said, Thou art the Christ, the Son of the living God. [17] And Jesus answered and said unto him, Blessed art thou, Simon Barjona: for flesh and blood hath not revealed *it* unto thee, but my Father which is in heaven. [18] And I say also unto thee, That thou art Peter, and upon this rock I will build my church; and the gates of hell shall not prevail against it. [19] And I will give unto thee the keys of the kingdom of heaven: and whatsoever thou shalt bind on earth shall be bound in heaven: and whatsoever thou shalt loose on earth shall be loosed in heaven. [20] Then charged he his disciples that they should tell no man that he was Jesus the Christ.

In the comments of Verses 5 – 12 we noted that there were three groups in Israel with false doctrine. The question now is: "Is there a group with the truth?" Jesus inquires of the disciples to bring out their faith. He asks "Who do men say that I the Son of man am?" That is a loaded question for He is drawing attention to the fact that He is a man. They answer with what they hear people speculate as to who He is. He then asks "But whom do ye say that I am?" Peter is quick to answer "Thou art the Christ, the Son of the living God." Peter gets it. The Lord tells Peter that he is blessed for having understood this. Peter did not learn this from men but by revelation from the Father (Note from Galatians 1:11-16 that Paul received his revelation from Christ). The Lord changes Peter's name from Simon Barjona (son of Jona) to Peter (Cephas, Peter, Rock) – i.e. a stone. The rock though is not Peter but Peter's confession that Jesus is the Christ. Christ is the one that is presented in Scripture as the Rock (Deut. 32:3, 4, 15-20, 30; 1Cor. 10:4; 1Peter 2:7; Acts 2:36; 8:37; John 20:31). The church here in Verse 18 is not the church which is Christ's Body that Paul speaks of. The church which is Christ's Body is built on the confession that Christ died for our sins according to the scriptures, was buried, and rose again the third day (1Cor. 15:1-4). The church that the Lord is referring to here is going to be built on the confession that Peter just made – that Jesus is the Christ the Messiah of Israel. This is the church that is being "added to" at Pentecost (Acts 2:47). There are two different churches being called out in the New Testament Scriptures. The church referred to here in Matthew 16 is the Messianic church that is being called out from the unbelieving nation of Israel to go into the promised Kingdom of Heaven under the headship of Peter. The other is the church of the present dispensation of grace that is being called out from the unbelieving masses of humanity to be raptured to heaven. The authority for the church of this dispensation is the apostle Paul through whom the Lord revealed the mystery – the body of doctrine by which it is called out and by which it operates.

The term "church" in the Bible refers to a called out assembly that belongs to the Lord. There are actually three different churches referred to in the New Testament Scriptures though only two of them are New Testament churches. In addition to the two being called out there is a church referred to by Stephen in Acts 7:38 – the church in the wilderness. That church was Israel being called out of Egypt as God's nation. In each of these three cases, one can identify what larger group they are called out from, who is being called out, what they are called out to, and what is the basis of their calling.

Let's apply these three questions to the three churches mentioned above.

Table 5: Three Bible Churches

Church	Called out from	Called out to	Called on basis of
Israel in the Wilderness (Acts 7:38)	Egypt	The Promised Land	The Abrahamic Covenant
The Messianic Church (Matt. 16:19)	Unbelieving Israel	The Kingdom of Heaven set up on Earth	That Jesus is the Messiah (i.e. the Christ)
The Church which is His Body (Col. 1:24)	The Unbelieving Masses of Humanity Today	Be Raptured to Heaven to Reign there	Christ Died for their Sins

In verse 19 the Lord gives Peter awesome authority. He gives Peter the keys to the Kingdom of Heaven. In John 20:23 we see that all of them had authority to remit sins. But here Peter is singled out as the leader of the twelve. The Lord is setting up an authority structure here and setting up bylaws by which the apostles could operate in His absence. He is giving Peter authority to act on His behalf using these keys.

- In Acts 1:22 he chooses Mathias to replace Judas. This was a case of binding something on earth and it was likewise bound in heaven.
- In Galatians 2:8 & 9 Peter used that authority to loose the twelve of their obligation to go to all of the world with the gospel of the kingdom when the twelve recognized the apostle Paul's ministry to the Gentiles under the mystery program. This was a case of loosing something on earth and it was loosed in heaven.

In Verse 20 He tells them to tell no one that he is the Christ. How different this is from Matthew 3:1-3 "¹ In those days came John the Baptist, preaching in the wilderness of Judaea, ² And saying, Repent ye: for the kingdom of heaven is at hand. ³ For this is he that was spoken of by the prophet Esaias, saying, The voice of one crying in the wilderness, Prepare ye the way of the Lord, make his paths straight." And Matthew 4:17 "¹⁷ From that time Jesus began to preach, and to say, Repent: for the kingdom of heaven is at hand." Or Matthew 10:7 "⁶ But go rather to the lost sheep of the house of Israel. ⁷ And as ye go, preach, saying, The kingdom of heaven is at hand." From here to the end of His earthly ministry the nation at large is being rejected for their unbelief and He focuses on the twelve.

A Startling Revelation to the Twelve

> **Matthew 16:21** "²¹ From that time forth began Jesus to shew unto his disciples, how that he must go unto Jerusalem, and suffer many things of the elders and chief priests and scribes, and be killed, and be raised again the third day.

This is a startling revelation to the twelve. This is the first time that He tells them that He is going to die. They do not understand it yet but the New Testament can not come to Israel until the death of the testator (Heb. 9:16-17).

> **Matthew 16:22** "²² Then Peter took him, and began to rebuke him, saying, Be it far from thee, Lord: this shall not be unto thee.

Peter is bewildered. Obviously, Peter did not preach the same gospel that Paul did. The Lord has sent the twelve out to preach "the gospel" – which they did do (Luke 9:1-6). However, they did not even know that

Christ would die let alone what he would die for. Even at Pentecost, Peter did not preach the cross as gospel (good news) but rather blamed Israel for crucifying her Messiah and appealed to them of repenting of that deed (Acts 2:22–23). Paul, on the other hand, preached the gospel as the fact that "Christ died <u>for</u> our sins." (1Cor.15:3 & 4).

> **Matthew 16:23** "²³ But he turned, and said unto Peter, Get thee behind me, Satan: thou art an offence unto me: for thou savourest not the things that be of God, but those that be of men."

The term "Satan" means adversary. Peter is being an adversary to the Lord here as the Lord considers what is ahead for Him in going to the cross. Here Peter is rebuked after just having received the keys to the kingdom of heaven. Peter has a long was to go yet before he can exercise those keys. The coming Holy Spirit will change things for Peter. We will see more on that later.

> **Matthew 16:24-27** "²⁴ Then said Jesus unto his disciples, If any *man* will come after me, let him deny himself, and take up his cross, and follow me. ²⁵ For whosoever will save his life shall lose it: and whosoever will lose his life for my sake shall find it. ²⁶ For what is a man profited, if he shall gain the whole world, and lose his own soul? or what shall a man give in exchange for his soul? ²⁷ For the Son of man shall come in the glory of his Father with his angels; and then he shall reward every man according to his works.

Condemned men in those days carried their cross to the place of execution. If one were to see a man carrying a cross one knew where he was going and what was to happen to him. What was ahead for the twelve (and what would have happened if the kingdom program was not interrupted) was the tribulation period. Getting into the kingdom (and having eternal life) was going to be an all out effort. He told them that He was going to die and in verse 27 He tells them that He will come back with His Holy angels. When He does, He will bring rewards for faithful service with Him.

> **Matthew 16:28** "²⁸ Verily I say unto you, There be some standing here, which shall not taste of death, till they see the Son of man coming in his kingdom."

This is a reference to the events of Chapter 17 where Peter, James, and John will see Him come in Kingdom glory at the transfiguration.

Chapter 16 Study Guide Questions:

1. What is the sign of the Prophet Jonah that the Lord talks about in Verse 4?

2. Verse 12 through 20 present much information regarding the Kingdom of Heaven and the leadership structure in it.

   a. Who does Peter say that Jesus is?
   b. From whom did Peter get this information?
   c. Is Peter a Rock?
   d. What is the rock on which the Lord will build His church?
   e. Is this the Church which is Christ's Body?
   f. What does the term "church" mean?
   g. What is the larger group from which the Messianic church is called out?
   h. Who are called out?
   i. What are those that are called out called out to?
   j. What is the larger group from which the church the Body of Christ is called out?
   k. What is the church the Body of Christ called to?

3. What authority does the Lord give Peter in Verse 19? What authority did the Lord give Peter in John 20:23? Who in the world has that authority today? How did Peter use that authority (c.f. Matt. 16:19) in the meeting with Paul in Galatians 2: 8 and 9?

4. Why does He instruct His disciples in Matthew 4:17 and 10:7 to tell people to repent for the kingdom of heaven is at hand but now in Verse 20 of this chapter to tell no one that He is the Christ?

5. Why does Peter begin to rebuke the Lord in Verse 22? Is there something that Peter does not understand yet?

6. What does the passage in Verses 24 to 26 say about the crisis point that Israel will be facing as far as getting into the kingdom of heaven and gaining eternal life is concerned?

7. Who is it that will not taste death until they see Christ coming? Did this happen?

MATTHEW 17:1-27

THE TRANSFIGURATION

Matthew 17:1-9 "¹ And after six days Jesus taketh Peter, James, and John his brother, and bringeth them up into an high mountain apart, ² And was transfigured before them: and his face did shine as the sun, and his raiment was white as the light. ³ And, behold, there appeared unto them Moses and Elias talking with him. ⁴ Then answered Peter, and said unto Jesus, Lord, it is good for us to be here: if thou wilt, let us make here three tabernacles; one for thee, and one for Moses, and one for Elias. ⁵ While he yet spake, behold, a bright cloud overshadowed them: and behold a voice out of the cloud, which said, This is my beloved Son, in whom I am well pleased; hear ye him. ⁶ And when the disciples heard *it*, they fell on their face, and were sore afraid. ⁷ And Jesus came and touched them, and said, Arise, and be not afraid. ⁸ And when they had lifted up their eyes, they saw no man, save Jesus only. ⁹ And as they came down from the mountain, Jesus charged them, saying, Tell the vision to no man, until the Son of man be risen again from the dead."

We saw in Matthew 16:21 that the Lord began to show to His disciples that he must suffer many things of the elders and the priests and scribes, and be killed, and be raised again the third day. The disciples were bewildered by that statement (Matt. 16:22). The thought of their Messiah being killed is beyond their comprehension at this point in their understanding. Therefore, the Lord takes the leaders (Peter, James and John) and gives them a glimpse of His kingdom glory. The events that follow can be set in order of occurrence by comparing Matthew 17:1-9 with Mark 9:1-10, and also with Luke 9:28-36. The orders of the events appear to be as follows:

1. They go up into a high mountain "apart" – away from the others.
2. They went up "to pray" (Luke 9:28-36).
3. As they prayed, two things happened – Peter, James, and John fall asleep and while they doze off to sleep the Lord was transfigured in the which:
   - His countenance was changed (Luke 9:29),
   - His raiment was white and glistening.
   - His raiment became shining, exceeding white as snow (Mark 9:3)
   - His face did shine as the sun (Matt. 17:2).
4. Moses and Elijah appear with Him talking to Him. They appear "in glory" speaking with Him of His decease which should be accomplished in Jerusalem.
5. Peter, James and John awake and find Jesus talking with Moses and Elijah.
6. Moses and Elijah begin to depart (Luke 9:32).
7. Peter speaks up and suggests that they build three tabernacles – one for Jesus, one for Moses, and one for Elijah. (Luke 9:33). Note from Verse 33 that Peter appears to be at a lost for words. While Peter is still speaking, a bright cloud comes over them (Matt. 17:5; Mark 9:7; Luke 9:30) and God speaks interrupting Peter.
8. They fall on their faces to the ground (Matt. 17:6) and were afraid as the cloud enveloped them (Luke 9:34).
9. A voice from the cloud said "This is my beloved Son, Hear him." (Matt 17:5; Mark 9:7; Luke 9:35).
10. Jesus touches them and calms them down (Matt. 17:7).
11. They look up and find everything back to normal (Luke 9:36; Matt. 17:8; Mark. 9:8).

12. Jesus tells them "Tell the vision to no man until the Son of man be risen again from the dead." (Matt. 17:9; Mark. 9:9).

13. The disciples did keep the secret until after the resurrection (Luke 9:36 cf 2Peter 1:16-19).

The purpose for the vision was to strengthen their faith in the face of what was ahead. They were given a glimpse of the coming glory (Ezek. 1:26-29; Isa. 60:19).

Why Moses and Elijah? There are several possible reasons:

1. Moses and Elijah are the two witnesses of Revelation 11:3 & 4 cf. John 1:21; Zechariah 4:3, 11-14.

2. Moses represented the Law and Elijah represented the prophets. The law will not be done away for Israel but will rather be written in their hearts and put in their minds under the New Covenant (Jer. 31:33). The prophets all pointed to the kingdom (Luke 1:70; Acts 3:21).

3. Moses represented those who have died and will be resurrected to go into the kingdom while Elijah represents those who will go into the kingdom without dying but are healed in the kingdom.

Why does Peter suggest building tabernacles? He was anticipating the kingdom. God's program for Israel culminates in the feast of tabernacles: Lets remember the Feast of the Lord as the calendar of Israel's prophetic future:

1. Passover (the cross – Lev. 23:2)
2. Unleavened bread (the putting away of sin by the cross)
3. First Fruits (Resurrection to go into the kingdom)
4. Weeks (the empowering of Israel to reach the world with the gospel of the kingdom)
5. Trumpets (the re-gathering of Israel)
6. Atonement (when Israel's sins are forgiven).
7. Tabernacles (God dwells with men – Rev. 21:3). This is the consummation of Israel's Redemption.

Elijah must first come and has already come

Matthew 17:10-13 "¹⁰ And his disciples asked him, saying, Why then say the scribes that Elias must first come? ¹¹ And Jesus answered and said unto them, Elias truly shall first come, and restore all things. ¹² But I say unto you, That Elias is come already, and they knew him not, but have done unto him whatsoever they listed. Likewise shall also the Son of man suffer of them. ¹³ Then the disciples understood that he spake unto them of John the Baptist.

The disciples want to know why Elijah must first come. He assures them saying Elijah shall come and has in fact come already (Matt. 11:14) in spirit in the person of John the Baptist. In the transfiguration, Elijah came in a vision with Moses. At the second coming, Elijah will come in person as one of the two witnesses (Rev. 11:3). The scribes and Pharisees understood this (Matt. 27:42-49) but they did not understand (or refused to understand) that Jesus is the Christ. Had Israel trusted Jesus Christ as Messiah, then John would have been Elijah and the Lord would have been the prophet like onto Moses (Deut. 18;5)

Matthew 17: 14-23 "¹⁴ And when they were come to the multitude, there came to him a *certain* man, kneeling down to him, and saying, ¹⁵ Lord, have mercy on my son: for he is lunatick, and sore vexed: for ofttimes he falleth into the fire, and oft into the water. ¹⁶ And I brought him to thy disciples, and they could not cure him. ¹⁷ Then Jesus answered and said, O faithless and perverse generation, how long shall I be with you? how long shall I suffer you? bring him hither to me. ¹⁸ And Jesus rebuked the devil; and he departed out of him: and the child was cured from that very hour. ¹⁹ Then came the disciples to Jesus apart, and said, Why could not we cast him out? ²⁰ And Jesus said unto them, Because of your unbelief: for verily I say unto you, If ye have faith as a grain of mustard seed, ye shall say unto this mountain, Remove hence to yonder place; and it shall remove; and nothing shall be impossible unto you. ²¹ Howbeit this kind goeth not out but by prayer and fasting. ²² And while they abode in Galilee, Jesus said unto them, The Son of man shall be betrayed into the hands of men: ²³ And they shall kill him, and the third day he shall be raised again. And they were exceeding sorry."

Here is a man whose son is what he calls a lunatic. The boy is apparently unable to control himself. The description is that of an epileptic person. We see that Jesus regarded the boy as being possessed of a devil (a demon). The Lord rebukes the disciples and then rebukes the devil. The Lord speaks to His disciples in terms expressing disappointment in them for their lack of faith. When they ask Him why they could not cast out the devil He tells them that the reason was their unbelief. We ask ourselves here "what was it that they did not believe?" The answer is in verse 23- they did not believe that He was going to die. He told them that He would in Matt. 16:21 but (as Peter's response in Matthew 16:22 & 23 would indicate) they did not believe it. They did understand that He is the Christ (Matt. 16:17- 20) but they did not understand that He would die and be raised again the third day. There is no documentation in scripture of any miracles that the disciples did from here on until Acts Chapter 2 when they fasted and prayed.

In Verse 23 it finally dawns on them that He is telling them about His death and resurrection but they do not understand why He would die (I.e. they were exceedingly sorrowful). It is not until we get to Paul's epistles that we find the cross presented as Good News. There is a lesson for us in this. Having the power of God in one's life depends upon believing all that God has said to us.

> **Matthew 17:24-27** "²⁴ And when they were come to Capernaum, they that received tribute *money* came to Peter, and said, Doth not your master pay tribute? ²⁵ He saith, Yes. And when he was come into the house, Jesus prevented him, saying, What thinkest thou, Simon? of whom do the kings of the earth take custom or tribute? of their own children, or of strangers? ²⁶ Peter saith unto him, Of strangers. Jesus saith unto him, Then are the children free. ²⁷ Notwithstanding, lest we should offend them, go thou to the sea, and cast an hook, and take up the fish that first cometh up; and when thou hast opened his mouth, thou shalt find a piece of money: that take, and give unto them for me and thee.

Here a customs official approaches Peter as they enter Capernaum asking if his master pays tribute. Peter responds saying 'Yes!' The Lord then asks Peter a question to get Him to think of the justice of the citizen of God's nation paying tribute.. His question was "Do kings take tribute from citizens or of non citizens?" Peter responds saying it is of strangers that they take tribute. The Lord then tells Peter "Then are the children free." The point that the Lord was trying to get Peter to realize was that the king of kings was there and He should not have to be paying tribute. Yet, because it was not His time to reign as king yet, He pays the tribute. He does so in a way that at once shows: He is God, He provides the tribute money, and He shows that He is the one who truly has dominion over the fish of the sea and all of creation (Gen. 1:26).

Chapter 17 Study Guide Questions:

1. Why does the Lord give Peter, James, and John the experience of the transfiguration?

2. Why did the Lord instruct them not to tell anyone about what they saw until the "Son of man be risen…"?

3. How does this event relate to Peter's words in 2Peter 1:16 – 19?

4. Why do you suppose Moses and Elijah were there at the transfiguration?

5. Why do you suppose Peter suggests building three tabernacles?

6. In Chapter 10 the disciples performed miracles to cast out devils and to heal. Here they are unable to cast out this devil. Why not?

7. What point is the Lord making with Peter in Verses 24 to 27?

8.

Matthew 18

MATTHEW 18:1-35

Matthew 18:1-6 "¹ At the same time came the disciples unto Jesus, saying, Who is the greatest in the kingdom of heaven? ² And Jesus called a little child unto him, and set him in the midst of them, ³ And said, Verily I say unto you, Except ye be converted, and become as little children, ye shall not enter into the kingdom of heaven. ⁴ Whosoever therefore shall humble himself as this little child, the same is greatest in the kingdom of heaven. ⁵ And whoso shall receive one such little child in my name receiveth me. ⁶ But whoso shall offend one of these little ones which believe in me, it were better for him that a millstone were hanged about his neck, and *that* he were drowned in the depth of the sea."

This is an interesting passage indeed. It sheds light on where these men were actually at as to their spiritual maturity. After having been with the Lord for over three years they can still be petty. They lack spiritual maturity as well as lacking in understanding. The Lord calls a child into the midst and tells them that unless they be converted (i.e. changed in their heart attitude) and become as little children they could not enter the kingdom of heaven. What is interesting is that the disciples are as yet not assured of entering the kingdom of heaven. The greatest in the kingdom would be one who humbles himself as a little child. Pride, arrogance, a haughty spirit, will exclude one from entering the kingdom.

Matthew 18:7-9 "⁷ Woe unto the world because of offences! for it must needs be that offences come; but woe to that man by whom the offence cometh! ⁸ Wherefore if thy hand or thy foot offend thee, cut them off, and cast *them* from thee: it is better for thee to enter into life halt or maimed, rather than having two hands or two feet to be cast into everlasting fire. ⁹ And if thine eye offend thee, pluck it out, and cast *it* from thee: it is better for thee to enter into life with one eye, rather than having two eyes to be cast into hell fire."

This passage is a repeat of the warning of Matthew 5:29-32. These people are still under the performance based acceptance system of the Law. We will see this in Matthew 23:1-4. To walk by faith under the Law was to keep the Law. To fail to keep the Law is to be excluded from entering the kingdom (Mark 9:47) and therefore to also fail to enter into life (Mark 9:43 & 45; Matt. 18:8 & 9). To fail to keep the Law would result in one who was under Law to be cast into hell (Matt. 18: 8 & 9; Matt 5:29 & 30; Mark 9 44).

Matthew 18:10 "¹⁰ Take heed that ye despise not one of these little ones; for I say unto you, That in heaven their angels do always behold the face of my Father which is in heaven.'

Angels watch over little children (at least they did in Israel). The Lord is looking beyond the little children to the humble believer who receives the kingdom of heaven as a little child (Verse 18:3). This is a reference to the Little Flock (See Luke 10:21 and 12:31 & 32). Angels were involved in protecting the children of Israel in the past and will be again in the Tribulation.

Angels in the Bible:
- Represent nations (Dan. 12: 1).
- Represent children (Matt. 18:10).

- Represent men (Acts 12:15).
- Represent churches (Rev. 1,2,3).
- Serve as representatives of God (Isa. 63:9).

Matthew 18:11-14 "[11] For the Son of man is come to save that which was lost. [12] How think ye? if a man have an hundred sheep, and one of them be gone astray, doth he not leave the ninety and nine, and goeth into the mountains, and seeketh that which is gone astray? [13] And if so be that he find it, verily I say unto you, he rejoiceth more of that *sheep*, than of the ninety and nine which went not astray. [14] Even so it is not the will of your Father which is in heaven, that one of these little ones should perish."

The Son of man came to seek and to save that which was lost. What was lost is man's right to reign in the earth. This was lost in Eden when Adam fell into sin and rebellion. Redeeming man is the salvation that the Lord is speaking of in this context. However, before a man can be saved, he has to be lost. The 99 in this text were not seeing themselves as lost. A man can't be saved until he is lost. Consider Ezekiel. 18:25-28 in light of this. "[25] Yet ye say, The way of the Lord is not equal. Hear now, O house of Israel; Is not my way equal? are not your ways unequal? [26] When a righteous *man* turneth away from his righteousness, and committeth iniquity, and dieth in them; for his iniquity that he hath done shall he die. [27] Again, when the wicked *man* turneth away from his wickedness that he hath committed, and doeth that which is lawful and right, he shall save his soul alive. [28] Because he considereth, and turneth away from all his transgressions that he hath committed, he shall surely live, he shall not die." Ezekiel 18:25-28 (KJV) Also compare this verse with Matthew 12:9 "They that be whole need not a physician but they that are sick."

Israel is seen in scripture as sheep (as they are here in Verse 12) and Christ as the shepherd of the sheep. We today in the dispensation of grace are in Christ and are regarded by God as sons (Romans 8:19).

- Psalm 22 – The Good Shepherd (John 10:11-16) lays down his life for the sheep. This is consistent with Christ as the Prophet.
- Psalm 23 – The Great Shepherd (Heb. 13:20) is raised from the dead. This is consistent with Christ as the High Priest of Israel.
- Psalm 24 – The Chief Shepherd (1Peter 5:4) reigns over Israel – This presents Christ as the King.

Matthew 18:14 is a passage on the salvation of children and the age of accountability. There are other such passages in the Bible.

- Romans 4:15 "…For where no law is, there is no transgression."
- Romans 5:13 "For until the law sin was in the world: but sin is not imputed when there is no law."
- Jonah 4:11 Those that can't tell their right hand from left are spared.
- 2Samuel 12:23 David regards his dead child saying "I shall go to him but he will not return to me." David expected to see his son (who died in infancy) in resurrection life with him.

Adults are personally accountable for their sins and can be saved by faith in Christ's work of redemption. But Christ can also save those that have not reached the age of personal accountability. Deuteronomy 1:39 illustrates the Bible principle of an age of accountability i.e. "…your children, which in that day had no knowledge between good and evil." The lack of the knowledge of good and evil is defined as innocence (Gen. 1-3).

Matthew 18:15-20 "[15] Moreover if thy brother shall trespass against thee, go and tell him his fault between thee and him alone: if he shall hear thee, thou hast gained thy brother. [16] But if he will not hear *thee, then* take with thee one or two more, that in the mouth of two or three witnesses every word may be established. [17] And if he shall neglect to hear them, tell *it* unto the church: but if he neglect to hear the church, let him be unto thee as an heathen man and a publican. [18] Verily I say unto you, Whatsoever ye shall bind on earth shall be bound in heaven: and whatsoever ye shall loose on earth shall be loosed in heaven. [19] Again I say unto you, That if two of you shall agree on earth as touching any thing that they shall ask, it shall be done for them of my Father which is in heaven. [20] For where two or three are gathered together in my name, there am I in the midst of them."

Jesus is giving instruction in dealing with problems between brethren.

"If thy brother…" – the brother being a fellow Israelite.

The term "Trespass against thee…" is referring to an offence – intentionally or otherwise.

Go and tell his fault between thee and him alone

> It might have been unintentional – you can then clear the matter.
>
> It might have been intentional
>
>> If he reconsiders and repents, you have won a friend.
>>
>> If he persist, it is time to take other brethren with you (Deut. 1:16 & 17; 1Cor. 6:5). It must be witnesses (Deut. 19:15; 2Cor. 13:1) people who know the facts.
>
> If he refuses to hear the witnesses, take it to the local assembly.
>
> If he refuses to hear the church, treat him as a heathen (Rom. 16:17; 1Cor. 5:9-13; 2Thess. 3:6).

The Lord is giving the Remnant authority to act in His absence based on the decision of a quorum of 2 or 3 (Verses 18-20).

Paul gives instructions regarding entertaining an accusation against an elder in 1Timothy 5:19 & 20 saying "Against an elder receive not an accusation, but before two or three witnesses. Them that sin rebuke before all, that others also may fear." Elders are very vulnerable people because of their position and their work. Elders can easily be targeted for accusation by those who the elder might have had to deal with in the course of him carrying out his duties of oversight of the church. Therefore, an accusation against an elder is not to be even considered unless it is witnessed by two or three people. The people (the witnesses) must not be the ones bringing the accusation but witnesses who know what really happened. If the elder in fact did something wrong, he is to be rebuked publically but the same is to be applied to those who bring a false accusation against the elder.

> **Matthew 19: 21-22** "[21] Then came Peter to him, and said, Lord, how oft shall my brother sin against me, and I forgive him? till seven times? [22] Jesus saith unto him, I say not unto thee, Until seven times: but, Until seventy times seven.

Peter's question is probably the result of the instructions that the Lord just gave in verse 15 and following. Peter asks how often he should forgive a brother who repents. The Lord's instruction to Peter in the verses that follow has great dispensational significance.

> **Matthew 18:23-32** " [23] Therefore is the kingdom of heaven likened unto a certain king, which would take account of his servants. [24] And when he had begun to reckon, one was brought unto him, which owed him ten thousand talents. [25] But forasmuch as he had not to pay, his lord commanded him to be sold, and his wife, and children, and all that he had, and payment to be made. [26] The servant therefore fell down, and worshipped him, saying, Lord, have patience with me, and I will pay thee all. [27] Then the lord of that servant was moved with compassion, and loosed him, and forgave him the debt. [28] But the same servant went out, and found one of his fellowservants, which owed him an hundred pence: and he laid hands on him, and took *him* by the throat, saying, Pay me that thou owest. [29] And his fellowservant fell down at his feet, and besought him, saying, Have patience with me, and I will pay thee all. [30] And he would not: but went and cast him into prison, till he should pay the debt. [31] So when his fellowservants saw what was done, they were very sorry, and came and told unto their lord all that was done. [32] Then his lord, after that he had called him, said unto him, O thou wicked servant, I forgave thee all that debt, because thou desiredst me: [33] Shouldest not thou also

have had compassion on thy fellowservant, even as I had pity on thee? [34] And his lord was wroth, and delivered him to the tormentors, till he should pay all that was due unto him. [35] So likewise shall my heavenly Father do also unto you, if ye from your hearts forgive not every one his brother their trespasses."

In Israel's program, believers are forgiven only if they first forgive. We saw this in Matthew 6:14 & 15. Today, we who live in the dispensation of grace are forgiven of all our sins at the moment that we first believe (Eph 4:32). However, the dispensational significance of forgiveness for Israel goes deeper. It should be noted that this parable is addressed to Peter:

- The King in this parable represents the Lord.
- The first servant who owed 10,000 talents (a large amount) is the nation at large. The nation will have been forgiven of a great debt of having crucified their Messiah (Luke 23:34; Acts 3:17).
- The second servant who owed the first 100 pence represents the little flock (100 pence is about 12.5 talents). The nation at large viewed the little flock as having offended the nation (represented by the leaders) but did not forgive that offence; rather they persecuted the little flock.
- The recompense to the nation for this failure to forgive will come at the Lord's return.

Chapter 18 Study Guide Questions:

1. What does the discussion of Verses 1 to 6 tell us about the spiritual maturity of the disciples at this point?

2. Are Verses 7 to 9 meant to be taken literally?

3. What is the hell fire in Verse 9 (Remember we studied that in Matthew 5:29)?

4. To fail to enter into the kingdom would be to fail to enter into what?

5. Verse 10 implies that the children of Israel have guardian angels. Do we today have such guardians? Has the ministry that angels serve changed with the change of the dispensations?

6. In Verses 11 to 14, Israelites are seen as sheep and Christ the shepherd. Are we seen as sheep today?

7. Verse 14 talks about little ones perishing. What does the Bible say about the age of accountability?

8. Verses 15 to 20 deal with settling disputes between brethren. What is the sequence of steps they were to follow? Compare that with 1Timothy 5:19 regarding an accusation against an elder.

9. Verse 18 is essentially the same as 16:19. Does this say something about the seriousness of an offence against a brother in the kingdom?

10. Verses 21 through 35 remind us of what we saw in 6:14 and 15 regarding the seriousness of not forgiving an offense. How is this different from Paul's instruction in Ephesians 4:32?

MATTHEW 19:1-30

The Ministry in Galilee Ends

Matthew 19:1 "¹ And it came to pass, *that* when Jesus had finished these sayings, he departed from Galilee, and came into the coasts of Judaea beyond Jordan;

This is another turning point in Mathew's gospel. Here in Mathew 19 the Lord leaves Galilee. He had been there since Matthew 4:12. He is now headed for Jerusalem where he will die.

Matthew 19:2-9 "² And great multitudes followed him; and he healed them there. ³ The Pharisees also came unto him, tempting him, and saying unto him, Is it lawful for a man to put away his wife for every cause? ⁴ And he answered and said unto them, Have ye not read, that he which made *them* at the beginning made them male and female, ⁵ And said, For this cause shall a man leave father and mother, and shall cleave to his wife: and they twain shall be one flesh? ⁶ Wherefore they are no more twain, but one flesh. What therefore God hath joined together, let not man put asunder. ⁷ They say unto him, Why did Moses then command to give a writing of divorcement, and to put her away? ⁸ He saith unto them, Moses because of the hardness of your hearts suffered you to put away your wives: but from the beginning it was not so. ⁹ And I say unto you, Whosoever shall put away his wife, except *it be* for fornication, and shall marry another, committeth adultery: and whoso marrieth her which is put away doth commit adultery.

Multitudes follow Him and He heals them. In spite of and in disregard of the mighty works and miracles that the Lord does, the Pharisees continue in their unbelief and try to discredit Him. Here they try to trick Him on the matter of divorce asking if it is lawful to put away one's wife for every cause. They are trying to trap Him on what He said in Matthew 5 31 & 32 when He was pressing the Law to its fullest intent. The Lord starts by going back to Genesis before sin entered humanity. They then ask why Moses allowed divorce (Deut. 24:1-4). Note from Jeremiah 3:7-8, that God had divorced Israel (the ten northern tribes) but had not divorced Judah (Isa. 50:1). Idolatry is spiritual fornication in the Bible. God will one day take Israel back (Ezek. 37:17). The Lord is making the point that now there is only one reason for divorce for an Israelite -- that being adultery.

It should be noted here that the issue of divorce has a dispensational consideration. Israel was a covenant people and God dealt with the nation of the bases of covenants. The Mosaic covenant controlled and dictated life in Israel under the Law. An Israelite was only to be married to another Israelite. However in the dispensation of grace, the situation of a believer married to an unbeliever could exist. Therefore Paul as the apostle of the Gentiles through whom the dispensation of grace was revealed allows divorce in the case where an unbelieving spouse is not content to live in peace with a believing mate (1Cor. 7:12 – 15)

Matthew 19:10-12 "¹⁰ His disciples say unto him, If the case of the man be so with *his* wife, it is not good to marry. ¹¹ But he said unto them, All *men* cannot receive this saying, save *they* to whom it is given. ¹² For there are some eunuchs, which were so born from *their* mother's womb: and there are some eunuchs, which were made eunuchs of men: and there be eunuchs, which have made themselves eunuchs for the kingdom of heaven's sake. He that is able to receive *it*, let him receive *it*."

The term "eunuch" here is a reference to a man who remains single. Celibacy is a choice that some people make so that they can devote more attention to the Lord's work (1Cor. 7:34). It is not something to be forced on anyone (1Tim. 4:3) as the Roman Catholic church does with regard to their clergy.

> **Matthew 19:13-15** "¹³ Then were there brought unto him little children, that he should put *his* hands on them, and pray: and the disciples rebuked them. ¹⁴ But Jesus said, Suffer little children, and forbid them not, to come unto me: for of such is the kingdom of heaven. ¹⁵ And he laid *his* hands on them, and departed thence."

The Lord is training His disciples to minister to little children and not to slight them because their innocence makes it easier for them to believe the gospel (remember Matt. 18:3).

Israel Still Under Law

> **Matthew 19:16-22** "¹⁶ And, behold, one came and said unto him, Good Master, what good thing shall I do, that I may have eternal life? ¹⁷ And he said unto him, Why callest thou me good? *there is* none good but one, *that is*, God: but if thou wilt enter into life, keep the commandments. ¹⁸ He saith unto him, Which? Jesus said, Thou shalt do no murder, Thou shalt not commit adultery, Thou shalt not steal, Thou shalt not bear false witness, ¹⁹ Honour thy father and *thy* mother: and, Thou shalt love thy neighbour as thyself. ²⁰ The young man saith unto him, All these things have I kept from my youth up: what lack I yet? ²¹ Jesus said unto him, If thou wilt be perfect, go *and* sell that thou hast, and give to the poor, and thou shalt have treasure in heaven: and come *and* follow me. ²² But when the young man heard that saying, he went away sorrowful: for he had great possessions."

The Lord starts His response to this questions by asking "Why callest thou me good?" He is inquiring to see if this man understands that He is speaking to the one who is God in the flesh. The Lord starts by telling him what an Old Testament person would have to do by faith – i.e. keep the commandments. The young man proudly claims to have kept them all from his youth and asks what else he lacks. He is interested in entering into life but does not see his inability to do so in and of himself. The Lord then adds the kingdom requirement – "Sell that thou hast, and give to the poor and thou shalt have treasure in heaven, and come and follow me." For these kingdom saints, to enter into the kingdom would be to enter into life and vice versa (Mark 9:43-47; Luke 18:28-30). The Old Testament saint kept the law by faith looking forward to entering into resurrection life into the kingdom (Dan. 12:2). They understood that few find the way that leads to life (Matt. 7:13 & 14). The Law was until John and now the kingdom is preached (Luke 16:16; Matt. 11:13). The young man's unbelief now manifested itself. Because of his unbelief, he is allowing his riches to prevent him from entering into eternal life (i.e. in the kingdom).

> **Matthew 19:23-25** "²³ Then said Jesus unto his disciples, Verily I say unto you, That a rich man shall hardly enter into the kingdom of heaven. ²⁴ And again I say unto you, It is easier for a camel to go through the eye of a needle, than for a rich man to enter into the kingdom of God.

Some commentators tell us that one of the gates to the city of Jerusalem was called "the eye of the needle" and that people had to unpack their camel and bring the camel through on its knees. That might or might not be true. But the point is that the only requirement to enter the kingdom was to divest one self of worldly possessions in order to get into the kingdom of heaven (Matt. 19:21; Mark 10:21; Luke 18:22; Acts 2:45). That would pose a problem for someone who has set his heart on riches of this world.

Matthew 19:25-26 "[25] When his disciples heard *it*, they were exceedingly amazed, saying, Who then can be saved? [26] But Jesus beheld *them*, and said unto them, With men this is impossible; but with God all things are possible.

The disciples were astonished at the statement in Verses 23 & 24. They ask "Who then can be saved?" They understand that to enter the kingdom is to be saved and vice versa. The Lord tells them that it is impossible for any man to be saved (i.e. to enter the kingdom) on his own but with God all things are possible. God can save any one but they need to have faith that God will bring them into the kingdom. For a rich man to part with his goods in order to enter the kingdom is difficult.

TWELVE APOSTLES, TWELVE THRONES, JUDGING THE TWELVE TRIBES

Matthew 19:27-30 "[27] Then answered Peter and said unto him, Behold, we have forsaken all, and followed thee; what shall we have therefore? [28] And Jesus said unto them, Verily I say unto you, That ye which have followed me, in the regeneration when the Son of man shall sit in the throne of his glory, ye also shall sit upon twelve thrones, judging the twelve tribes of Israel. [29] And every one that hath forsaken houses, or brethren, or sisters, or father, or mother, or wife, or children, or lands, for my name's sake, shall receive an hundredfold, and shall inherit everlasting life. [30] But many *that are* first shall be last; and the last *shall be* first.

Peter tells the Lord "We have forsaken all and followed thee, what shall we have therefore?" There is a wealth of information in the Lord's response to Peter's question:

- "Ye which have followed me..." i.e. His statement is limited to them alone.
- "In the regeneration when the Son of Man shall sit in the throne of His glory..." i.e. the regeneration (new beginning) is defined as the time when the kingdom is established.
- The twelve who had followed Him (from the baptism of John unto the ascension – Acts 1:22).
- They will sit on twelve thrones (as twelve princes over the twelve tribes just as in David's day when there were princes ruling over the twelve tribes -- 1Chronicles 27:16-22).
- They will be judging the twelve tribes of Israel in fulfillment of Isaiah 1:26-27.
  "[26] And I will restore thy judges as at the first, and thy counselors as at the beginning: afterward thou shalt be called, The city of righteousness, the faithful city. [27] Zion shall be redeemed with judgment, and her converts with righteousness."
- God will restore the judges according to Isaiah 1:25-26; cf Numbers 1:16.
- The Throne of His glory will not be established until He shall come in His glory to set up the kingdom (Matt. 25:31).
- His throne of glory will be the throne of His father David (Luke 1:30-33).

A good question here is "Who will be king – David or Christ?" There are passages that speak of David being raised up from the dead to be their king (Jer. 30:9; Ezek. 37:24; Hos. 3:5). There are other passages that speak of Christ sitting on David's throne. We understand that there are no contradictions in the Bible. Obviously both are true -- but how? The structure of the government of the Kingdom of Heaven can be understood as follows:

- Jesus Christ will be King of Kings and Lord of Lords (Matt. 25:3; Jer. 14:2; Luke 1:30. Rev. 17:12).
- David will be the king over the Judges of Israel – Jeremiah 30:9; Ezekiel 34:23-26; Isaiah 31:1; 55: 3-4; and Hosea 3:4-5).
- The twelve apostles will be the restored judges (Isa. 1:25-26; Matt. 19:28).
- There will be a twelve fold division of the earth with each of the twelve tribes reigning over one of the divisions (Deut. 32:8).

But there is more to the government in the Kingdom of God than in what is happening in the earth when the Kingdom of Heaven is set up on earth. There is something very interesting when we come to Paul's epistles. In the Pauline epistles we find believers who will one day reign with Christ (2Tim. 2:8-12) but not over the earth (2Cor. 5:1). In Paul's epistles we find God reconciling all things to Himself through Christ – not just the things in the earth but also the things in heaven. (Col. 1:20). We understand from what we have been studying in Matthew's gospel that it is through Israel that Christ will set up a kingdom on earth and reconcile the earth to Himself. However, in Paul's epistles, we find that the same Christ (through the same shed blood) will also reconcile another body of believers to Himself called the church the Body of Christ (Eph. 2:15; 5:23; Col. 1:18, 24) which shall one day judge the world of angels. The church of this present dispensation of grace will be caught up to meet the Lord in the air (i.e. the unseen realm of heaven) where we shall be ever with the Lord (1Thess. 4:17). (Note: 2Cor. 5:1 & 2). Paul as "the apostle of the Gentiles talks about a Gentile church (Israel being temporarily set aside as God's unique nation today is also regarded as a Gentile nation today). He talks about us members of the Body of Christ one day having celestial bodies capable of functioning up there (1Cor. 15:40) in the heavens.

Angels will have an interesting part in God's plan for the ages. Angels will have a part in Christ establishing His kingdom on the Earth (Matt. 13:49; 25:31; Mark 8:38; Luke 9:26; etc.). However, God has not intended that the world to come be in subjection to angels. Rather, he has determined (before the world began- 2Tim. 1:9) that His creation will one day be in the hands of man as the eternal custodians of God's creation (Heb. 2:5-17). It will however be only those of the human race who find the fulfillment of God's plan in the redeeming work of Jesus Christ on Calvary who will be a part of that eternal kingdom.

Angels will have an interesting role in the eternal kingdom. In Genesis 28:12 and John 1:15 we see angels ascending from the earth and descending again. This would imply that the earth will be the center of the government of the universe and the Lord Jesus Christ will rule both from the earth. Angels will be the messengers to carry communication between the earth and the heavens. Who are the messages sent to? When we study the Pauline epistles – especially Ephesians and Colossians, we learn that we will reign with Christ (2Tim. 2:12) in the Heavens (2Cor. 5:1).

Chapter 19 Study Guide Questions:

1. There was a turning point in Matthew's gospel in Chapter 13. There is a second turning point here. What is it?

2. Comparing Verse 2 to Verse 9 regarding marriage, is there a difference between what we might call Kingdom Law and the Law of Moses? Which is the higher standard?

3. In Verses 16 to 22 we see a requirement of the rich young ruler to sell his possessions in order to get into the kingdom of Heaven. Why is that not a requirement for us today?

4. According to Verse 27, did Peter and the twelve give up all? What will they have in return?

5. Lay out what the structure of the government of the kingdom will be.

MATTHEW 20:1-34

Laborers for His Vineyard

Matthew 20:1-16 "¹ For the kingdom of heaven is like unto a man *that is* an householder, which went out early in the morning to hire labourers into his vineyard. ² And when he had agreed with the labourers for a penny a day, he sent them into his vineyard. ³ And he went out about the third hour, and saw others standing idle in the marketplace, ⁴ And said unto them; Go ye also into the vineyard, and whatsoever is right I will give you. And they went their way. ⁵ Again he went out about the sixth and ninth hour, and did likewise. ⁶ And about the eleventh hour he went out, and found others standing idle, and saith unto them, Why stand ye here all the day idle? ⁷ They say unto him, Because no man hath hired us. He saith unto them, Go ye also into the vineyard; and whatsoever is right, *that* shall ye receive. ⁸ So when even was come, the lord of the vineyard saith unto his steward, Call the labourers, and give them *their* hire, beginning from the last unto the first. ⁹ And when they came that *were hired* about the eleventh hour, they received every man a penny.
¹⁰ But when the first came, they supposed that they should have received more; and they likewise received every man a penny. ¹¹ And when they had received *it*, they murmured against the goodman of the house, ¹² Saying, These last have wrought *but* one hour, and thou hast made them equal unto us, which have borne the burden and heat of the day. ¹³ But he answered one of them, and said, Friend, I do thee no wrong: didst not thou agree with me for a penny? ¹⁴ Take *that* thine *is*, and go thy way: I will give unto this last, even as unto thee. ¹⁵ Is it not lawful for me to do what I will with mine own? Is thine eye evil, because I am good? ¹⁶ So the last shall be first, and the first last: for many be called, but few chosen."

The Lord is giving a lesson on service. He began it in Matthew 19:30 with the words "And many that are last shall be first…" and will continue talking about service through to 20:16. This parable teaches a lesson on service, one's motivation for service, and on God's grace. Let's look at it verse by verse:

Verse 1 The householder went out early to hire laborers for his vineyard (a type of Israel – Psa. 80:8).

Verse 2 He agrees with the laborers for a penny per day and sent them to his vineyard.

Verses 3 & 4 The third hour (about 9:00 a.m.) he saw more standing idle in the market place. He sends them promising to pay them "whatsoever is right."

Verse 5 He went out the sixth hour (noon) and the ninth hour (3:00 p.m.) and did the same.

Verses 6 & 7 He went out the eleventh hour (5:00 p.m. – almost quitting time) and does the same thing promising to pay whatsoever is right.

Verses 8 & 9 - When even came (6:00 p.m.) He had the steward give each laborer his hire beginning with the last (who worked one hour) to the first (who labored all day- 12 hours).

Verse 12 - Those who had worked 12 hours complained that they received what those that worked only one hour.

Verse 13ff - The good man of the household answered:

- I do you no wrong. You agreed to a penny. I paid you that.
- Is it not lawful for me to do what I want with my own?
- Is thy eye evil because I am good?
- The last shall be first and the first shall be last.

To understand this parable we must note the context. We note:
1. The parable is not about salvation but about service.

2. The service is service to the Lord in His vineyard – Israel is His vineyard.
3. The Lord chooses who will do service (John 15:16).
4. This is a continuation of the Lord's instruction to Peter in 19:28. There were many who had labored in Israel from Moses and Aaron on through the prophets, priests and kings. However, the twelve were blessed above them in that he labored at the 11th hour. Also, there will be laborers yet to come (the 144,000 of Revelation 7:14ff and those beheaded for their testimony in the tribulation period) who will reign with Christ 1,000 years (Rev. 20:4-6).
5. This parable teaches that God will not be indebted to anyone for His mercy and grace or for who He calls into service (e.g. Rom 9:11).
6. The closer in time people are to the kingdom, the more blessed they be (see Matt. 11:11 on this).
7. God is looking at the heart motivation for service (Matt. 20:16). We will see this concept again in Chapter 22 (Matt. 22:14).

Jesus Again Foretells of His Death

Matthew 20:17-19 "[17] And Jesus going up to Jerusalem took the twelve disciples apart in the way, and said unto them, [18] Behold, we go up to Jerusalem; and the Son of man shall be betrayed unto the chief priests and unto the scribes, and they shall condemn him to death, [19] And shall deliver him to the Gentiles to mock, and to scourge, and to crucify *him*: and the third day he shall rise again."

The Lord is on His way to Jerusalem to be crucified; to accomplish redemption by the Sacrifice of Himself. He takes them aside in the way to tell them now the third time (16:21 was the first and 17:23 was the second) that He will die and rise again the third day. However, as before, it does not seem to register with them.

Matthew 20:20-28 "[20] Then came to him the mother of Zebedee's children with her sons, worshipping *him*, and desiring a certain thing of him. [21] And he said unto her, What wilt thou? She saith unto him, Grant that these my two sons may sit, the one on thy right hand, and the other on the left, in thy kingdom. [22] But Jesus answered and said, Ye know not what ye ask. Are ye able to drink of the cup that I shall drink of, and to be baptized with the baptism that I am baptized with? They say unto him, We are able. [23] And he saith unto them, Ye shall drink indeed of my cup, and be baptized with the baptism that I am baptized with: but to sit on my right hand, and on my left, is not mine to give, but *it shall be given to them* for whom it is prepared of my Father. [24] And when the ten heard *it*, they were moved with indignation against the two brethren. [25] But Jesus called them *unto him*, and said, Ye know that the princes of the Gentiles exercise dominion over them, and they that are great exercise authority upon them. [26] But it shall not be so among you: but whosoever will be great among you, let him be your minister; [27] And whosoever will be chief among you, let him be your servant: [28] Even as the Son of man came not to be ministered unto, but to minister, and to give his life a ransom for many.

This passage teaches a lesson on humility and on what the heart of a true servant really is. Zebedee's wife; the mother of his sons James and John comes to the Lord to request that they might sit one on the right side and the other on the left of Christ in the kingdom. The Lord tells them they do not know what they are asking for and asks them "are ye able to drink of the cup that I shall drink of and to be baptized with the baptism that I am baptized with?" They answer Him that they can. He tells them then they will drink of that cup and be baptized with that baptism (i.e. death by martyrdom) but he tells them that His Father will determine who sits on His right and on His left. Going back to Chapter 17, we might well conclude that it will be Moses (representing the Law) and Elijah (representing the prophets) who will fill those positions. The other ten were indignant that these two would seek to elevate themselves so. The Lord uses this as an occasion to teach an important lesson about the nature of the kingdom.

The Lesson: The kingdom will be set up on different principles than the operating principles of the Gentile world system. In the Gentile world (the world that we live in today) the princes (those in charge) exercise dominion over those under them. Those in high positions exercise authority over those under them (i.e. by throwing their weight around). But the Lord tells them that it will not be that way among them. The one who would be great is to be "the servant" of all (Mark 9:35; 10:44). This is the way truly effective godly leadership works. This is the example that the Lord set for us (Verse 28 cf. 1Tim. 2:6).

"A ransom for many…" in Verse 28 speaks of a limited atonement. However, in 1Timothy 2:6 Paul (the apostle of the Gentiles) says that he gave Himself a ransom for all. What is the difference? In the four Gospels (Matt., Mark, Luke, and John) the Lord during His earthly ministry is not sent but to the lost sheep of the house of Israel (Matt. 10:6; 15:24). In the Pauline epistles, He is the Savior of the whole world wherein all can come freely to a salvation that is apart from Israel and apart from the Law of Moses. Today the imputed righteousness that people need to get to heaven and eternal life is "…unto all, and upon all that believe." (Rom. 3: 22)

> **Matthew 20:29-34** "[29] And as they departed from Jericho, a great multitude followed him. [30] And, behold, two blind men sitting by the way side, when they heard that Jesus passed by, cried out, saying, Have mercy on us, O Lord, *thou* Son of David. [31] And the multitude rebuked them, because they should hold their peace: but they cried the more, saying, Have mercy on us, O Lord, *thou* Son of David. [32] And Jesus stood still, and called them, and said, What will ye that I shall do unto you? [33] They say unto him, Lord, that our eyes may be opened. [34] So Jesus had compassion *on them*, and touched their eyes: and immediately their eyes received sight, and they followed him."

They depart from Jericho. Jericho is the city of the curse (Joshua 6:26). Two blind men callout to the Lord and the Lord hears them and give them what they seek – their sight. This is the last miracle that the Lord does in His earthly ministry (as far as the record of scripture is concerned). It is interesting that He does it in Jericho. These two men are a type of those in the tribulation period who receive spiritual vision from the Lord to know Him and to follow Him out of the sin cursed world into the kingdom.

On to Jerusalem and Passion Week

The close of Chapter 20 and the start of Chapter 21 mark a definite change in Matthew's gospel. The events in Chapter 21:1 thru Chapter 28:20 all occur in one week of time. Chapters 21 thru 28 all cover the last week of our Lord's earthly ministry.

Chapter 20 Study Guide Questions:

1. Identify what is the vineyard in the parable in Verses 1 through 16. What lesson is being taught? Who is the householder in Verse 1? Who are they that labored in the vineyard?

2. In Verses 17 to 19, the Lord tells the disciples for the third time that He will die and rise again. Does it seem that they are finally getting it?

3. What lesson is being taught in Verses 20 to 28? What does it say about how to be an effective, godly leader?

4. Explain why Verse 28 is presenting the Lord giving of His life as a ransom for many while in 1Timothy 2:6 is a ransom for all.

5. Who might the two blind men who received their sight in Verses 29 to 34 be a type of?

Chapter 21

MATTHEW 21:1-46

The Lord Fulfilling Prophecy

Matthew 21:1-11 "[1] And when they drew nigh unto Jerusalem, and were come to Bethphage, unto the mount of Olives, then sent Jesus two disciples, [2] Saying unto them, Go into the village over against you, and straightway ye shall find an ass tied, and a colt with her: loose *them*, and bring *them* unto me. [3] And if any *man* say ought unto you, ye shall say, The Lord hath need of them; and straightway he will send them. [4] All this was done, that it might be fulfilled which was spoken by the prophet, saying, [5] Tell ye the daughter of Sion, Behold, thy King cometh unto thee, meek, and sitting upon an ass, and a colt the foal of an ass."

The Lord is here demonstrating His deity by His foreknowledge of future events and at the same time fulfilling prophecy.

Matthew 21:6-11 "[6] And the disciples went, and did as Jesus commanded them, [7] And brought the ass, and the colt, and put on them their clothes, and they set *him* thereon. [8] And a very great multitude spread their garments in the way; others cut down branches from the trees, and strawed *them* in the way. [9] And the multitudes that went before, and that followed, cried, saying, Hosanna to the Son of David: Blessed *is* he that cometh in the name of the Lord; Hosanna in the highest. [10] And when he was come into Jerusalem, all the city was moved, saying, Who is this? [11] And the multitude said, This is Jesus the prophet of Nazareth of Galilee."

The Lord enters Jerusalem riding on an ass. This is in fulfillment of Zechariah 9:9. He enters Jerusalem from the Mount of Olives. He will do this again when He returns the second time. However, then He will be riding on a white charger to do battle against His enemies (Zech. 14:4; Rev. 19:11). The first entry to Jerusalem is in humiliation as the Passover lamb as a sacrifice for sin. The second is as the king who will sit on the Throne of David. Israel is looking for the second but they do not see that the lamb who takes away sin must come first. The crowd "…cried, saying, Hosanna to the Son of David: Blessed *is* he that cometh in the name of the Lord; Hosanna in the highest." Most of professing Christianity calls this the triumphant entry. However, triumph can not come until sin is defeated. This is not a triumphant entry but a humiliating entry when the creator was "made to be sin for us…" so that "…we might be made the righteousness of God in Him." (2Cor. 5:20 & 21).

Up until Chapter 12, the Lord and John were proclaiming the "the kingdom of heaven is at hand…" (Matt. 3:2; 4:17; 10:17). However, now (in Chapters 21 thru 28) He tells His disciples "that they should tell no man that he was Jesus the Christ (Matt. 16:20). Clearly, the Lord is not going to offer the kingdom to Israel again until after redemption is accomplished. The kingdom will not be offered again to Israel until Peter and the twelve (with Mathias replacing Judas) again offers the kingdom to Israel in Acts Chapters 2, 3, and 4. Note Peter's messages in Acts:

Acts 2:38-39 "[38] Then Peter said unto them, Repent, and be baptized every one of you in the name of Jesus Christ for the remission of sins, and ye shall receive the gift of the Holy Ghost. [39] For the promise is unto you, and to your children, and to all that are afar off, *even* as many as the Lord our God shall call.

Acts 3:19-21 "[19] Repent ye therefore, and be converted, that your sins may be blotted out, when the times of refreshing shall come from the presence of the Lord; [20] And he shall send Jesus Christ, which before was preached unto you: [21] Whom the heaven must receive until the times of restitution of all things, which God hath spoken by the mouth of all his holy prophets since the world began.

Comparing Matthew 21:9 with Luke 19:11-13 we see that the crowd thought that the kingdom would "immediately appear…" The Lord gave them a parable to teach them (or to enable them to understand later) that there are other events that have to unfold and that there will be a delay in the kingdom being set up. In that parable (in Luke 19) the nobleman is Christ, the far country is heaven, the kingdom is "the Kingdom…" the ten servants are the little flock. The citizens are citizens of the nation of Israel that would not have Christ reign over them. The Lord will reward faithfulness for the little flock by having them reigning with Him on earth [just as member of the Body of Christ will be rewarded for faithfulness by reigning with Christ (2Tim. 2:10-12) in the heavens (2Cor. 5:1-5)].

Matthew 21:8 describes what the majority of professing Christendom calls "Palm Sunday." This marks the beginning of the week that is the feast of the Passover (cf. John 12:1 & 2). It was during this week that the Jews would select the Passover lamb. They would select the lamb on the 14th of the month and kill it on the 19th (Exodus 12:3-6). This was six days before the Passover when the Lord entered Jerusalem. However, it should be noted that there is no indication in anything that is said in the scripture concerning this event that he is presenting Himself as the king. Rather, what He is doing is presenting Himself as the Passover lamb. The Lamb was to be observed for three days to look for imperfections (Exodus 12:3-6). In Luke 22:20 we find the leaders of Israel doing that very thing to the Lord not realizing that they were a part of the real Passover activity. They were blinded by unbelief as many are today when they hear the gospel that Christ died for their sins.

In Verse 11 we see the multitude viewing Christ as a prophet but do not see Him as the true Messiah. The prophet that the people see Him as is the "prophet like unto Moses…" of which Deuteronomy 18:15-19 speaks.

JESUS PURGES THE TEMPLE

Matthew 21:12-13 "[12] And Jesus went into the temple of God, and cast out all them that sold and bought in the temple, and overthrew the tables of the moneychangers, and the seats of them that sold doves, [13] And said unto them, It is written, My house shall be called the house of prayer; but ye have made it a den of thieves."

It was not wrong to sell doves for sacrifice (Deut. 14:24-26). What was wrong was to do so in the Temple. Also, it is apparent from Mark 11:17 that they were over charging the people. The temple was to be a house of prayer for all people (Isa. 56:7). Anyone in the world (Jew or Gentile) could come and bring a sacrifice and embrace Israel's covenant and have access to God. This same disregard for the temple that the Lord saw was present in Jeremiah's day (Jer. 7:11) and was one of the reasons for the deportation.

Matthew 21:14-17 "[14] And the blind and the lame came to him in the temple; and he healed them. [15] And when the chief priests and scribes saw the wonderful things that he did, and the children crying in the temple, and saying, Hosanna to the Son of David; they were sore displeased, [16] And said unto him, Hearest thou what these say? And Jesus saith unto them, Yea; have ye never read, Out of the mouth of babes and sucklings thou hast perfected praise? [17] And he left them, and went out of the city into Bethany; and he lodged there.

Wow! How hard the unbelieving heart can get to be. The chief priests and scribes see the mighty works that the Lord does and yet refuse to allow themselves to even consider the possibility that this is their promised Messiah. Such is the blindness that religious tradition brings on people. Here in Verse 16 the Lord is quoting Psalm 8:2.

The Cursing of the Fig Tree

Matthew 21:18-20 "[18] Now in the morning as he returned into the city, he hungered. [19] And when he saw a fig tree in the way, he came to it, and found nothing thereon, but leaves only, and said unto it, Let no fruit grow on thee henceforward for ever. And presently the fig tree withered away. [20] And when the disciples saw *it*, they marvelled, saying, How soon is the fig tree withered away!"

The Lord walks up to a fig tree and finds no fruit on it; only leaves. The fig tree is first found in the Bible in Genesis 3 where Adam and Eve covered their loss of innocence with fig leaves. This fig tree is a type of what religion does. The fig tree when used in scripture as a type is a type of religion (see Jeremiah Chapter 24 on the two baskets of figs). This tree had leaves so it had the appearance of life but it could not produce fruit. So it is with religion. Religion has a form of godliness but it lacks the power to produce real spiritual vitality. This is the state of our society today as men turn away from Bible truth to traditions (2Tim. 3:1-5). But why did the Lord pronounce such a curse on this particular fig tree that no fruit will grow on it forever? It is because the religion of Israel is coming to an end and something new is coming to replace it. Israel had the only God ordained religion that the world has ever known. That is the ceremonial portion of the Old Covenant that God made with Israel through Moses. The Lord was in effect cursing the religion of Israel in that it could not and did not produce the fruit of true righteousness. We will see in Matthew 24 that the fig tree (Israel's religious system) will one day bud again and have the appearance of life but it will not produce fruit. However the Lord will make a New Covenant with them whereby He will do for them what they could not do for themselves.

There is another instructive parable on the fig tree in Luke 13:6-9. There a certain man (Christ) had a fig tree (a religious system) planted in his vineyard (the nation of Israel is the Lord's vineyard – Psalm 80:8) and he came (during His earthly ministry) and sought fruit thereon (i.e. he sought Israel's faith) and found none (i.e. He was rejected by Israel). Then He said to the dresser of the vineyard (that being the Holy Spirit) "Behold these three years I came seeking fruit on this fig tree, and find none; cut it down (i.e. set Israel aside); why cumbereth the ground?" (i.e. the space could be used for something more profitable). And he (i.e. the Holy Spirit) answering said unto him, Lord, let it alone this year also (i.e. give it one more chance), till I shall dig about it, and dung it (i.e. the miraculous testimony of the Little flock via the Holy Spirit at Pentecost); And if it bear fruit (i.e. if Israel repent and believe) well; and if not, then after that thou shalt cut it down. (cf Rom. 9:30-33). Luke 13:8 is the year between the crucifixion of Jesus and the stoning of Stephen when Israel was set aside for having committed the unpardonable sin – that of blaspheming the Holy Spirit.

Matthew 21:21-22 "[21] Jesus answered and said unto them, Verily I say unto you, If ye have faith, and doubt not, ye shall not only do this *which is done* to the fig tree, but also if ye shall say unto this mountain, Be thou removed, and be thou cast into the sea; it shall be done. [22] And all things, whatsoever ye shall ask in prayer, believing, ye shall receive."

In the kingdom, the believers will be able to do that which we can only think possible in our wildest imagination. However, they must first get into the kingdom by faith.

Matthew 21:23-27 "[23] And when he was come into the temple, the chief priests and the elders of the people came unto him as he was teaching, and said, By what authority doest thou these things? and who gave thee this authority? [24] And Jesus answered and said unto them, I also will ask you one thing, which if ye tell me, I in like wise will tell you by what authority I do these things. ^{25} The baptism of John, whence was it? from heaven, or of men? And they reasoned with themselves, saying, If we shall say, From heaven; he will say unto us, Why did ye not then believe him? ^{26} But if we shall say, Of men; we fear the people; for all hold John as a prophet. ^{27} And they answered Jesus, and said, We cannot tell. And he said unto them, Neither tell I you by what authority I do these things.

Here Jesus turns the question back on these religious leaders of Israel to expose their willful unbelief. Had they simply turned to the scriptures and the prophecies of the Messiah they would have understood that John was sent as a forerunner to Himself and that He and John came by means of the same authority. In John 12:42-50 we see this phenomenon of willful unbelief. Note the importance of confession of faith in Israel's program. "Nevertheless among the chief rulers also many believed on him; but because of the Pharisees they did not confess him, lest they should be put out of the synagogue: For they loved the praise of men more than the praise of God." (John 12:42-43) For these Israelites, to not confess Christ is to reject Christ (John 12:45ff) and to miss out on salvation and eternal life. Romans 10:9-10 states what the formula for salvation would be in Israel's program during the gospel era and in the early Acts period. With the heart man believes unto righteousness and with the mouth confession is made unto salvation in Israel's program. Romans Chapter 10 addresses the question as to why Israel is in her present state. They refused to confess Jesus Christ as their Messiah. The chief rulers refuse to answer because they would have exposed their willful unbelief. The Lord would not let them off with a "no answer" response.

He proceeds to give them three parables that clearly state their spiritual condition and also sets the stage for the transfer of authority in Israel from the then rulers to the little flock.

The first Parable

> **Matthew 21:28-32** ". ^{28} But what think ye? A *certain* man had two sons; and he came to the first, and said, Son, go work to day in my vineyard. ^{29} He answered and said, I will not: but afterward he repented, and went. ^{30} And he came to the second, and said likewise. And he answered and said, I *go*, sir: and went not. ^{31} Whether of them twain did the will of *his* father? They say unto him, The first. Jesus saith unto them, Verily I say unto you, That the publicans and the harlots go into the kingdom of God before you. ^{32} For John came unto you in the way of righteousness, and ye believed him not: but the publicans and the harlots believed him: and ye, when ye had seen *it*, repented not afterward, that ye might believe him.

The nobleman with two sons (vss. 26-32)

To the first son he says: "Go work in my vineyard." This is representative of the remnant. They refuse the request to work in the vineyard (the vineyard being representative of the nation of Israel). He gives the same request to the second son (representative of the scribes and Pharisees) they agree to do so but they did not work in the vineyard. The Lord then points to the ministry of John the Baptist who had called Israel to repentance. The publicans and sinners repented but the rulers of the nation did not. Water baptism was a required ordinance (a part of the law – Numbers 19) that demonstrated faith in the message that John brought concerning the kingdom being at hand (Luke 7:29-30). The scribes and Pharisees refusal to be baptized was a statement of pride (i.e. too proud to admit that they need to repent – to think differently) and willful disobedience. The vineyard in this passage is Israel and the owner of the vineyard is the Father (Isa. 5: 1-10).

In the parable the first son represented the publicans and sinners. They at first did not go into the vineyard to labor. But then repented and did go. The second represented the scribes and Pharisees who viewed themselves as serving God in leading Israel. They were the leaders of Israel but they were not faithful to lead Israel to her Messiah.

The Second Parable

Matthew 21:33-46 "³³ Hear another parable: There was a certain householder, which planted a vineyard, and hedged it round about, and digged a winepress in it, and built a tower, and let it out to husbandmen, and went into a far country: ³⁴ And when the time of the fruit drew near, he sent his servants to the husbandmen, that they might receive the fruits of it. ³⁵ And the husbandmen took his servants, and beat one, and killed another, and stoned another. ³⁶ Again, he sent other servants more than the first: and they did unto them likewise. ³⁷ But last of all he sent unto them his son, saying, They will reverence my son. ³⁸ But when the husbandmen saw the son, they said among themselves, This is the heir; come, let us kill him, and let us seize on his inheritance. ³⁹ And they caught him, and cast *him* out of the vineyard, and slew *him*. ⁴⁰ When the lord therefore of the vineyard cometh, what will he do unto those husbandmen? ⁴¹ They say unto him, He will miserably destroy those wicked men, and will let out *his* vineyard unto other husbandmen, which shall render him the fruits in their seasons. ⁴² Jesus saith unto them, Did ye never read in the scriptures, The stone which the builders rejected, the same is become the head of the corner: this is the Lord's doing, and it is marvellous in our eyes? ⁴³ Therefore say I unto you, The kingdom of God shall be taken from you, and given to a nation bringing forth the fruits thereof. ⁴⁴ And whosoever shall fall on this stone shall be broken: but on whomsoever it shall fall, it will grind him to powder. ⁴⁵ And when the chief priests and Pharisees had heard his parables, they perceived that he spake of them. ⁴⁶ But when they sought to lay hands on him, they feared the multitude, because they took him for a prophet.

The murder of the Son (vss. 33 – 42)

- A certain householder (the Father) planted a vineyard (i.e. Israel).
- The husbandmen are the men of Israel
- The time of the harvest was the time then at hand when the kingdom was being offered to Israel.
- The fruit sought was belief and obedience by Israel.
- The first servants are the Old Testament prophets.
- The second group of servants represents John and the twelve apostles.
- The householder's son is Christ.
- Verse 38 is a clear statement on the willfulness of the disobedience and rebellion that was in the hearts of these men – the scribes and Pharisees. They understand that "This is the heir." And then add "Let us kill Him and seize his inheritance." Matthew 11:12 tells about how the violent (the scribes and the Pharisees) will try to take the kingdom by force instead of appropriating it by faith in Christ.)
- In Verses 39 – 41 He asks them a question and in their answer, they indict and condemn themselves.
- Verse 42 is a quote from Psalm 118:22&23. Christ as the stone:
  - Rejected by the builders
    - The leaders (Acts 4:8,10,11)
    - The people (Acts 3:13)
  - He will be the chief corner stone.
  - He is the rock of salvation (1Cor. 10:1-4).
  - He is a stone of stumbling and a rock of offence (Rom. 9:33).
  - He is a rock cut out without hands (Dan. 2: 34, 44).
  - But He is a precious stone to believers (1Pet. 2:6 & 7).

The Rejected Stone that becomes the corner Stone

In Verse 43 the Lord tells the leaders of the nation that the kingdom will be taken away from them and given to a nation bringing forth the fruits (i.e. belief and repentance) of it (of the kingdom). That nation is the little flock (Luke 12: 32). The "other sheep…" of John 10:16 are not the Gentiles but the rest of Israel (those scattered throughout the world). See Ezekiel 37 on the two sticks representing the divided nation that becomes one under the reign of the Messiah. In Verse 44 we see that, though they might reject this stone, it will one day grind them to powder.

Chapter 21 Study Guide Questions

1. What is the Lord riding on when He comes to the Mount of Olives in Verse 1? Is this what one would expect the entrance of a King to be like? What will He ride when He comes the second time to the Mount (Rev. 19:11)?

2. Would you call the entrance to be a Triumphant Entrance?

3. Would you consider this event the offer of the kingdom to Israel? Or will that offer come after His death, burial, and resurrection?

4. How does the humble entrance of the Lord relate to the Passover feast?

5. According to Verse 11, how does the multitude see Jesus – i.e. in what capacity?

6. What does the fig tree in Verses 18 to 20 represent? Why did the Lord curse this particular fig tree? How would this relate to the fig tree in Luke 13:6-9?

7. Based on verses 23 to 25, who sent John the Baptist to Israel with his message?

8. Based on verses 23 to 25 and comparing it with John 12:42 to 50 and Romans 10: 9 & 10, what is the consequence of failing to openly express faith in Christ?

9. Identify who the two sons in the parable in Verses 6 to 32 represent.

10. What is the vineyard in the parable of Verses 33 to 42? Who are the first servants? Who are the second? Who is the son?

Matthew 22

MATTHEW 22:1-46

JESUS THE PASSOVER LAMB

Matthew 22:1-14 "¹ And Jesus answered and spake unto them again by parables, and said, ² The kingdom of heaven is like unto a certain king, which made a marriage for his son, ³ And sent forth his servants to call them that were bidden to the wedding: and they would not come. ⁴ Again, he sent forth other servants, saying, Tell them which are bidden, Behold, I have prepared my dinner: my oxen and *my* fatlings *are* killed, and all things *are* ready: come unto the marriage. ⁵ But they made light of *it*, and went their ways, one to his farm, another to his merchandise: ⁶ And the remnant took his servants, and entreated *them* spitefully, and slew *them*. ⁷ But when the king heard *thereof*, he was wroth: and he sent forth his armies, and destroyed those murderers, and burned up their city. ⁸ Then saith he to his servants, The wedding is ready, but they which were bidden were not worthy. ⁹ Go ye therefore into the highways, and as many as ye shall find, bid to the marriage. ¹⁰ So those servants went out into the highways, and gathered together all as many as they found, both bad and good: and the wedding was furnished with guests. ¹¹ And when the king came in to see the guests, he saw there a man which had not on a wedding garment: ¹² And he saith unto him, Friend, how camest thou in hither not having a wedding garment? And he was speechless. ¹³ Then said the king to the servants, Bind him hand and foot, and take him away, and cast *him* into outer darkness; there shall be weeping and gnashing of teeth. ¹⁴ For many are called, but few *are* chosen.

THE PARABLE OF THE WEDDING FEAST

Here the kingdom is likened to a wedding feast that the Father prepared for Christ His Son. There are three calls to the wedding.

- The first call is in verse 3. This is the call made by John the Baptist and the twelve.
- The second call is in verse 4. This is the call issued to Israel in the Book of Acts.
    - My Oxen and fatlings are killed (representing Christ's sacrifice).
    - All things are ready: "Come to the wedding."
    - They made light of it (vs. 5)
    - Those that didn't make light of it mistreated and killed the Pentecostal believers (vs. 6).
    - Verse 7 speaks of the then coming destruction of Jerusalem. This will be the fulfillment of Daniel 9:26 "And after three score and two weeks shall Messiah be cut off, but not for himself: and the people of the prince that shall come shall destroy the city and the sanctuary; and the end shall be with a flood, unto the end of the war desolations are determined.' Luke 21:12-24 speaks of a destruction of Jerusalem. Note though that Luke 21:12 starts with "But before all these…" speaking of the nation against nation, and earthquakes, famine, pestilences, fearful sights, and great signs…from heaven in Luke 21:10-11. This suggests that there is yet another destruction of Jerusalem coming.
- In Verses 8–18 we see the third call to the wedding. This is the call that is given in the coming tribulation period. The third group of servants is the 144,000 who go into all the world and call Israel from the four corners of the earth. Those that respond are "…a chosen generation, a royal priesthood, an holy nation, and a peculiar people…which in times past were not a people but are now the people of God: which had not obtained mercy but now [in the kingdom] have obtained mercy." (1Pet. 2:9 & 10 cf. Hosea 2:23). Today however, Gentiles are obtaining mercy through Israel's unbelief under the mystery program (Rom. 11:30 & 31). Those that respond to the third call are those in Revelation 7:9-17. "¹⁴ And I said unto him, Sir, thou knowest. And he said to me, These

are they which came out of great tribulation, and have washed their robes, and made them white in the blood of the Lamb." (Rev. 7:14). Those in Verses 11-12 without the proper wedding garb are the religionist in Israel who would come to the wedding trusting in their good works. They are described in Romans 10:2 &3 "² For I bear them record that they have a zeal of God, but not according to knowledge. ³ For they being ignorant of God's righteousness, and going about to establish their own righteousness, have not submitted themselves unto the righteousness of God."

Matthew 22:15 "¹⁵ Then went the Pharisees, and took counsel how they might entangle him in *his* talk.

The Examination of the Passover Lamb

They try from here through the end of the chapter to entangle Him in the choice of words that He uses. This is a common ploy of political demagogues. What they are actually doing but do not realize is they are examining the real Passover Lamb for any flaws in fulfillment of the type of the Passover.

Herodians Examine the Passover Lamb

Matthew 22:16-22 "¹⁶ And they sent out unto him their disciples with the Herodians, saying, Master, we know that thou art true, and teachest the way of God in truth, neither carest thou for any *man*: for thou regardest not the person of men. ¹⁷ Tell us therefore, What thinkest thou? Is it lawful to give tribute unto Caesar, or not? ¹⁸ But Jesus perceived their wickedness, and said, Why tempt ye me, *ye* hypocrites? ¹⁹ Shew me the tribute money. And they brought unto him a penny. ²⁰ And he saith unto them, Whose *is* this image and superscription? ²¹ They say unto him, Caesar's. Then saith he unto them, Render therefore unto Caesar the things which are Caesar's; and unto God the things that are God's. ²² When they had heard *these words*, they marvelled, and left him, and went their way.

The Pharisees get together with another sect in Israel (the Herodians) to try to trick him. The Herodians were a political group that supported Herod who was a non-Israeli king (an Edomite) whom Caesar put on the throne to reign over Israel. Their trickery was evident to the Lord: They ask (after first trying to throw Him off by flattery): "Is it lawful to give tribute to Caesar or not?" If He would answer "No" He would be in rebellion to the government. If He would answer "Yes" He would be denying His right to the throne. He is the Messiah who will sit on the throne of David over Israel and is in fact the rightful king. He again turns the trickery back on them. They were under Gentile dominion because of their (the nation's) sin and rebellion. God allowed Caesar's rule over them because of their own doing. To show this, He asks for a coin with which they had to pay the tribute. The coin bore Caesar's image. He tells them to give Caesar what is rightfully his (the tribute money) and to God what is rightfully His (i.e. their worship and obedience). They were paying tribute money to Caesar because they did not (as a nation) pay worship and obedience to God. Had they trusted Jesus as Messiah, they would soon no longer be paying tribute to Caesar but vice versa (Isa. 61:6). They marvel at how He caught them in their trickery and went away realizing that they were not dealing with an ordinary man.

Examined by the Sadducees

Matthew 22:23-33 "²³ The same day came to him the Sadducees, which say that there is no resurrection, and asked him, ²⁴ Saying, Master, Moses said, If a man die, having no children, his brother shall marry his wife, and raise up seed unto his brother. ²⁵ Now there were with us seven brethren: and the first, when he had married a wife, deceased, and, having no issue, left his wife unto his brother: ²⁶ Likewise the second also, and the third, unto the seventh. ²⁷ And last of all the woman died also. ²⁸ Therefore in the resurrection whose wife shall she be of the seven? For they all had her. ²⁹ Jesus answered and said unto them, Ye do err, not knowing the scriptures, nor the power of God.

[30] For in the resurrection they neither marry, nor are given in marriage, but are as the angels of God in heaven. [31] But as touching the resurrection of the dead, have ye not read that which was spoken unto you by God, saying, [32] I am the God of Abraham, and the God of Isaac, and the God of Jacob? God is not the God of the dead, but of the living. [33] And when the multitude heard *this*, they were astonished at his doctrine."

The Sadducees saw that He had put to flight the Herodians and so they come to try their hand at tricking Him with Words. They cite instruction given by Moses in Deuteronomy 25:5-10. Ruth 1:11 alludes to this practice. He tells them in Verse 29 "You do err, not knowing the scripture, nor the power of God." The scripture teaches that Abraham, Isaac and Jacob will rise again. The Power of God will raise them by His Word (John 5:28 & 29). John says "When he shall appear, we shall be like Him " (1John 3:2). Revelation 5:9-11 speaks of the resurrection life of the believers of Israel in which they will reign in the earth. Paul speaks of our (members of the church which is Christ's Body) in passages as 2Timothy 2:18 and 1Corinthians 15:12-14 but does so with regard to us reigning in the heavens (2Tim 2:12 cf 2Cor 5:1-5).

Lastly -- Examined by the Pharisees

Matthew 22:34-40 "[34] But when the Pharisees had heard that he had put the Sadducees to silence, they were gathered together. [35] Then one of them, *which was* a lawyer, asked *him a question*, tempting him, and saying, [36] Master, which *is* the great commandment in the law? [37] Jesus said unto him, Thou shalt love the Lord thy God with all thy heart, and with all thy soul, and with all thy mind. [38] This is the first and great commandment. [39] And the second *is* like unto it, Thou shalt love thy neighbour as thyself. [40] On these two commandments hang all the law and the prophets."

This is almost humorous. The Pharisees seeing that the Lord had silenced the Sadducees take their turn at trying to trick Him. A lawyer of the Pharisees asks which is the greatest of the commandments. This could have been prompted by the Lord's instruction to the rich young ruler in Matthew 19:18 & 19. The Lord quotes Deut. 65:5 & 10:12 saying, "Thou shalt love the Lord thy God with all thy heart and with all thy soul, and with all thy mind." He then cites Leviticus 19:18 as to love for neighbor saying "Thou shalt love thy neighbor as thyself." In Matthew 19:19 He cited only love for neighbor. For us today, love for God is not based on a command but rather on the natural response of the heart of believers to the love that God has for us (2Cor. 5:14).

One More Question!

Matthew 22: 41-46 "[41] While the Pharisees were gathered together, Jesus asked them, [42] Saying, What think ye of Christ? whose son is he? They say unto him, *The Son* of David. [43] He saith unto them, How then doth David in spirit call him Lord, saying, [44] The LORD said unto my Lord, Sit thou on my right hand, till I make thine enemies thy footstool? [45] If David then call him Lord, how is he his son? [46] And no man was able to answer him a word, neither durst any *man* from that day forth ask him any more *questions*."

While the Lord has their attention, He asks a pointed question to point out the real issue; their steadfast refusal to believe that He is the Messiah. He asks them whose son is the Messiah? They answer that He is the Son of David. This would make Him a man. However, the Lord presses the point asking further. How then does David in spirit call Him Lord, saying "The LORD said to my Lord, sit thou at my right hand, till I make thine enemies thy footstool? If David then calls him Lord, how is he his son?" This is a reference to Psalm 110:1. Peter will later apply this definitively to Christ in Acts 2:34. The answer is that Christ is the Son of David (as man) but the Son of God in His essence. They accused Him of blasphemy in John 10:33 "…because that thou, being a man, makes thyself God." God always has an answer for man. However, man will not be able to answer God in the day that God judges man (Psalm 51:4; Rom. 3:4, 19).These men were standing in the presence of the one and the only one who can and will execute judgment and justice in the earth (Jer. 23:5).

The Passover lamb was to be observed for three days to be sure that it was without spot. Do you see any connection with the three sects who comprised the then current leadership in Israel with the examining of the Passover lamb?

Chapter 22 Study Guide Questions

1. What does the wedding feast represent in the parable of Verses 1 through 14?

2. In the parable of Verses 1 through 14, identify who is making each of the three calls to the wedding feast.

3. Explain how the Lord tuned the trickery of the Herodians back on themselves.

4. What trickery do the Sadducees use to try to catch the Lord with words?

5. How in Verses 41 to 45 did the Lord turn the Pharisees trickery back on them?

Chapter 23

MATTHEW 23:1-39

JESUS, THE KINGDOM, AND THE LAW

Matthew 23:1-12 "¹ Then spake Jesus to the multitude, and to his disciples. ² Saying, The scribes and the Pharisees sit in Moses' seat: ³ All therefore whatsoever they bid you observe, *that* observe and do; but do not ye after their works: for they say, and do not. ⁴ For they bind heavy burdens and grievous to be borne, and lay *them* on men's shoulders; but they *themselves* will not move them with one of their fingers. ⁵ But all their works they do for to be seen of men: they make broad their phylacteries, and enlarge the borders of their garments, ⁶ And love the uppermost rooms at feasts, and the chief seats in the synagogues, ⁷ And greetings in the markets, and to be called of men, Rabbi, Rabbi. ⁸ But be not ye called Rabbi: for one is your Master, *even* Christ; and all ye are brethren. ⁹ And call no *man* your father upon the earth: for one is your Father, which is in heaven. ¹⁰ Neither be ye called masters: for one is your Master, *even* Christ. ¹¹ But he that is greatest among you shall be your servant. ¹² And whosoever shall exalt himself shall be abased; and he that shall humble himself shall be exalted."

The Bible has much to say about religion, religious leaders and the Law. The following might be studied as a sample: Galatians 6:12 & 13; Matthew 12:36-42; Luke 20: 46-47; 3John 9 & 10; Job 32: 21-22; Judges 17 & 18; Exodus 18:13-27.

This passage is addressed to the multitude and to the disciples. He is telling them in no uncertain terms that they are to keep the Law given by Moses. At this point in the Lord's ministry to Israel the Law of Moses was still fully in effect. The scribes and Pharisees are part of the Sanhedron – the ruling body in Israel. This body grew out of the system that Moses set up in Israel as a result of the advice that Jethro gave Moses in Exodus 18:22-27. These religious leaders were to be respected for the position that they occupied. However, they were not to be respected for their conduct – for "…they say and do not." The Lord referred to these people in Matthew 15:8 "This people draweth high unto me with their mouth, and honoureth me with their lips; but their heart is far from me…" (cf. Isa. 29:13). The Lord will change the leadership in Israel (Luke 21:43) but He will not take Israel out from under the Law (Acts 21:20) but instead He will put the Law in their inward parts (Jer. 31:33) and write it in their hearts and cause them to keep it (Ezek. 36:27).

This is what religion does. It seeks to control people for its personal gain. Note that in Verse 4 that they bind heavy burdens and grievous to be borne. They lay them on men's shoulders but they will not lift a little finger to help bear the burden. They do their works to be seen of men (Gal. 6:12 – to make a fair show in the flesh). In Verse 5 they wear special garments that single them out and separate themselves from the ordinary man (Matt. 12:38-42; Luke 20:46 & 47; 3John. 9&10). The Lord instructs the disciples to avoid that prideful arrogance. They were not to take religious titles of any kind. It is interesting to note that the disciples (except for political leaders – Acts 26:25) put a title on only one person – that being the Lord Jesus Christ. Other than that, the disciples were on a first name basis with every man. Job says "²¹ Let me not, I pray you, accept any man's person, neither let me give flattering titles unto man. ²² For I know not to give flattering titles; *in so doing* my maker would soon take me away." (Job 32:21-22) The title 'Father' is the title of a false priesthood (Judges 17:1-5) in Israel. Leaders in the ministry must always remember the point that the Lord makes in Verse 8 that we all (all believers) are brethren. Verse 11 refers back to Matthew 20:26 on the servant leader. Verse 12 should be a word of caution to all who are in leadership in the Lord's work. The one who exalts himself will be humbled and vice versa.

Matthew 23:13-34 ""13 But woe unto you, scribes and Pharisees, hypocrites! for ye shut up the kingdom of heaven against men: for ye neither go in *yourselves*, neither suffer ye them that are entering to go in. 14 Woe unto you, scribes and Pharisees, hypocrites! for ye devour widows' houses, and for a pretence make long prayer: therefore ye shall receive the greater damnation. 15 Woe unto you, scribes and Pharisees, hypocrites! for ye compass sea and land to make one proselyte, and when he is made, ye make him twofold more the child of hell than yourselves. 16 Woe unto you, *ye* blind guides, which say, Whosoever shall swear by the temple, it is nothing; but whosoever shall swear by the gold of the temple, he is a debtor! 17 *Ye* fools and blind: for whether is greater, the gold, or the temple that sanctifieth the gold? 18 And, Whosoever shall swear by the altar, it is nothing; but whosoever sweareth by the gift that is upon it, he is guilty. 19 *Ye* fools and blind: for whether *is* greater, the gift, or the altar that sanctifieth the gift? 20 Whoso therefore shall swear by the altar, sweareth by it, and by all things thereon. 21 And whoso shall swear by the temple, sweareth by it, and by him that dwelleth therein. 22 And he that shall swear by heaven, sweareth by the throne of God, and by him that sitteth thereon. 23 Woe unto you, scribes and Pharisees, hypocrites! for ye pay tithe of mint and anise and cummin, and have omitted the weightier *matters* of the law, judgment, mercy, and faith: these ought ye to have done, and not to leave the other undone. 24 *Ye* blind guides, which strain at a gnat, and swallow a camel. 25 Woe unto you, scribes and Pharisees, hypocrites! for ye make clean the outside of the cup and of the platter, but within they are full of extortion and excess. 26 *Thou* blind Pharisee, cleanse first that *which is* within the cup and platter, that the outside of them may be clean also. 27 Woe unto you, scribes and Pharisees, hypocrites! for ye are like unto whited sepulchres, which indeed appear beautiful outward, but are within full of dead *men's* bones, and of all uncleanness. 28 Even so ye also outwardly appear righteous unto men, but within ye are full of hypocrisy and iniquity. 29 Woe unto you, scribes and Pharisees, hypocrites! because ye build the tombs of the prophets, and garnish the sepulchres of the righteous, 30 And say, If we had been in the days of our fathers, we would not have been partakers with them in the blood of the prophets. 31 Wherefore ye be witnesses unto yourselves, that ye are the children of them which killed the prophets. 32 Fill ye up then the measure of your fathers. 33 *Ye* serpents, *ye* generation of vipers, how can ye escape the damnation of hell? 34 Wherefore, behold, I send unto you prophets, and wise men, and scribes: and *some* of them ye shall kill and crucify; and *some* of them shall ye scourge in your synagogues, and persecute *them* from city to city: "

Verses 13 thru 39 lists nine woes that the Lord pronounces on the scribes and Pharisees because they have prevented Israel from trusting in her Messiah and thus receiving the promised kingdom. Compare these nine woes with the nine blessings (beatitudes) that will come on Israel when the kingdom is established in the table below.

Matthew 23:35 "35 That upon you may come all the righteous blood shed upon the earth, from the blood of righteous Abel unto the blood of Zacharias son of Barachias, whom ye slew between the temple and the altar.

From Abel in Genesis (the first innocent blood shed) to Zacharias the son of Barachias the last prophet sent to Israel (See 2nd Chronicles 24:20-22), all of the righteous blood shed will come upon that generation. Why upon that generation? That generation in rejecting the kingdom bears the responsibility for their refusal because all of the Old Testament history was about bringing Israel to this point of getting into the Kingdom.

Table 6: Comparing the Blessings (Beatitudes) with the Woes.

Matthew 5 Blesseings	Matthew 23 Woes
Verse 3. Blessed are the poor in spirit for theirs is the Kingdom of Heaven.	Verse 13. Ye shut up the kingdom …ye don't go in yourselves…you don't let others in either.
Verse 4. Blessed are they that mourn …They shall be comforted.	Verse 14. Ye devour widows houses and for a pretense make long prayers.
Verse 5.Blessed are the meek…they shall inherit the earth.	Verse 15. Ye make proselytes only to make them worse than yourselves.
Verse 6. Blessed are they who hunger and thirst for righteousness …they shall be filled.	Verses 16-22. Place value on appearance and not on spiritual substance.
Verse 7. Blessed are the merciful …they shall obtain mercy.	Verses 23-24 Make expensive gifts to the altar but the money for them came from causing suffering to others.
Verse 8. Blessed are the pure in heart … they shall see God.	Verses 25-28 Outward show of righteousness but hypocrisy in the heart.
Verse 9. Blessed are the peacemakers for they shall be called the children of God.	Verses 29 – 35 Make war against the peacemakers.
Verse 10. Blessed are they who are persecuted for righteousness sake: for theirs is the kingdom of heaven.	Verses 36–39 The kingdom is not established because there is no righteousness.
Verse 11. Blessed are ye when men shall revile you and persecute you and shall say all manner of evil against you…	Verse 38. Israel's house is left to them desolate – i.e. "your house" compare this with "my Father's house" in Matt. 21:13

Matthew 23:36-39 "[36] Verily I say unto you, All these things shall come upon this generation. [37] O Jerusalem, Jerusalem, *thou* that killest the prophets, and stonest them which are sent unto thee, how often would I have gathered thy children together, even as a hen gathereth her chickens under *her* wings, and ye would not! [38] Behold, your house is left unto you desolate. [39] For I say unto you, Ye shall not see me henceforth, till ye shall say, Blessed *is* he that cometh in the name of the Lord.

Israel's house is the temple (Matt. 21:13). It was God's house but it is now left desolate because God was walking out as the Lord walked out of it (Matt. 24:1). Verse 39 will be fulfilled when the Lord returns in glory to re-enter the temple. The temple will not see Christ again until he comes to be recognized as Israel's Messiah. Then Zechariah 12:10 will be fulfilled: "[10] And I will pour upon the house of David, and upon the inhabitants of Jerusalem, the spirit of grace and of supplications: and they shall look upon me whom they have pierced, and they shall mourn for him, as one mourneth for *his* only *son*, and shall be in bitterness for him, as one that is in bitterness for *his* firstborn." Then it will come to pass that "..all Israel shall be saved…" (Rom 11:26). However, until that day come, "…there remaineth the same veil untaken away in the reading of the old testament: which veil is done away in Christ." The desolation of the city is foretold in Zechariah 14:1 & 2.

In Matthew 27:50-51 we will see of a truth that the temple is left desolate without the presence of God. When the Lord gave up His spirit on Calvary, the veil of the temple was torn from top to bottom. Had God been in the Holy place, all who were before the veil would have died. But God was on the cross and had departed from the earth by way of death.

In Verse 36 all of Israel's rejection of God was coming on this last generation that was rejecting one who is more than a prophet; the very Son of God. Israel's day of reckoning had come (Ezek. 12:21-28). Verse 37 shows the Lord's heart desire for the conversion and salvation of Jerusalem. Jeremiah 6:8 is Jehovah speaking but it is fulfilled in Christ leaving Jerusalem. The Lord would have gathered and nurtured the city if she would only have turned to Him. However, she would not (Jer. 2:30) turn to Christ. The Lord demonstrated His loving concern for the nation when He brought Israel out of Egypt (Deut. 32:9-12)

Note that the first few verses of Matthew 24 relate to these closing verses of Matthew 23. As the Lord leaves the temple with his disciples, they are captivated by the beauty and the grandeur of the buildings. They totally miss the point that the Lord had just made that their house is left to them desolate by Him walking out. The Lord is the purpose for the building and He is now leaving it -- not to return to it until He returns to set up His kingdom. Without the Messiah, the temple's meaning is lost to Israel. Israel "...hath forgotten his Maker, and buildeth temples; and Judah hath multiplied fenced cities..." but God "...will send a fire upon his cities, and it shall devour the palaces thereof." (Hos. 8:14) People do the same thing today. They build impressive buildings and in them develop elaborate forms of godliness but they deny the power of true godliness (2Tim. 3:15). This is what constitutes dead religion. The Lord would have us function with a living faith in the working of His Spirit through his Word.

Chapter 23 Study Guide Questions

1. What does Matthew 23: 1 through 12 indicate when viewed with Matthew 28:20 regarding the Law of Moses and the Kingdom of Heaven? Will the Law be preached in the Kingdom?

2. Should any man ever take a religious title according to Verses 8 to 11?

3. Is there a point by point contrast of the eight woes of Matthew 23 when compared with the eight blessings of Matthew 5? Who turned the potential blessings of Matthew 5 into the woes of Matthew 23?

4. In what sense is Israel's house left desolate in Verse 38?

5. When will Verse 39 be fulfilled?

Chapter 24

MATTHEW 24:1-51

Matthew 24:1-2 "¹ And Jesus went out, and departed from the temple: and his disciples came to *him* for to shew him the buildings of the temple. ² And Jesus said unto them, See ye not all these things? verily I say unto you, There shall not be left here one stone upon another, that shall not be thrown down."

The Lord tells the disciples that the temple will be destroyed and taken down stone by stone. This was prophesied in Micah 3:12 that "Zion would be ploughed as a field, and Jerusalem shall become heaps." (See Jeremiah 25:18 where Jeremiah quotes from Micah). Note that the prophecy from Micah was given in the days of Hezekiah. It appears clear that Jeremiah 25:18 refers to the destruction during the Babylonian captivity. However, as is often the case, prophecy has both a near and far fulfillment. The temple was destroyed in 70 A.D. In Matthew 21:13, the temple was "My house…" but to the Lord's perspective, it was then "your house." (Matt. 23:38) Without Christ in the temple, it no longer had meaning or purpose. Having no longer any purpose, God will destroy it. This was fulfilled when the Romans took it down stone by stone looking for the gold that was purported to have been hid in the walls.

There is yet another reason for the destruction of the temple that needs to be considered. The temple represented the Law of Moses – the Old Covenant that God made with Israel. The Old Covenant was to be done away (Heb. 8:13; 9: 9). Christ ratified the New Covenant in His own blood (Heb. 9:12) in a temple not made with hands (Heb. 9:11). See the author's book *A Study in Hebrews – Israel and the new Covenant*.

The route that the Lord took when he left the temple is interesting in that it is the same route that the Shekinah glory took when it left the temple in Ezekiel's day (Ezek. 10:17-19; 11:22,23). In Ezekiel 8:6-18 we see the abominations that prompted the Lord to leave the temple. The Lord said through the prophet Hosea "…Yea, woe also to them when I depart from them." (Hos. 9:12).

Regarding the destruction of the temple, it should be noted that it will be rebuilt again. Daniel 9:26-27 implies that the temple will be standing during the seventieth week of Daniel. It will obviously be rebuilt. Probably the covenant that Israel makes with the antichrist (what Isaiah calls "a covenant with death" in Isaiah 28:15 and 28:18) will include the commissioning of the rebuilding of it. It will be rebuilt only to be profaned by the antichrist and again made desolate (2Thess. 2:4). In Ezekiel 40 and 41 we see yet another temple (the millennial temple) being measured by the angel in the kingdom. .

The Lord told Solomon in regard to the temple: "…if ye shall at all turn from following me, ye or your children…Then will I cut off Israel out of the land which I have given them; and this house which I have hallowed for my name, will I cast out of my sight…And this house which is high, every one that passeth by it shall be astonished, and shall hiss and they shall say, Why hath the LORD done thus unto this land, and to this house (1Kings 9:7-8).

THE OLIVET DISCOURSE

Matthew 24:3 "³ And as he sat upon the mount of Olives, the disciples came unto him privately, saying, Tell us, when shall these things be? and what *shalt be* the sign of thy coming, and of the end of the world?"

The Mount of Olives is a favorite place for the Lord to rest as it overlooks the temple site. When He ascends to heaven (Acts 1:9-12), He will do so from this mount. When He returns, He will return to this site (Zech. 14:4). Here the disciples ask Him three questions. The rest of Chapter 24 answers those questions. Note that He answers these questions in reverse order.

1. When shall these things be? The answer is given in Matthew 24:32-51.
2. What shall be the sign of thy coming? The answer is given in Matthew 24:25-31.
3. What shall be the end of the world? He answers this in Matthew 24: 4-24.

These questions are now coming out as the disciples consider all of the instruction that the Lord has been giving since Matthew 13 with the parables of the mysteries of the kingdom in which the kingdom will be preached without the King being present. They are finally starting to get the idea that the establishing of the kingdom is a ways off yet.

The term "the end of the world" is a reference to the end of the world system as it was then under the dominion of the Gentiles. This is what is called the "times of the Gentiles" in Luke 21:24. The times of the Gentiles began when Jerusalem was taken captive by Babylon and will continue until the time when "the kingdoms of this world are become the kingdoms of our Lord and of His Christ." (Rev. 11:15).

> **Matthew 24:4-10** "[4] And Jesus answered and said unto them, Take heed that no man deceive you. [5] For many shall come in my name, saying, I am Christ; and shall deceive many. [6] And ye shall hear of wars and rumours of wars: see that ye be not troubled: for all *these things* must come to pass, but the end is not yet. [7] For nation shall rise against nation, and kingdom against kingdom: and there shall be famines, and pestilences, and earthquakes, in divers places. [8] All these *are* the beginning of sorrows. [9] Then shall they deliver you up to be afflicted, and shall kill you: and ye shall be hated of all nations for my name's sake. [10] And then shall many be offended, and shall betray one another, and shall hate one another.

The Lord answers the last question: "What shall be the sign of the end of the world?" in Verses 4 thru 24. The key verse is Verse 15: "When ye therefore shall see the abomination of desolation spoken of by Daniel the prophet stand in the holy place…" This takes us back to Daniel 9:27 "And he [the antichrist] shall confirm the covenant with many for one week [one week = seven years – Gen. 29:27] and in the midst of the week he shall cause the sacrifice and the oblation to cease, and for the overspreading of abominations he shall make it desolate, even until the consummation, and that determined shall be poured out upon the desolate." Paul speaks of this event in 2Thessalonians 2: 3-4 "…and that man of sin be revealed. The son of perdition: who opposeth and exalteth himself above all that is called God, or that is worshipped; so that he as God sitteth in the temple of God, shewing himself that he is God." It is when the antichrist goes into the temple (which at that time will have been rebuilt) and claims to be God that Israel (the believing remnant) will know where they are in the prophetic program. From there until the end of the tribulation will be 1290 days until Christ returns (Dan. 12:11). The resurrection of the Old Testament saints will occur 45 days after that (1235 days cf. Dan. 12:12 & 13).

The events of Matthew 24:9ff are not events that will be seen today during the Dispensation of Grace. This present dispensation was a secret not revealed until Saul of Tarsus became saved and was commissioned as the apostle of the Gentiles. There are the phenomena of Matthew 24: 6-7 evident today but these are just the natural phenomena that will occur as long as the times of the Gentiles continue. Once the kingdom is established there will be no more wars, famines, pestilences and earthquakes. In Verse 6 we see that wars and rumors of wars are not necessarily a part of the end times. However, Verse 8 looks back to the famines, pestilences, and earthquakes in Verse 7 as "the beginning of sorrows – i.e. they are events that will occur in the first 3.5 years of the tribulation period. (See the first 6 seals of the Revelation Chapter 6 listed below). See the author's book *A Study in the Revelation / Tiry 2024* on the career of the antichrist.

Revelation 6:1-17 The First Six Seals of Revelation Chapter Six is the antichrist and the result of his career.

1. In Revelation 6:1 & 2 the White horse has a rider with a bow but no arrows. The Daniel 8:5 says of the antichrist he shall "By peace he shall destroy many." Daniel 11:21 says of him "…He shall come in peaceably and obtain the kingdom by flatteries. Paul tells us "Satan himself is transformed into an angel of light." (2Cor. 11:14). Many think that this rider is Christ. Christ appears riding a white horse too but that is in Revelation 19 11. The antichrist imitates Christ in many ways. Satan's method is to counterfeit God. The comparison is presented in Table 7 below.

2. Revelation 6:3 & 4 presents the antichrist riding a red horse. As the rider of the red horse, he takes peace from the earth. The earth was at peace when he rides the red horse. This is the war and rumors of war and the nations rising up against each other of which the passage in Matthew 24:7 speaks. It is the result of the antichrist efforts while riding the red horse. In Revelation 6:4 the rider of the red horse is given a great sword which he uses to take peace from the earth and to cause people to kill one another. In Revelation 19:15 the Lord also has a great sword with which He smites the nations.

3. Revelation 6:5 & 6 presents the antichrist riding a black horse with a set of balances in his hand. The balance is the symbol of justice and commerce. He controls commerce and administers what should be justice but is not. The result of his ride on the black horse is that there is famine in the earth. This is the famine that the Lord speaks of in Matthew 24:7. Famine is the natural aftermath of war.

4. Revelation 6: 7 & 8 present the antichrist riding a pale horse. His title as the rider of the pale horse is Death. This is an appropriate title in that Satan has the power of death (Heb. 2:14). In Isaiah 28: 14 and 17 Israel's covenant with the antichrist is said to be a covenant with death. As the rider of the pale horse he has power to kill one fourth of the earth's population with the sword, with hunger, with the beasts of the field and with death. Hell followed after the rider of the pale horse. Hell is gathering the souls of the lost who are being killed. The souls of the believers who are killed during the tribulation go to Paradise – which at that time will be in the third heaven (Rev. 6:9).

5. In Revelation 6: 9-11 we see the souls of the martyred saints asking the Lord how long it will be before He avenges their blood on them that live on earth.

6. Revelation 6:12-17 speaks of a great earthquake. This would be a partial fulfillment of Matthew 24: 7. Isaiah 24:17 – 23 speaks of a time when the "…earth shall reel to and fro like a drunkard…the Lord shall punish the hosts of the high ones…they shall be gathered as prisoners are gathered… then the moon shall be confounded and the sun ashamed…" These are events and phenomena that occur during the first half of the tribulation period.

Table 7: Satan and Christ Compared

God desires worship	Satan desires worship
Christ is a prince	Satan is a prince
Christ is called a lion (Rev. 5:5)	Satan is called a lion (1Peter 5:8)
Christ marks and seals His people (Rev. 7:3; Eph 1:13)	Satan marks his people (Rev. 13:16)
Christ has ministers (Romans 15:16; 1Cor. 4:1)	Satan has ministers (2Cor. 11:15)
Christ was raised from the dead (Matt. 17:9; 28:7)	Antichrist had a deadly wound that was healed. (Rev. 13:3)
Christ went to Hades and returned (Matt. 12:40)	Antichrist goes to the bottomless pit and returns (Rev. 11:7)
Christ is the way (John 14:6)	Satan is the broad way (Matt. 7:13)
Christ is the rock (1Cor. 10:4)	Satan is a rock (Deut 32:1-30)
Christ is the true shepherd (John 10:2)	Satan is the idol shepherd (Zech 11:17)
Christ has a throne (Matt. 19:28; 25:31; Luke. 1:23; Heb. 1:8)	Satan has a throne. (Isa. 14:13)
Christ will ride a white horse (Rev. 19:11)	Antichrist will ride a white horse (Rev. 6:2)

Matthew 24:9 speaks of a time when the nation of Israel is hated of <u>all</u> nations for the name of Christ. There has never been a time yet when Israel is hated of all nations. The persecution against the remnant will be intense:

- "…whosoever killeth you will think that he doeth God service." (John 16:2).
- "If ye were of the world, the world would love his own but because ye are not of the world, but I have chosen you out of the world, therefore the world hateth you." (John 15:19).
- They killed James (Acts 12:2 & 3).
- They stoned Stephen (Acts 7:59).
- They tried to kill Paul (Acts 21:31).
- The religious leaders of the day said of Christianity "that every where it is spoken against." (Acts 28:22).

Matthew 24:10 says that "…then shall many be offended, and shall betray one another, and shall hate one another…" We ask "at what would they be offended?" We can understand this by studying passages as John 6:60-68 where even some of the disciples that followed the Lord were offended at some of His sayings. For example He tells them "Whoso eateth my flesh, and drinketh my blood, hath eternal life; and I will raise him up at the last day." (John 6:54) In Verse 60 we then see "Many therefore of his disciples, when they had heard this said, This is an hard saying; who can hear it?" And then in Verse 66 we read "From that time many of his disciples went back, and walked no more with him." They were offended in Him because they could not understand His words. In Matthew 11:6 we read: "And blessed is *he*, whosoever shall not be offended in me." In Matthew 13:56 we see people offended in Christ because He had wisdom beyond natural wisdom and they were offended because they were challenged to consider that He was no ordinary man. He tells them that on the night of His betrayal "All ye shall be offended because of me this night…" because He would not defend Himself. During the tribulation period, many will be offended because of Christ in that there will be a price to be paid to stand for the truth when the lie will be reigning in the person of the antichrist. Micah Chapter 7 talks about the times when no one can be trusted because of the betrayal of family and friends.

> **Matthew 24:11-15** "[11] And many false prophets shall rise, and shall deceive many. [12] And because iniquity shall abound, the love of many shall wax cold. [13] But he that shall endure unto the end, the same shall be saved. [14] And this gospel of the kingdom shall be preached in all the world for a witness unto all nations; and then shall the end come. [15] When ye therefore shall see the abomination of desolation, spoken of by Daniel the prophet, stand in the holy place, (whoso readeth, let him understand:)"

Matthew 24:11 speaks of many false prophets that shall arise in that day to deceive many. Deception is an all too common thing even today in the dispensation of grace. Paul warns the Ephesian elders of some of their own speaking perverse things to draw away disciples to themselves. Paul tells us "…some shall depart from the faith giving heed to seducing spirits…" (1Tim. 4:1) That deception will be even more acute when the church the body of Christ is gone from the earth.

Matthew 24:12 speaks of the love of many waxing cold. The love in view here is love for the Lord. The Lord writes to the church at Ephesus "thou hast left thy first love…" This love turning cold is due to iniquity abounding. It is only those who will endure in love to the end that will be saved (Matt. 24:13).

The gospel of the kingdom (i.e. that Jesus Christ is the Messiah of Israel) will be preached in all of the world for a witness to all nations and then shall the end come. It will be the 144,000 who will call out the remnant of Israel and then they (the remnant) will preach the Gospel of the Kingdom. Doubtless the gift of tongues will again be in effect for this to be accomplished.

Matthew 24:15 refers to the abomination of desolation spoken of by Daniel the prophet. This is spoken of in Daniel 9:27 where we see the antichrist will make a covenant with many in Israel for one week (7 years). In the midst of the week he shall cause the sacrifice and the oblation to cease, and for the overspreading of abominations he shall make it desolate, even until the consummation…" We see it spoken of again in 12:11 of Daniel "And from the time that the daily sacrifice shall be taken away, and the abomination that maketh desolate set up, there shall be a thousand two hundred and ninety days."

> 360 x 3.5 years = 1260 days
> 1290 – 1260 = 30 days
> 1335 – 1260 = 75 days (see Dan. 12: 12 & 13 on the time of Daniel's resurrection)

The abomination is also spoken of in 2Thessalomnians 2:2-4 "…and that man of sin be revealed, the son of perdition; who opposeth and exalteth himself above all that is called God, or that is worshipped; so that he as God sitteth in the temple of God, shewing himself that he is God."

The parenthesis at the end of Verse 15 is important. "Whoso ever readeth, let him understand…" is pressing the importance of understanding what God says. We find this admonition often in scripture.
- "I am come to show thee…therefore understand…" (Dan 9:23,25)
- "…Thou didst set thine heart to understand…I am come to give thee understanding." (Dan. 10: 12-14)
- "…We ought to give heed to the things we have heard…" Heb. 2:1)
- "Blessed is he that readeth, and they that hear the words of this prophecy." (Rev 1:3)
- He that hath an ear to hear let him hear." (Rev. 3:22)

Matthew 24:16-20 "[16] Then let them which be in Judaea flee into the mountains: [17] Let him which is on the housetop not come down to take any thing out of his house: [18] Neither let him which is in the field return back to take his clothes. [19] And woe unto them that are with child, and to them that give suck in those days! [20] But pray ye that your flight be not in the winter, neither on the sabbath day: elect.

Verse 16 talks about fleeing to the mountains. Zechariah 13:4-6 speaks of the Mount of Olives being cleaved to form a valley where the remnant can be hid safely. Just as Lot was instructed to flee to avoid the destruction of the city and for his own protection (Gen. 19:15-17), so will the believers in Jerusalem be instructed to flee when the destruction of the city is close at hand.

Matthew 24:21-24 "[21] For then shall be great tribulation, such as was not since the beginning of the world to this time, no, nor ever shall be. [22] And except those days should be shortened, there should no flesh be saved: but for the elect's sake those days shall be shortened. [23] Then if any man shall say unto you, Lo, here *is* Christ, or there; believe *it* not. [24] For there shall arise false Christs, and false prophets, and shall shew great signs and wonders; insomuch that, if *it were* possible, they shall deceive the very elect.

Matthew 24:21 "For then [immediately after the abomination of desolation is set up] shall be great tribulation…" This is the second half of the week of Daniel 9:27. This tribulation will be frighteningly intense. It will be "great tribulation such as was not since the beginning of the world to that time, no, nor ever shall be." There are many prophetic passages that describe that tribulation.

- **Joel 2:2**
  [2] A day of darkness and of gloominess, a day of clouds and of thick darkness, as the morning spread upon the mountains: a great people and a strong; there hath not been ever the like, neither shall be any more after it, *even* to the years of many generations.

- **Zechariah 14:2-3**
  [2] For I will gather all nations against Jerusalem to battle; and the city shall be taken, and the houses rifled, and the women ravished; and half of the city shall go forth into captivity, and the residue of the people shall not be cut off from the city.
  [3] Then shall the LORD go forth, and fight against those nations, as when he fought in the day of battle.

- **Isaiah 65:1**
  [1] I am sought of *them that* asked not *for me*; I am found of *them that* sought me not: I said, Behold me, behold me, unto a nation *that* was not called by my name.

- **Isaiah 66:5-6 (KJV)**
  [5] Hear the word of the LORD, ye that tremble at his word; Your brethren that hated you, that cast you out for my name's sake, said, Let the LORD be glorified: but he shall appear to your joy, and they shall be ashamed.
  [6] A voice of noise from the city, a voice from the temple, a voice of the LORD that rendereth recompence to his enemies.

There are also prophetic words of comfort as well:
- **Isaiah 66:10-13**
  [10] Rejoice ye with Jerusalem, and be glad with her, all ye that love her: rejoice for joy with her, all ye that mourn for her:
  [11] That ye may suck, and be satisfied with the breasts of her consolations; that ye may milk out, and be delighted with the abundance of her glory.
  [12] For thus saith the LORD, Behold, I will extend peace to her like a river, and the glory of the Gentiles like a flowing stream: then shall ye suck, ye shall be borne upon *her* sides, and be

dandled upon *her* knees.

[13] As one whom his mother comforteth, so will I comfort you; and ye shall be comforted in Jerusalem.

- **Daniel 12:1**

  [1] And at that time shall Michael stand up, the great prince which standeth for the children of thy people: and there shall be a time of trouble, such as never was since there was a nation *even* to that same time: and at that time thy people shall be delivered, every one that shall be found written in the book.

Verse 22 says "Except those days be shortened, there should no flesh be saved:"; The existence of life itself on earth would be in jeopardy of coming to an end if it were not that the Lord Jesus Christ came to put an end to the tribulation. The verse goes on to say: "…but for the elects sake those days will be shortened." The elect in view here is the believing remnant. There has always been a remnant in every dispensation and every time on earth. There was a remnant that returned from the Babylonian captivity (Isa. 6:13). There is a remnant being saved today in the present dispensation of grace. There will be a remnant of Israel saved during the tribulation period (Zech. 13:8). Romans 11:26 speaks of those that survive the tribulation period as a remnant.

Matthew 24:23 & 24 are key passages to understanding the nature of that time. There will be many false Christs and false prophets in the tribulation period (Luke 17: 23 & 24; 21:8). The true prophets will reveal themselves because they will be those who confess that Jesus Christ has already come in the flesh and that those claiming to be Christ are imposters (1John 4:2). The deception exerted by the imposters will be very convincing. (Rev. 13:13 & 14; 19:20) The real test though will be "what sayeth the scriptures" The admonition of Deuteronomy 13:1-3 will again be in effect: "[1] If there arise among you a prophet, or a dreamer of dreams, and giveth thee a sign or a wonder, [2] And the sign or the wonder come to pass, whereof he spake unto thee, saying, Let us go after other gods, which thou hast not known, and let us serve them; [3] Thou shalt not hearken unto the words of that prophet, or that dreamer of dreams: for the LORD your God proveth you, to know whether ye love the LORD your God with all your heart and with all your soul."

The words "…if it were possible…" in Verse 24 are encouraging. There is a point in time in the tribulation period that the believers will be secure in Christ and will not be able to be deceived. John 6:37-39 and 10:28-30 implies this as does 1Peter 1:3-5 and 1John 5:18 where John talks about a sin unto death.

Matthew 24:25-28 "[25] Behold, I have told you before. [26] Wherefore if they shall say unto you, Behold, he is in the desert; go not forth: behold, *he is* in the secret chambers; believe *it* not. [27] For as the lightning cometh out of the east, and shineth even unto the west; so shall also the coming of the Son of man be. [28] For wheresoever the carcase is, there will the eagles be gathered together.

"Behold I have told you before." That is, I have told you future events before they happened. In Isaiah 48:5 & 6 we are given the reason for Bible Prophecy; "[3] I have declared the former things from the beginning; and they went forth out of my mouth, and I shewed them; I did *them* suddenly, and they came to pass. [4] Because I knew that thou *art* obstinate, and thy neck *is* an iron sinew, and thy brow brass; [5] I have even from the beginning declared *it* to thee; before it came to pass I shewed *it* thee: lest thou shouldest say, Mine idol hath done them, and my graven image, and my molten image, hath commanded them."

The Lord is telling the tribulation saints what to look for so that they are not deceived by any false Messiah. When He returns, he will not be in the desert as John the Baptist was (Isa. 40:3; Luke 3:2). When He returns, His coming will be as dramatic and as striking as lightening is when it lights up the entire sky. As Revelation 1:7 says "Behold he cometh with clouds; and every eye shall see him and they also which pierced him: and all kindreds of the earth shall wail because of him." His appearance will be visible to everyone on the earth. That will be one time when He will have the whole world's attention.

149

The amazing verse in Job 37:1-5 is prophetic of this event: "At this also my heart trembleth, and is moved out of his place. ² Hear attentively the noise of his voice, and the sound *that* goeth out of his mouth. ³ He directeth it under the whole heaven, and his lightning unto the ends of the earth. ⁴ After it a voice roareth: he thundereth with the voice of his excellency; and he will not stay them when his voice is heard. ⁵ God thundereth marvellously with his voice; great things doeth he, which we cannot comprehend."

Also Isaiah 30:30-31 "³⁰And the LORD shall cause his glorious voice to be heard, and shall shew the lighting down of his arm, with the indignation of *his* anger, and *with* the flame of a devouring fire, *with* scattering, and tempest, and hailstones. ³¹ For through the voice of the LORD shall the Assyrian be beaten down, *which* smote with a rod."

The Reference to the Assyrian is apparently a reference to the antichrist. In Acts Chapter 7 Stephen refers to the Pharaoh of Egypt that oppressed Israel as the Assyrian.

Matthew 24:28 "Wheresoever the carcase is, there will the eagles be gathered." This speaks of the carnage that will result from the Lord's return when the Gentile nations come to join the antichrist to fight against the Lord to prevent His return. Amos 9:1-4 talks about how thorough the Lord will be in venting His wrath upon his enemies in that day. Jeremiah 16:13-16 speaks of that time when God gathers the elect of Israel and fights against his enemies.

> **Matthew 24:29-30** "²⁹ Immediately after the tribulation of those days shall the sun be darkened, and the moon shall not give her light, and the stars shall fall from heaven, and the powers of the heavens shall be shaken: ³⁰ And then shall appear the sign of the Son of man in heaven: and then shall all the tribes of the earth mourn, and they shall see the Son of man coming in the clouds of heaven with power and great glory."

The tribulation period closes with phenomenal cosmic events.
- The sun darkened.
- The moon shall not give her light.
- The stars shall fall from heaven. This is apparently in connection with Revelation 12.
- The powers of heaven shall be shaken.

The tribulation closes with the Lord's return to defeat the antichrist (Dan. 7:11). The antichrist is slain by being cast alive into the Lake of Fire (Rev. 19:20).

There are many prophetic passages on these cosmic disturbances:
- Amos 8:9
- Amos 5:18-20
- Joel 2:10-13
- Joel 2: 30,31; cf Acts 2:19 & 20
- Isaiah 13:9-13
  ⁹ Behold, the day of the LORD cometh, cruel both with wrath and fierce anger, to lay the land desolate: and he shall destroy the sinners thereof out of it. ¹⁰ For the stars of heaven and the constellations thereof shall not give their light: the sun shall be darkened in his going forth, and the moon shall not cause her light to shine. ¹¹ And I will punish the world for *their* evil, and the wicked for their iniquity; and I will cause the arrogancy of the proud to cease, and will lay low the haughtiness of the terrible. ¹² I will make a man more precious than fine gold; even a man than the golden wedge of Ophir. ¹³ Therefore I will shake the heavens, and the earth shall remove out of her place, in the wrath of the LORD of hosts, and in the day of his fierce anger.

Listed below are some of the prophetic passages regarding the Day of the Lord.

- Isaiah 24:20-23 "[20] The earth shall reel to and fro like a drunkard, and shall be removed like a cottage; and the transgression thereof shall be heavy upon it; and it shall fall, and not rise again. [21] And it shall come to pass in that day, *that* the LORD shall punish the host of the high ones *that are* on high, and the kings of the earth upon the earth. [22] And they shall be gathered together, *as* prisoners are gathered in the pit, and shall be shut up in the prison, and after many days shall they be visited. [23] Then the moon shall be confounded, and the sun ashamed, when the LORD of hosts shall reign in mount Zion, and in Jerusalem, and before his ancients gloriously."

- Ezekiel 32:7 & 8 [7] And when I shall put thee out, I will cover the heaven, and make the stars thereof dark; I will cover the sun with a cloud, and the moon shall not give her light. [8] All the bright lights of heaven will I make dark over thee, and set darkness upon thy land, saith the Lord GOD.

- Zephaniah 1:14-18 "[14] The great day of the LORD *is* near, *it is* near, and hasteth greatly, *even the* voice of the day of the LORD: the mighty man shall cry there bitterly. [15] That day *is* a day of wrath, a day of trouble and distress, a day of wasteness and desolation, a day of darkness and gloominess, a day of clouds and thick darkness, [16] A day of the trumpet and alarm against the fenced cities, and against the high towers. [17] And I will bring distress upon men, that they shall walk like blind men, because they have sinned against the LORD: and their blood shall be poured out as dust, and their flesh as the dung. [18] Neither their silver nor their gold shall be able to deliver them in the day of the LORD'S wrath; but the whole land shall be devoured by the fire of his jealousy: for he shall make even a speedy riddance of all them that dwell in the land.

- Revelation 6:12-14 speaks of a day of a great earthquake and great cosmic disturbances "[12] And I beheld when he had opened the sixth seal, and, lo, there was a great earthquake; and the sun became black as sackcloth of hair, and the moon became as blood; [13] And the stars of heaven fell unto the earth, even as a fig tree casteth her untimely figs, when she is shaken of a mighty wind. [14] And the heaven departed as a scroll when it is rolled together; and every mountain and island were moved out of their places.

- 2 Peter 3:10 ff looks past these events to the time some 1000 years later when the Lord makes all things new "[10] But the day of the Lord will come as a thief in the night; in the which the heavens shall pass away with a great noise, and the elements shall melt with fervent heat, the earth also and the works that are therein shall be burned up."

It should be noted that these prophetic passages tend to lump the events in the day of the Lord together. The Day of the Lord Starts when He begins the ministry of the two witness and continues until He has defeated the last enemy (that being death). There will be cosmic disturbances in the middle of the seventieth week and again at the end of the week. In the middle of the week they will be associated with the war in heaven of which Revelation 12:7 speaks. There will also be such disturbances immediately after the tribulation.

THE RE-GATHERING OF ISRAEL

Matthew 24:31 "[31] And he shall send his angels with a great sound of a trumpet, and they shall gather together his elect from the four winds, from one end of heaven to the other."

His elect here is the nation of Israel. This is not the rapture of the church which is Christ's body. When this gathering of the elect of Israel will have occurred, the rapture will happened seven plus years earlier. In the rapture (the catching away of the Body of Christ to heaven), it will be the Lord Himself who descends to catch away the church which is His body. Here He sends His angels to gather the outcasts of Israel. This too will be in fulfillment of many Old Testament passages:

> Isaiah 11:12 [12] And he shall set up an ensign for the nations, and shall assemble the outcasts of Israel, and gather together the dispersed of Judah from the four corners of the earth.

> Isaiah 27:13 [13] And it shall come to pass in that day, *that* the great trumpet shall be blown, and they shall come which were ready to perish in the land of Assyria, and the outcasts in the land of Egypt, and shall worship the LORD in the holy mount at Jerusalem.

> Isaiah 43:5-7 [5] Fear not: for I *am* with thee: I will bring thy seed from the east, and gather thee from the west; [6] I will say to the north, Give up; and to the south, Keep not back: bring my sons from far, and my daughters from the ends of the earth; [7] *Even* every one that is called by my name: for I have created him for my glory, I have formed him; yea, I have made him.

> Isaiah 60:1-4 [1] Arise, shine; for thy light is come, and the glory of the LORD is risen upon thee. [2] For, behold, the darkness shall cover the earth, and gross darkness the people: but the LORD shall arise upon thee, and his glory shall be seen upon thee. [3] And the Gentiles shall come to thy light, and kings to the brightness of thy rising. [4] Lift up thine eyes round about, and see: all they gather themselves together, they come to thee: thy sons shall come from far, and thy daughters shall be nursed at *thy* side.

The Lord will send His angels to gather the elect to bring them back to the land. But He will also send His angel to gather the unbelievers out of the nation (Matt. 13:41). This will fulfill what John the Baptist said regarding the Lord's work in Matthew 3:10-12 regarding the chaff and the wheat.

THE PARABLE OF THE FIG TREE

> **Matthew 24:32-35** "[32] Now learn a parable of the fig tree; When his branch is yet tender, and putteth forth leaves, ye know that summer *is* nigh: [33] So likewise ye, when ye shall see all these things, know that it is near, *even* at the doors. [34] Verily I say unto you, This generation shall not pass, till all these things be fulfilled. [35] Heaven and earth shall pass away, but my words shall not pass away."

It is important to understand the Biblical symbolism of the fig tree. The fig tree represents works righteousness. Israel is the only nation that had a divinely given system that involved works righteousness – the Law of Moses. The Law had a system of justification by works wherein faith had to be demonstrated by works (James 2:20-24). There are various trees that represent Israel. The fig tree represents the religious life of Israel. The olive represents for Israel the means of access to God when Israel was God's elect agency for the salvation of men (Rom. 11:17-24). The vine represents Israel as a nation. Most of evangelical Christianity sees the establishment of Israel as a nation in 1948 as the fulfillment of this prophecy. However, the budding of the fig tree will not happen until Israel's sacrificial system is re-inaugurated. That will not happen until the antichrist makes a covenant with Israel to allow them to reinstitute the sacrificial system of the Law. It will be the generation that sees the budding of the fig tree that will not pass away until all of the things spoken of here in Chapter 24 and 25 are fulfilled. This budding of the fig tree will happen early in the tribulation period. We who live in this dispensation of grace will not witness this event.

One Taken and Another Left

> **Matthew 24:36-41** "[36] But of that day and hour knoweth no *man*, no, not the angels of heaven, but my Father only. [37] But as the days of Noe *were*, so shall also the coming of the Son of man be. [38] For

as in the days that were before the flood they were eating and drinking, marrying and giving in marriage, until the day that Noe entered into the ark, [39] And knew not until the flood came, and took them all away; so shall also the coming of the Son of man be. [40] Then shall two be in the field; the one shall be taken, and the other left. [41] Two *women shall be* grinding at the mill; the one shall be taken, and the other left."

Verses 36 thru 39 suggest that the day when the Lord will send his angels for the elect of Israel will come as a complete surprise for the unbelieving nation. There are many Bible passages that speak of the day of the Lord coming as a thief in the night (1Thess. 5:2; 2Pet. 3:10). Scripture indicates that when this happens, there will be life as usual on earth. It should be also noted that the roundness of the earth is implied in that there will be both day time activity and night time activity going on at the same time.

Verses 40 and 41 speaks of the threshing of Israel in which the believers are gathered to go into the kingdom while the unbelievers are gathered out of the nation to go into unquenchable fire. John the Baptist talked about this in Matthew 3: 10-12. Note that the rapture (spoken of in the Pauline passages as 1Thessalonians 4:16 and 1Corinthians 15:51) refers to the believers (members of the Body of Christ being taken out of the earth to a home in heaven while the unbelievers are left on earth to go into the tribulation that will thereafter come on the earth. Here, in Matthew 24, it is the unbelievers who are taken to be removed from the earth while the believers are left to go into the kingdom that will be set up on the earth. There are two different elect agencies involved because God is reconciling two different spheres of glory to Himself. His eternal purpose for the Gentile church (the church which is His body) and the mystery program is to reconcile the heavenly places to Himself. His eternal purpose for the Redeemed Nation of Israel is to be the means of reconciling the earth to Himself. I quote Colossians 1:16-20 on this important point.

"[16] For by him were all things created, that are in heaven, and that are in earth, visible and invisible, whether *they be* thrones, or dominions, or principalities, or powers: all things were created by him, and for him: [17] And he is before all things, and by him all things consist. [18] And he is the head of the body, the church: who is the beginning, the firstborn from the dead; that in all *things* he might have the preeminence. [19] For it pleased *the Father* that in him should all fulness dwell; [20] And, having made peace through the blood of his cross, by him to reconcile all things unto himself; by him, *I say*, whether *they be* things in earth, or things in heaven. (Colossians 1:16-20)

Watching as if for the Thief in the Night

Matthew 24:42-44 "[42] Watch therefore: for ye know not what hour your Lord doth come. [43] But know this, that if the goodman of the house had known in what watch the thief would come, he would have watched, and would not have suffered his house to be broken up. [44] Therefore be ye also ready: for in such an hour as ye think not the Son of man cometh."

This figure of speech is a bit of a paradox. The Lord is the thief in this parable while the "Goodman" of the house is the unbelieving nation under the antichrist. The believers of Israel are to watch for the Lord who will come as a thief in the night.

Matthew 24:45-51 "[45] Who then is a faithful and wise servant, whom his lord hath made ruler over his household, to give them meat in due season? [46] Blessed *is* that servant, whom his lord when he cometh shall find so doing. [47] Verily I say unto you, That he shall make him ruler over all his goods. [48] But and if that evil servant shall say in his heart, My lord delayeth his coming; [49] And shall begin to smite *his* fellowservants, and to eat and drink with the drunken; [50] The lord of that servant shall come in a day when he looketh not for *him*, and in an hour that he is not aware of, [51] And shall cut him asunder, and appoint *him* his portion with the hypocrites: there shall be weeping and gnashing of teeth.

In Verses 45 thru 51 we see that there is not only a reward system that the Lord will administer to the tribulation saints when He returns but also we see a performance based acceptance system. The Lord will reward the servant (i.e. the Tribulation saints-Reveation 1:1) who He finds faithfully serving when He returns. In Luke 19: 12 – 27 we see this same concept presented. The servant whose pound brought ten pounds will receive authority over ten cities (on earth), The servant whose pound had gained five pounds will have authority over five cities. However, the servant who did not invest the pound lost the pound that he was originally given.

Chapter 24 Study Guide Questions:

1. Was what the Lord told the disciples in Verse 1 and 2 prophesied in the Old Testament? Where?

2. Are there Old Testament passages that talk about the Temple being rebuilt again?

3. What three questions do the disciples ask the Lord in Verse 37?

4. What does the term "end of the world" in Verse 3 refer to?

5. What is the key event in Verse 15 that will let Israel know where they are in the clock of Bible Prophecy? Is there a passage in Daniel 9 that relates to this?

6. Are the prophesied things in Verse 9 through 15 things we should look for today? Why Not?

7. Verse 16 speaks of fleeing to the mountain. Is there an Old Testament passage that tells them what mountain to flee to?

8. How is the true prophet to be identified according to Verse 23 and 24? Does 1John 4:2 relate to this?

9. List the cosmic disturbances that will immediately follow the tribulation.

10. What does the fig tree (Verse 32) have to do with the events in the tribulation period?

11. Who are those "taken" in Verses 40 and 41? Does Matthew 3: 10 to 12 address this also?

12. Identify who the person (or people) is who is represented as the "faithful and wise servant" in Verses 45 to 48?

Chapter 25

MATTHEW 25:1-46

The Ten Virgins

Matthew 25:1-13 "¹ Then shall the kingdom of heaven be likened unto ten virgins, which took their lamps, and went forth to meet the bridegroom. ² And five of them were wise, and five *were* foolish. ³ They that *were* foolish took their lamps, and took no oil with them: ⁴ But the wise took oil in their vessels with their lamps. ⁵ While the bridegroom tarried, they all slumbered and slept. ⁶ And at midnight there was a cry made, Behold, the bridegroom cometh; go ye out to meet him. ⁷ Then all those virgins arose, and trimmed their lamps. ⁸ And the foolish said unto the wise, Give us of your oil; for our lamps are gone out. ⁹ But the wise answered, saying, *Not so*; lest there be not enough for us and you: but go ye rather to them that sell, and buy for yourselves. ¹⁰ And while they went to buy, the bridegroom came; and they that were ready went in with him to the marriage: and the door was shut. ¹¹ Afterward came also the other virgins, saying, Lord, Lord, open to us. ¹² But he answered and said, Verily I say unto you, I know you not. ¹³ Watch therefore, for ye know neither the day nor the hour wherein the Son of man cometh.

This is a difficult passage to understand in that there is much symbolism in it. There are a lot of questions that come to mind as one studies it. Questions like:

- Why "virgins"?
- Who are the virgins?
- Why are there ten?
- What is the significance of the oil?
- Who is the bridegroom?
- What are the consequences of running out of oil?
- What is the time frame of the parable?

I offer the following as a possible explanation in answer to these questions. Based on the context of this and the preceding chapter, we see (we assume) that the time frame is the tribulation period.

Who is the Bridegroom? The Bridegroom would be Christ coming to establish His kingdom through Israel.

Who are the virgins? The virgins would be Israelites. The reference to virgins reminds us of the 144,000 who minister to Israel in the tribulation period (Rev. 14:3) who are said to be virgins. The 144,000 are virgins in a spiritual sense in that they keep themselves from being defiled with the system of worship that the antichrist will be promoting through the false prophet (Rev. 14:4). In the coming Tribulation Period there will be a system of worship under the antichrist that involves women as priestesses and prophetesses. Paul speaks in regard to women who would involve themselves in teaching ministries saying that "I suffer not a woman to teach, nor to usurp authority over the man, but to be in silence. For Adam was first formed, then Eve. And Adam was not deceived, but the woman being deceived was in the transgression." Women are not to be in a teaching capacity in the Lord's work. We would understand from passages as Hebrews 13:4 that mere sexual intercourse with women does not defile men as long as it is in the context of marriage. The defiling is obviously of a spiritual nature. In Revelation 2:20 we see the Lord warning Israel about a woman named Jezebel who calls herself a prophetess. She seduces the Lord's servants to commit fornication and to eat things sacrificed unto idols. The adultery and fornication is a spiritual adultery involving eating food sacrificed to idols.

Who are these virgins and why ten? The number ten has some scriptural significance in that it represents a sample from a multitude. It is also the number for the Gentiles. We would conclude then that these virgins are probably Israelites who not only keep themselves free from being defiled by the worship of the antichrist but who also are faithful to maintain a testimony to reach out to the Gentiles during the Tribulation Period.

What is the significance of the oil? Based on the Lord's words in Matthew 10:22 ("…he that endureth to the end shall be saved…") we conclude that the oil represents faith that enables endurance of the tribulation through to the end. Oil is also used in connection with the Holy Spirit. Scripture tells us that faith cometh by hearing and hearing by the Word of God (Rom. 10:17). These Hebrew people will acquire faith from the Word of God.

What is the significance of running out of oil? If indeed, "he that endureth [in faith] to the end [of the tribulation] shall be saved…," then one must have sufficient faith from the word of God to do that. Let's think about where and how these people will be introduced to the Word of God. In Revelation 11:3-6 we meet two witnesses who maintain a powerful witness to the Word of God during the first half of the tribulation period. Revelation 11:4 refers to them as the two olive trees standing before the God of the earth. This takes us to Zechariah 4 where we see a candle stick with seven lamps and two olive trees filling the lamps. The two witnesses are likely Moses and Elijah (the two who were on either side of Christ in the mount of the transfiguration). They minister to Israel during the first half of the Tribulation period and serve to introduce the believing remnant of Israel to the New Testament Scripture – particularly the books of Hebrews through the Revelation. During the Dispensation of Grace while Israel is in unbelief, the Holy Spirit is using the books of Romans through Philemon to call out the church which is Christ's Body. The unbelieving nation of Israel today does not recognize the New Testament Scriptures. The two witnesses introduce the nation to the New Testament. In the middle of the Tribulation Period, these two witnesses are slain by the antichrist (Rev. 11:7-12). They lay in the streets for three and a half days and are then raised and taken up to haven. At that point the believing remnant of Israel will be on their own in the world. They will have to have acquired enough faith (represented by the oil) from the witness of these witnesses and the Word of God to take them through to the end – i.e. "to endure to the end".

THE TALENTS

Matthew 25:14-30 "¹⁴ For *the kingdom of heaven is* as a man travelling into a far country, *who* called his own servants, and delivered unto them his goods. ¹⁵ And unto one he gave five talents, to another two, and to another one; to every man according to his several ability; and straightway took his journey. ¹⁶ Then he that had received the five talents went and traded with the same, and made *them* other five talents. ¹⁷ And likewise he that *had received* two, he also gained other two. ¹⁸ But he that had received one went and digged in the earth, and hid his lord's money. ¹⁹ After a long time the lord of those servants cometh, and reckoneth with them. ²⁰ And so he that had received five talents came and brought other five talents, saying, Lord, thou deliveredst unto me five talents: behold, I have gained beside them five talents more. ²¹ His lord said unto him, Well done, *thou* good and faithful servant: thou hast been faithful over a few things, I will make thee ruler over many things: enter thou into the joy of thy lord. ²² He also that had received two talents came and said, Lord, thou deliveredst unto me two talents: behold, I have gained two other talents beside them. ²³ His lord said unto him, Well done, good and faithful servant; thou hast been faithful over a few things, I will make thee ruler over many things: enter thou into the joy of thy lord. ²⁴ Then he which had received the one talent came and said, Lord, I knew thee that thou art an hard man, reaping where thou hast not sown, and gathering where thou hast not strawed: ²⁵ And I was afraid, and went and hid thy talent in the earth: lo, *there* thou hast *that is* thine. ²⁶ His lord answered and said unto him, *Thou* wicked and slothful servant, thou knewest that I reap where I sowed not, and gather where I have not strawed: ²⁷ Thou oughtest therefore to have put my money to the exchangers, and *then* at my coming I should have received mine own with usury. ²⁸ Take therefore the talent from him, and give *it* unto him which hath ten talents. ²⁹ For unto every one that hath shall be given, and he shall have abundance: but from him that hath not shall be taken away even that which he hath. ³⁰ And cast ye the unprofitable servant into outer darkness: there shall be weeping and gnashing of teeth.

The introductory phrase "For *the kingdom of heaven is* as..." tells us that this is a figure of speech that we call a simile. The man traveling into a far country is the Lord returning to heaven after His death, burial and resurrection. The servants are the citizens of Israel. The goods are the souls of men – souls that are to be won to Christ by the gospel of the kingdom. The talents are areas of responsibility which the Lord gives to His saints according to their ability. When the man in Verse 14 (i.e. the Lord) returns, we see Him judging the servants according to their performance. This is a hard parable for us who are Pauline in our understanding and have an appreciation of justification by grace through faith apart from works to understand in that it expresses a performance based acceptance system. To be cast in to outer darkness is to be excluded from the kingdom and excluded from eternal life. The servant who did nothing with the talent that the Lord had given him lost everything. Those that invested the talents and thereby gained other were rewarded with again as much as they were given.

THE JUDGMENT OF THE NATIONS

Matthew 25:31-46 "³¹ When the Son of man shall come in his glory, and all the holy angels with him, then shall he sit upon the throne of his glory: ³² And before him shall be gathered all nations: and he shall separate them one from another, as a shepherd divideth *his* sheep from the goats: ³³ And he shall set the sheep on his right hand, but the goats on the left. ³⁴ Then shall the King say unto them on his right hand, Come, ye blessed of my Father, inherit the kingdom prepared for you from the foundation of the world: ³⁵ For I was an hungred, and ye gave me meat: I was thirsty, and ye gave me drink: I was a stranger, and ye took me in: ³⁶ Naked, and ye clothed me: I was sick, and ye visited me: I was in prison, and ye came unto me. ³⁷ Then shall the righteous answer him, saying, Lord, when saw we thee an hungred, and fed *thee*? or thirsty, and gave *thee* drink? ³⁸ When saw we thee a stranger, and took *thee* in? or naked, and clothed *thee*? ³⁹ Or when saw we thee sick, or in prison, and came unto thee? ⁴⁰ And the King shall answer and say unto them, Verily I say unto you, Inasmuch as ye have done *it* unto one of the least of these my brethren, ye have done *it* unto me. ⁴¹ Then shall he say also unto them on the left hand, Depart from me, ye cursed, into everlasting fire, prepared for the devil and his angels: ⁴² For I was an hungred, and ye gave me no meat: I was thirsty, and ye gave me no drink: ⁴³ I was a stranger, and ye took me not in: naked, and ye clothed me not: sick, and in prison, and ye visited me not. ⁴⁴ Then shall they also answer him, saying, Lord, when saw we thee an hungred, or athirst, or a stranger, or naked, or sick, or in prison, and did not minister unto thee? ⁴⁵ Then shall he answer them, saying, Verily I say unto you, Inasmuch as ye did *it* not to one of the least of these, ye did *it* not to me. ⁴⁶ And these shall go away into everlasting punishment: but the righteous into life eternal."

Verses 31 thru 46 addresses the matter of the Lord judging the Gentiles when He returns to set up His kingdom. The Lord's brethren in this passage are the believing remnant of Israel. Based on what we learn from this teaching, the only Gentiles that will get into the kingdom when it is set up will be those who have treated the believing remnant of Israel well during that time when the antichrist was warring against them. We see that warfare described in Revelation 12:17. The sheep on the right are the Gentiles who protected the believing remnant during that time of Jacob's trouble while the goats on the left are those who did not believe that Jesus was the true Messiah of Israel and thus betrayed the believing remnant into the hands of the antichrist.

There is much to be said regarding this event and these Gentiles who do go into the kingdom. They go into the earthly kingdom as flesh and blood people in that they are believers but not people who have been changed as we members of the Body of Christ will have been some seven plus years earlier when we were caught up to heaven before the Tribulation Period started (1Cor. 15:51& 52; 1Thess. 4:15-17). In the Revelation Chapter 20 we see that Satan is bound for a thousand years while the Gentiles who had gone into the kingdom procreate children who had not been subjected to the deception of Satan. After the thousand years are expired, Satan is released and deceives the nations again. Many of the Gentiles born during that thousand years are not converted to faith in Israel's Messiah. This is only to prove that even under the best of conditions, man still proves to be a failure in and of himself. (Rev. 20:7).

Chapter 25 Study Guide Questions:

1. Who are the virgins in Matthew 25: 1-12? What is the oil representative of?
2. Is the passage in Verses 14 – 30 grace based or law based?
3. Identify who do the sheep and the goats in Verses 31 thru 46 represent.
4. When will the separation of the sheep and the goats take place?

MATTHEW 26:1-75

THE FEAST OF THE PASSOVER

Matthew 26:1-2 "¹ And it came to pass, when Jesus had finished all these sayings, he said unto his disciples, ² Ye know that after two days is *the feast of* the passover, and the Son of man is betrayed to be crucified."

Here the Lord tells the disciples that he will be betrayed and be crucified. He is preparing to both take part in the Passover and also be the Passover sacrifice.

Matthew 26:3-5 "³ Then assembled together the chief priests, and the scribes, and the elders of the people, unto the palace of the high priest, who was called Caiaphas, ⁴ And consulted that they might take Jesus by subtilty, and kill *him*. ⁵ But they said, Not on the feast *day*, lest there be an uproar among the people."

Here we see religious hypocrisy in action. They plan to shed innocent blood but have political sense to not do in on the feast day – not for decency sake but for political expediency.

Matthew 26:6-13 "⁶ Now when Jesus was in Bethany, in the house of Simon the leper, ⁷ There came unto him a woman having an alabaster box of very precious ointment, and poured it on his head, as he sat *at meat*. ⁸ But when his disciples saw *it*, they had indignation, saying, To what purpose *is* this waste? ⁹ For this ointment might have been sold for much, and given to the poor. ¹⁰ When Jesus understood *it*, he said unto them, Why trouble ye the woman? for she hath wrought a good work upon me. ¹¹ For ye have the poor always with you; but me ye have not always. ¹² For in that she hath poured this ointment on my body, she did *it* for my burial. ¹³ Verily I say unto you, Wheresoever this gospel shall be preached in the whole world, *there* shall also this, that this woman hath done, be told for a memorial of her."

What a wonderful scene. Here they are enjoying fellowship with a man who was once a leper but now is apparently healed. Leprosy was connected with sin. The Lord had apparently healed this man of sin and this man was now enjoying sweet fellowship with the Lord. While the religious leaders of the nation were out planning to shed innocent blood, this man was enjoying fellowship with the one who can save from sin and give life.

This woman is also interesting. The Lord had been telling His disciples that He was going to be killed but they refuse to believe it. This woman apparently does believe it. She probably does not understand why He will die but she does know that He will and anoints Him for His burial. As it turns out, she is the only one who does have this opportunity.

Mathew 26:14-16 "¹⁴ Then one of the twelve, called Judas Iscariot, went unto the chief priests, ¹⁵ And said *unto them*, What will ye give me, and I will deliver him unto you? And they covenanted with him for thirty pieces of silver. ¹⁶ And from that time he sought opportunity to betray him."

Zechariah 11:12-13 is an interesting passage in that it relates to this action by Judas. It was prophesied that the Lord would be valued for a price of thirty pieces of silver. "And I said unto them, If ye think good, give *me* my price; and if not, forbear. So they weighed for my price thirty *pieces* of silver. And the LORD said unto me, Cast it unto the potter: a goodly price that I was prised at of them. And I took the thirty *pieces* of silver, and cast them to the potter in the house of the LORD."

Matthew 26:17-25 "[17] Now the first *day* of the *feast of* unleavened bread the disciples came to Jesus, saying unto him, Where wilt thou that we prepare for thee to eat the passover? [18] And he said, Go into the city to such a man, and say unto him, The Master saith, My time is at hand; I will keep the passover at thy house with my disciples. [19] And the disciples did as Jesus had appointed them; and they made ready the passover. [20] Now when the even was come, he sat down with the twelve. [21] And as they did eat, he said, Verily I say unto you, that one of you shall betray me. [22] And they were exceeding sorrowful, and began every one of them to say unto him, Lord, is it I? [23] And he answered and said, He that dippeth *his* hand with me in the dish, the same shall betray me. [24] The Son of man goeth as it is written of him: but woe unto that man by whom the Son of man is betrayed! it had been good for that man if he had not been born. [25] Then Judas, which betrayed him, answered and said, Master, is it I? He said unto him, Thou hast said."

Here the Lord demonstrates His supernatural knowledge as he did with the colt of the ass in Matthew 21:2-3. He tells them that one of them will betray Him and they begin to consider that they each could be the one that would do it. Judas who knew that he would betray Him asks the same question in an attempt cover his quilt.

Matthew 26:26-29 "[26] And as they were eating, Jesus took bread, and blessed *it*, and brake *it*, and gave *it* to the disciples, and said, Take, eat; this is my body. [27] And he took the cup, and gave thanks, and gave *it* to them, saying, Drink ye all of it; [28] For this is my blood of the new testament, which is shed for many for the remission of sins. [29] But I say unto you, I will not drink henceforth of this fruit of the vine, until that day when I drink it new with you in my Father's kingdom."

The Lord presents to Israel a memorial of the death, burial and resurrection that He will go through. He will later give this memorial to Paul in 1Corinthians 11:17-34 for us today living in the dispensation of grace. Our salvation is based on the same broken body and same shed blood that will bring the New Covenant to Israel.

Matthew 26:30-35 "[30] And when they had sung an hymn, they went out into the mount of Olives. [31] Then saith Jesus unto them, All ye shall be offended because of me this night: for it is written, I will smite the shepherd, and the sheep of the flock shall be scattered abroad. [32] But after I am risen again, I will go before you into Galilee. [33] Peter answered and said unto him, Though all *men* shall be offended because of thee, *yet* will I never be offended. [34] Jesus said unto him, Verily I say unto thee, That this night, before the cock crow, thou shalt deny me thrice. [35] Peter said unto him, Though I should die with thee, yet will I not deny thee. Likewise also said all the disciples."

The Lord is quoting Zechariah 13:7 here in Verse 31. He tells them that all of them will be offended because of Him that night. They each assure Him that they would be willing to die to not deny Him. How week the flesh is though the spirit is willing. How different a man is once the work of the Holy Spirit is in the life of a believer.

Matthew 26:36-45 "[36] Then cometh Jesus with them unto a place called Gethsemane, and saith unto the disciples, Sit ye here, while I go and pray yonder. [37] And he took with him Peter and the two sons of Zebedee, and began to be sorrowful and very heavy. [38] Then saith he unto them, My soul is exceeding sorrowful, even unto death: tarry ye here, and watch with me. [39] And he went a little further, and fell on his face, and prayed, saying, O my Father, if it be possible, let this cup pass from me: nevertheless not as I will, but as thou *wilt*. [40] And he cometh unto the disciples, and findeth them asleep, and saith unto Peter, What, could ye not watch with me one hour? [41] Watch and pray, that ye enter not into temptation: the spirit indeed *is* willing, but the flesh *is* weak. [42] He went away again the second time, and prayed, saying, O my Father, if this cup may not pass away from me, except I drink it, thy will be done. [43] And he came and found them asleep again: for their eyes were heavy. [44] And he left them, and went away again, and prayed the third time, saying the same words. [45] Then cometh he to his disciples, and saith unto them, Sleep on now, and take *your* rest: behold, the hour is at hand, and the Son of man is betrayed into the hands of sinners."

The men who had assured Him that they would die before denying Him can not even stay awake to pray with Him. The Lord is here looking into the cup that He will have to drink of and see the horror of the sin of the world being laid on Him who had lived the only perfectly righteous life that had ever been lived only to have to surrender that life as full payment for the sins of the rest of humanity. Three times he goes off to pray by Himself to ask that the cup pass from Him. It is finally after the third time that He comes back with the resolve to go through with it.

THE BETRAYAL BY JUDAS

Matthew 26:46-50 "[46] Rise, let us be going: behold, he is at hand that doth betray me. [47] And while he yet spake, lo, Judas, one of the twelve, came, and with him a great multitude with swords and staves, from the chief priests and elders of the people. [48] Now he that betrayed him gave them a sign, saying, Whomsoever I shall kiss, that same is he: hold him fast. [49] And forthwith he came to Jesus, and said, Hail, master; and kissed him. [50] And Jesus said unto him, Friend, wherefore art thou come? Then came they, and laid hands on Jesus, and took him."

Here is Judas still trying to look innocent. He is about to commit the worst atrocity committed by man of betraying the only truly righteous man that ever lived and he does it with a kiss.

Matthew 26:51-54 "[51] And, behold, one of them which were with Jesus stretched out *his* hand, and drew his sword, and struck a servant of the high priest's, and smote off his ear. [52] Then said Jesus unto him, Put up again thy sword into his place: for all they that take the sword shall perish with the sword. [53] Thinkest thou that I cannot now pray to my Father, and he shall presently give me more than twelve legions of angels? [54] But how then shall the scriptures be fulfilled, that thus it must be?

From John 18:10 we know that it was Peter who drew the sword. Peter is out to prove something. The Lord had just told him that he was going to deny Him three times that night. Peter is out to prove that he is truly willing to die defending the Lord. The Lord tells him to put his sword away. The Lord did not need anyone's sword for protection. He could have called for twelve legions of angels. Why the number twelve? Well twelve is the number for Israel and we are dealing with Israel and Israel's Messiah. The Lord could have asked the Father to forgo the whole thing and call it off and the Father would have granted His request. The only problem would have been that we (every member of Adam's fallen race) would have been doomed to an eternity separated form God and His kingdom.

Matthew 26:55-57 "[55] In that same hour said Jesus to the multitudes, Are ye come out as against a thief with swords and staves for to take me? I sat daily with you teaching in the temple, and ye laid no hold on me. [56] But all this was done, that the scriptures of the prophets might be fulfilled. Then all the disciples forsook him, and fled. [57] And they that had laid hold on Jesus led *him* away to Caiaphas the high priest, where the scribes and the elders were assembled."

The Lord is actually the one in charge of the entire proceedings from here on through to the end. He is fulfilling the scriptures that prophesy of this event. We will see Him doing so all the way through.

PETER'S DENIAL

> **Matthew 26:58-65** "⁵⁸ But Peter followed him afar off unto the high priest's palace, and went in, and sat with the servants, to see the end. ⁵⁹ Now the chief priests, and elders, and all the council, sought false witness against Jesus, to put him to death; ⁶⁰ But found none: yea, though many false witnesses came, *yet* found they none. At the last came two false witnesses, ⁶¹ And said, This *fellow* said, I am able to destroy the temple of God, and to build it in three days. ⁶² And the high priest arose, and said unto him, Answerest thou nothing? what *is it which* these witness against thee? ⁶³ But Jesus held his peace. And the high priest answered and said unto him, I adjure thee by the living God, that thou tell us whether thou be the Christ, the Son of God. ⁶⁴ Jesus saith unto him, Thou hast said: nevertheless I say unto you, Hereafter shall ye see the Son of man sitting on the right hand of power, and coming in the clouds of heaven. ⁶⁵ Then the high priest rent his clothes, saying, He hath spoken blasphemy; what further need have we of witnesses? behold, now ye have heard his blasphemy."

What deceit is in these proceedings! They could not find witnesses that could bring a legitimate charge of wrongdoing against Him so they take a true statement that He made and twist it to make it say something that he did not say. What irony! They seek false witnesses and end up crucifing Him for making a true statement.

> **Matthew 26:66-68** "⁶⁶ What think ye? They answered and said, He is guilty of death. ⁶⁷ Then did they spit in his face, and buffeted him; and others smote *him* with the palms of their hands, ⁶⁸ Saying, Prophesy unto us, thou Christ, Who is he that smote thee?"

The creator of the universe stands before these men and they do not know it. They treat Him in a manner that should not be put upon any fellow member of the human race but the Lord willingly submitted Himself to such treatment at the hands of fallen man in order that He might redeem men to Himself.

> **Matthew 26:69-75** "⁶⁹ Now Peter sat without in the palace: and a damsel came unto him, saying, Thou also wast with Jesus of Galilee. ⁷⁰ But he denied before *them* all, saying, I know not what thou sayest. ⁷¹ And when he was gone out into the porch, another *maid* saw him, and said unto them that were there, This *fellow* was also with Jesus of Nazareth. ⁷² And again he denied with an oath, I do not know the man. ⁷³ And after a while came unto *him* they that stood by, and said to Peter, Surely thou also art *one* of them; for thy speech betrayeth thee. ⁷⁴ Then began he to curse and to swear, *saying*, I know not the man. And immediately the cock crew. ⁷⁵ And Peter remembered the word of Jesus, which said unto him, Before the cock crow, thou shalt deny me thrice. And he went out, and wept bitterly."

What turmoil anger, frustration and bewilderment must have been going on within Peter here. What anguish must have gone on within him as he fulfilled the prophecy given by the Lord that before the cock would crow he would deny Him three times.

Chapter 26 Study Guide Questions

1. Verses 6 through 13 have many contrasts. And what we might call "human interest".
    a. What is leprosy a type of in the Bible?
    b. What does the healing of the Leper in Verses 6 to 13 symbolize?
    c. What is the ointment for?
    d. Dose it register with them yet that He will actually die?

2. What Old Testament Prophecy is fulfilled by Verses 14 to 16?

3. What memorial does the Lord establish in Verses 26 to 29?

4. In Verses 30 to 35 we see the frailty of these men. What will happen at Pentecost that will change that?

5. In Verses 36 through 45, how many times did the Lord go to the Father in prayer before He was committed to go through with the cross?

    a. Would the Father have accepted His decision if He decided not to go through with the cross?
    b. What would have happened to Old Testament believers (and us) if He decided not to go to the cross?

6. Based on Verses 51 through 56, who on the scene was really in charge of the whole event?

7. Why did Jesus not say a word in defense of Himself when falsely accused?

8. What emotion do you think was going through Peter's mind in Verses 8 to 25? Is this the same Peter that stood up with such confidence later in the Book of Acts? What changed?

Chapter 27

MATTHEW 27:1-66

Matthew 27:1-2 "¹ When the morning was come, all the chief priests and elders of the people took counsel against Jesus to put him to death: ² And when they had bound him, they led *him* away, and delivered him to Pontius Pilate the governor."

Judas has Remorse but not Repentance

Matthew 27:3-5 "³ Then Judas, which had betrayed him, when he saw that he was condemned, repented himself, and brought again the thirty pieces of silver to the chief priests and elders, ⁴ Saying, I have sinned in that I have betrayed the innocent blood. And they said, What *is that* to us? see thou *to that*. ⁵ And he cast down the pieces of silver in the temple, and departed, and went and hanged himself."

Here again we see the fulfillment of Zachariah 11:12 & 13

Matthew 27:6-10 "⁶ And the chief priests took the silver pieces, and said, It is not lawful for to put them into the treasury, because it is the price of blood. ⁷ And they took counsel, and bought with them the potter's field, to bury strangers in. ⁸ Wherefore that field was called, The field of blood, unto this day. ⁹ Then was fulfilled that which was spoken by Jeremy the prophet, saying, And they took the thirty pieces of silver, the price of him that was valued, whom they of the children of Israel did value; ¹⁰ And gave them for the potter's field, as the Lord appointed me."

The passage in Verse 9 is alluded to in Jeremiah 18:1-11 and 19:1-3 with regard to the potter's field. In the Jeremiah passage, the Lord is reaching out to Israel to repent. In Jeremiah 18:12 we see Israel's answer to that call for repentance saying "we will walk after our own devices…" The potter's field is where the potter destroyed defective pots. The Lord would make every Israelite a vessel unto honor but not every Israelite would yield to the hand of the potter (the Lord). Judas, because of unbelief became a vessel onto dishonor and was destroyed. It is also referenced more clearly in Zechariah 11:12-13 where Jeremiah is quoted again. Here the King of Israel and the Creator of the universe is valued at the going price of a slave – thirty shekels of silver (Exodus 21:32). Judas is there in the judgment hall when Jesus is brought in. Judas repented in the he had remorse for what he did but he did not seek forgiveness. He could have sought forgiveness from the Lord and would have been forgiven but he did not. The Lord was there to die for the sins of the world – including Judas' sin. Instead of seeking forgiveness, he addresses the chief priests and elders with whom he dealt in the betrayal.

Matthew 27:11-14 "¹¹ And Jesus stood before the governor: and the governor asked him, saying, Art thou the King of the Jews? And Jesus said unto him, Thou sayest. ¹² And when he was accused of the chief priests and elders, he answered nothing. ¹³ Then said Pilate unto him, Hearest thou not how many things they witness against thee? ¹⁴ And he answered him to never a word; insomuch that the governor marvelled greatly.

165

The Lord's answer: "Thou Sayest" means literally "It is as you say." He answered the Gentile governor but not thr chief priest and the elders. We might ask "Why did the Lord not defend Himself?" But we know why. He could have put all of them present to shame with His answers but He was not there to defend Himself but to be crucified.

Release of Barabbas

Matthew 27:15-23 "¹⁵ Now at *that* feast the governor was wont to release unto the people a prisoner, whom they would. ¹⁶ And they had then a notable prisoner, called Barabbas. ¹⁷ Therefore when they were gathered together, Pilate said unto them, Whom will ye that I release unto you? Barabbas, or Jesus which is called Christ? ¹⁸ For he knew that for envy they had delivered him. ¹⁹ When he was set down on the judgment seat, his wife sent unto him, saying, Have thou nothing to do with that just man: for I have suffered many things this day in a dream because of him. ²⁰ But the chief priests and elders persuaded the multitude that they should ask Barabbas, and destroy Jesus. ²¹ The governor answered and said unto them, Whether of the twain will ye that I release unto you? They said, Barabbas. ²² Pilate saith unto them, What shall I do then with Jesus which is called Christ? *They* all say unto him, Let him be crucified. ²³ And the governor said, Why, what evil hath he done? But they cried out the more, saying, Let him be crucified."

The governor knew that these religious hypocrites were motivated by envy. Hypocrisy is difficult to hide. He also knew that this was an innocent man who they were demanding be crucified.

Jesus Condemned

Matthew 27:24-30 "²⁴ When Pilate saw that he could prevail nothing, but *that* rather a tumult was made, he took water, and washed *his* hands before the multitude, saying, I am innocent of the blood of this just person: see ye *to it*. ²⁵ Then answered all the people, and said, His blood *be* on us, and on our children. ²⁶ Then released he Barabbas unto them: and when he had scourged Jesus, he delivered *him* to be crucified. ²⁷ Then the soldiers of the governor took Jesus into the common hall, and gathered unto him the whole band *of soldiers*. ²⁸ And they stripped him, and put on him a scarlet robe. ²⁹ And when they had platted a crown of thorns, they put *it* upon his head, and a reed in his right hand: and they bowed the knee before him, and mocked him, saying, Hail, King of the Jews! ³⁰ And they spit upon him, and took the reed, and smote him on the head. ³¹ And after that they had mocked him, they took the robe off from him, and put his own raiment on him, and led him away to crucify *him*.

Pilate tried to wash his hands in an attempt to cover his guilt in allowing an innocent man to be put to death. Once Pilate gave Him over to be crucified, He was turned over to the soldiers and they could now do what they wanted with Him. Being that He was to be crucified, they could now have fun with Him in the cruelest way that they might see fit. Doubtless the beatings that He sustained here left him unrecognizable. Isaiah 52:14 prophesied of this: "¹⁴ As many were astonied at thee; his visage was so marred more than any man, and his form more than the sons of men:" The creator of the universe is mocked as not even a normal human would be and marred by abuse that is worse than what evil men would put on even a normal man.

Matthew 27:32-34 "³² And as they came out, they found a man of Cyrene, Simon by name: him they compelled to bear his cross. ³³ And when they were come unto a place called Golgotha, that is to say, a place of a skull, ³⁴ They gave him vinegar to drink mingled with gall: and when he had tasted *thereof*, he would not drink.

Simon of Cyrene is named elsewhere in scripture. In Mark 15:21 we find that he is the father of Alexander and Rufus. In Romans 16:13 Paul tells the Romans to salute one Rufus chosen in the Lord.

Jesus is Crucified

Matthew 27:35-37 "³⁵ And they crucified him, and parted his garments, casting lots: that it might be fulfilled which was spoken by the prophet, They parted my garments among them, and upon my vesture did they cast lots. ³⁶ And sitting down they watched him there; ³⁷ And set up over his head his accusation written, THIS IS JESUS THE KING OF THE JEWS."

There are many events that transpired at the crucifixion that are not covered in Mathews account. To get the full picture, all four accounts must be studied and compared to put the events in order. In John's account (John 19:22) we find that Pilate put the words THIS IS JESUS THE KING OF THE JEWS over the cross.

Two Thieves

Matthew 27:38-44 "³⁸ Then were there two thieves crucified with him, one on the right hand, and another on the left. ³⁹ And they that passed by reviled him, wagging their heads, ⁴⁰ And saying, Thou that destroyest the temple, and buildest *it* in three days, save thyself. If thou be the Son of God, come down from the cross. ⁴¹ Likewise also the chief priests mocking *him*, with the scribes and elders, said, ⁴² He saved others; himself he cannot save. If he be the King of Israel, let him now come down from the cross, and we will believe him. ⁴³ He trusted in God; let him deliver him now, if he will have him: for he said, I am the Son of God. ⁴⁴ The thieves also, which were crucified with him, cast the same in his teeth."

The salvation of the believing thief is not addressed in Matthew's account. It is apparent that both thieves who were crucified with Him at first mocked Him but one of them later repented and recognized Him for who He is (cf. Mark 15:27-32; Luke 23:32-43; John 19:18). That believing thief ended up gaining eternal life as a result of his faith and his petition to Israel's Messiah.

Jesus Surrenders His Spirit to the Father

Matthew 27:45-50 "⁴⁵ Now from the sixth hour there was darkness over all the land unto the ninth hour. ⁴⁶ And about the ninth hour Jesus cried with a loud voice, saying, Eli, Eli, lama sabachthani? that is to say, My God, my God, why hast thou forsaken me? ⁴⁷ Some of them that stood there, when they heard *that*, said, This *man* calleth for Elias. ⁴⁸ And straightway one of them ran, and took a spunge, and filled *it* with vinegar, and put *it* on a reed, and gave him to drink. ⁴⁹ The rest said, Let be, let us see whether Elias will come to save him. ⁵⁰ Jesus, when he had cried again with a loud voice, yielded up the ghost."

At His last breath, He was still able to cry out with a loud voice. Unlike other men who die, He could not (and would not) die until He willingly yielded up His spirit. The question that the Lord asks in Verse 47 is a quote form Psalm 22:1. The question is answered in Psalm 22:3 "But thou art holy thou that inhabitest the praises of Israel." The Father's holiness compelled Him to turn His back on His beloved Son when the Son was "made to be sin for us..." (2Cor. 5:21). See also Psalm 71:11, Isaiah 53:10, and Laminations 1:12 on the thoughts that went through the minds of both the Father and the Son on that fateful day on Calvary.

Isaiah 53:10-12 (KJV)

[10] Yet it pleased the LORD to bruise him; he hath put *him* to grief: when thou shalt make his soul an offering for sin, he shall see *his* seed, he shall prolong *his* days, and the pleasure of the LORD shall prosper in his hand.

[11] He shall see of the travail of his soul, *and* shall be satisfied: by his knowledge shall my righteous servant justify many; for he shall bear their iniquities.

[12] Therefore will I divide him *a portion* with the great, and he shall divide the spoil with the strong; because he hath poured out his soul unto death: and he was numbered with the transgressors; and he bare the sin of many, and made intercession for the transgressors.

The Temple Veil Torn

Matthew 27:51-53 "[51] And, behold, the veil of the temple was rent in twain from the top to the bottom; and the earth did quake, and the rocks rent; [52] And the graves were opened; and many bodies of the saints which slept arose, [53] And came out of the graves after his resurrection, and went into the holy city, and appeared unto many."

The tearing of the veil in the temple from the top to the bottom is significant here. The fact that it was tore from the top down is proof that God did this. The fact that those on the front side of the veil were not killed is also significant in that it proved that God was no longer behind that veil in the earthly temple. God was out on Calvary's hill paying sin's debt for every man as the real sacrifice for sin.

After His resurrection, Jesus went into heaven into the true tabernacle, which the Lord pitched, and not man. (Heb. 8:3) When He did, He "…Neither by the blood of goats and calves, but by his own blood he entered in once into the holy place, having obtained eternal redemption *for us*." (Hebrews 9:12) Jesus went into the real tabernacle in heaven as Israel's High Priest to obtain eternal redemption for Israel. When Jesus revealed the mystery through Paul, He revealed that the redeeming shed blood of Christ also provides for our redemption for us members of the Body of Christ.

The opening of the graves is also interesting. This is not a resurrection of these people but a restoration to life. Those saints who arose would have died again. These people would have been people who had recently died who could have testified that they had seen the Lord in Hades in the heart of the earth just a few days earlier. How the Lord gave infallible proofs of His resurrection!

Jesus' Burial

Matthew 27:54-61 " [54]Now when the centurion, and they that were with him, watching Jesus, saw the earthquake, and those things that were done, they feared greatly, saying, Truly this was the Son of God. [55] And many women were there beholding afar off, which followed Jesus from Galilee, ministering unto him: [56] Among which was Mary Magdalene, and Mary the mother of James and Joses, and the mother of Zebedee's children. [57] When the even was come, there came a rich man of Arimathaea, named Joseph, who also himself was Jesus' disciple: [58] He went to Pilate, and begged the body of Jesus. Then Pilate commanded the body to be delivered. [59] And when Joseph had taken the body, he wrapped it in a clean linen cloth, [60] And laid it in his own new tomb, which he had hewn out in the rock: and he rolled a great stone to the door of the sepulchre, and departed. [61] And there was Mary Magdalene, and the other Mary, sitting over against the sepulchre.

In verse 56 we see these two women being faithful and stayed at the cross while the disciples fled.

Matthew 27:62-66 "[62] Now the next day, that followed the day of the preparation, the chief priests and Pharisees came together unto Pilate, [63] Saying, Sir, we remember that that deceiver said, while he was yet alive, After three days I will rise again. [64] Command therefore that the sepulchre be made sure until the third day, lest his disciples come by night, and steal him away, and say unto the people, He is risen from the dead: so the last error shall be worse than the first. [65] Pilate said unto them, Ye have a watch: go your way, make *it* as sure as ye can. [66] So they went, and made the sepulchre sure, sealing the stone, and setting a watch."

The chief priest and Pharisees wanted to make sure that the body stayed in the grave and to special precautions to be sure no one took the body to feign a resurrection. However the presence of the soldiers served only add great witness to the fact of the resurrection.

Chapter 27 Study Guide Questions

1. Where in the Old Testament do we find references to the thirty pieces of silver that we paid to Judas? What according to Zechariah 11:12 & 13 was that the price of in human terms?

2. Judas realizes in Verse 3 that Jesus is going to die because of him. Could he have turned to Jesus to seek forgiveness? Could he have been forgiven?

3. Why could the money not be put back into the treasury?

4. What (according to Verse 18) was their motive for bringing Christ to Pilate?

5. According to Verses 15 through 18, how did Pilate see Jesus? Did he know that some regarded Him as Messiah?

6. What awful oath did the leaders of Israel make inverse 25? Does the nation still bear the consequences of that oath?

7. What Old Testament passage answers the Lord's question in Verse 45?

8. What Old Testament passage is fulfilled in Verses 48 & 49?

9. What is the significance of the temple veil being torn from top to bottom when the Lord said "It is finished"?

10. What is the significance of the amazing incident of some graves of saints being opened and these dead saints arose? They would have been in Paradise. What would they have witnessed there?

11. What effect did the presence of the soldiers guarding the tomb have to witness to the fact of the resurrection?

Chapter 28

MATTHEW 28:1-20

THE EMPTY TOMB

Matthew 28:1-7 "¹ In the end of the sabbath, as it began to dawn toward the first *day* of the week, came Mary Magdalene and the other Mary to see the sepulchre. ² And, behold, there was a great earthquake: for the angel of the Lord descended from heaven, and came and rolled back the stone from the door, and sat upon it. ³ His countenance was like lightning, and his raiment white as snow: ⁴ And for fear of him the keepers did shake, and became as dead *men*. ⁵ And the angel answered and said unto the women, Fear not ye: for I know that ye seek Jesus, which was crucified. ⁶ He is not here: for he is risen, as he said. Come, see the place where the Lord lay. ⁷ And go quickly, and tell his disciples that he is risen from the dead; and, behold, he goeth before you into Galilee; there shall ye see him: lo, I have told you."

It appears from this account that the women came to the sepulcher before the angel rolled the stone away. The angel of the Lord rolled the stone away so that the women could see that the grave was empty. When the Lord arose, He left the tomb without moving the stone. In His resurrection body He could pass through solid objects as we will see when He walked through closed doors (Luke 24:36ff). We would note here that the angel of the Lord is not the Lord as some suggest. The Lord Himself had left to go to Galilee as the angel spoke to the women..

Matthew 28:8-10 "⁸ And they departed quickly from the sepulchre with fear and great joy; and did run to bring his disciples word. ⁹ And as they went to tell his disciples, behold, Jesus met them, saying, All hail. And they came and held him by the feet, and worshipped him. ¹⁰ Then said Jesus unto them, Be not afraid: go tell my brethren that they go into Galilee, and there shall they see me.

The Lord is directing them to send His disciples to a predefined place in Galilee where He would meet with them.

Matthew 28:11-15 "¹¹ Now when they were going, behold, some of the watch came into the city, and shewed unto the chief priests all the things that were done. ¹² And when they were assembled with the elders, and had taken counsel, they gave large money unto the soldiers, ¹³ Saying, Say ye, His disciples came by night, and stole him *away* while we slept. ¹⁴ And if this come to the governor's ears, we will persuade him, and secure you. ¹⁵ So they took the money, and did as they were taught: and this saying is commonly reported among the Jews until this day."

How hard unbelief can be! These men should have investigated if indeed this is true so that they can come to God who did such a work for their personal salvation. Here they try to cover up their deed and dig the hole that they were in even deeper. Eventually the truth comes out as in the case here "…this saying is commonly reported among the Jews until this day."

Matthew 28:16-20 "¹⁶ Then the eleven disciples went away into Galilee, into a mountain where Jesus had appointed them. ¹⁷ And when they saw him, they worshipped him: but some doubted." ¹⁸ And Jesus came and spake unto them, saying, All power is given unto me in heaven and in earth. ¹⁹ Go ye therefore, and teach all nations, baptizing them in the name of the Father, and of the Son, and of the Holy Ghost: ²⁰ Teaching them to observe all things whatsoever I have commanded you: and, lo, I am with you alway, *even* unto the end of the world.

Mathew's gospel closes with the commission to teach all nations, baptizing them in the name of the triune God. He commissions them to teach all things that He had taught them during His earthly ministry with them. This includes the keeping of the Law of Moses (Matt. 5:17; 23:1-4; etc.)

Chapter 28 Study Guide Questions

1. Why do you suppose the angel rolled the stone away from the tomb?

2. Can you imagine a heart so hard as to remain in unbelief after such evidence as Verses 11 through 14 reveal?

3. The Lord gives a post resurrection commission to the twelve in Verses 16 to 20. Did this commission involve the Law being taken out of the way as Paul said was under the commission given to him in Colossians 2:14 Romans 6:14; Galatians 3:10; and 5:18?

CONCLUSION

The Kingdom of Heaven and Geopolitics of the World Today

"Then shall the King say unto them on his right hand, Come, ye blessed of my Father, inherit the kingdom prepared for you from the foundation of the world:" (Matthew 25:34)

In *Matthew's Gospel - A Study of the King and His Kingdom*, we studied what life on earth will be like under the reign of the Lord Jesus Christ as Israel's Messiah in the Kingdom of Heaven. From the very foundation of the world, God had in mind that kingdom that He will establish on this earth. These words (Verse 34 above) were spoken by our Lord Jesus Christ at the close of His earthly ministry. The context is Matthew 25:31- 46 where we see the Lord speaking prophetically of judging the Gentile nations after the close of the Tribulation Period. The Gentiles in this context would be called to go into the promised Kingdom of Heaven when the entire world would be blessed through Abraham's multiplied seed – the redeemed nation of Israel. This would be the fulfillment of the Covenant that God made with Abraham in Genesis 18:18 and 22:18. What is significant about this statement in Matthew 25:34 is that the Kingdom was in God's mind "…from the foundation of the world." In fact, everything He had done up to that point in history was for the purpose of establishing that kingdom in the earth. We note however, that kingdom has still not been established on earth some 2,000 years after He spoke these words. What we find in the Book of Acts is that God Himself temporarily interrupted the program of Prophecy under which He would have set up that kingdom. He interrupted it to start a new program involving a new elect agency by bringing in a new dispensation which, by its nature, had to be kept a secret until the time was right to reveal.

The term "the Kingdom of Heaven" is used 32 times in Matthew's gospel but nowhere else in the Bible. It is a reference to the kingdom that will be set up on the earth when Jesus Christ returns to the earth at the close of the Tribulation period. Under that kingdom, this earth will have its finest hour under the reign of Christ. Jesus will reign over redeemed Israel and Israel will reign over the earth. Israel will be under the New Covenant by which the nation will finally be in such a spiritual condition whereby she shall be the means whereby Abraham's seed will truly be a blessing to the world.

Much of Christianity today views the church which is the Body of Christ as having started in Chapter 2 of the Book of Acts. They hold this view because the Holy Spirit who forms the church of this present dispensation came into prominence there in Acts Chapter 2. However, the fact is that the promised kingdom was actually officially offered to the nation Israel in the first chapters of the Book of Acts. The sin of blaspheming the Holy Ghost that the Lord spoke about occurred as He (the Holy Spirit) witnessed to that nation through Peter and the twelve apostles (with Matthias having replaced Judas) at Pentecost. Israel's official rejection of Jesus Christ as her Messiah did not occur at the cross but rather in the Book of Acts when the nation rejected the resurrected Christ as her Messiah. The nation committed the unpardonable sin by rejecting the call made by the Holy Spirit through the twelve apostles to Israel at Pentecost in Acts Chapters 2 through 7.

As we saw in our study of Matthew's gospel, God made two different appeals to Israel during the Lord's earthly ministry regarding the Kingdom of Heaven. The first appeal to Israel came with the ministry of John the Baptist.

> "1 In those days came John the Baptist, preaching in the wilderness of Judaea, 2 And saying, Repent ye: for the kingdom of heaven is at hand. 3 For this is he that was spoken of by the prophet Esaias, saying, The voice of one crying in the wilderness, Prepare ye the way of the Lord, make his paths straight." (Matthew 3:1-3)

This appeal by John the Baptist is actually God the Father's appeal to Israel to get ready for her Messiah and the Kingdom. That Matthew 3 passage actually sets the course for the four gospel accounts of our Lord's earthly ministry. The issue was a kingdom that is called "The Kingdom of Heaven." The kingdom in view here is not to be understood as a kingdom in heaven. This Kingdom was to be set up upon the earth. His kingdom will be set up on earth by the God of Heaven – therefore the name "the Kingdom of Heaven." Matthew is the account of our Lord's earthly ministry in which He is presented as the seed of David who will sit on the Throne of David in that Kingdom that was promised in the Old Testament Scriptures. We see it described in Daniel 2:44.

> "And in the days of these kings shall the God of heaven set up a kingdom, which shall never be destroyed: and the kingdom shall not be left to other people, but it shall break in pieces and consume all these kingdoms, and it shall stand for ever." (Daniel 2:44)

That kingdom is called the "Kingdom of Heaven" not only because the God of Heaven sets it up but also because, when it is set up, God's will is going to be done on earth as it is in heaven. "After this manner therefore pray ye: Our Father which art in heaven, Hallowed be thy name, Thy kingdom come. Thy will be done in earth, as it is in heaven." (Matthew 6:9-10)

After John is put in prison, the Lord Himself takes up the appeal to Israel. We saw the appeal of the Father and here we see the second appeal being made by the Son to Israel.

> "12 Now when Jesus had heard that John was cast into prison, he departed into Galilee; 13 And leaving Nazareth, he came and dwelt in Capernaum, which is upon the sea coast, in the borders of Zabulon and Nephthalim: 14 That it might be fulfilled which was spoken by Esaias the prophet, saying,15 The land of Zabulon, and the land of Nephthalim, by the way of the sea, beyond Jordan, Galilee of the Gentiles; 6 The people which sat in darkness saw great light; and to them which sat in the region and shadow of death light is sprung up. 17 *From that time Jesus began to preach, and to say, Repent: for the kingdom of heaven is at hand.*" (Matthew 4:12-17 emphasis added)

In the first ten chapters of Matthew's gospel, we saw the calling out of the twelve disciples who become the twelve apostles. They then continue the appeal to the nation to repent because the Kingdom of Heaven is at hand. "At hand" meaning that it is ready to be set up. Note that they were not to go to the Gentiles or even to the Samaritans but only to the house of Israel. They were sent out with supernatural powers to demonstrate that this was a serious call to Israel.

> "5 These twelve Jesus sent forth, and commanded them, saying, Go not into the way of the Gentiles, and into any city of the Samaritans enter ye not: 6 But go rather to the lost sheep of the house of Israel. 7 And as ye go, preach, saying, *The kingdom of heaven is at hand.* 8 Heal the sick, cleanse the lepers, raise the dead, cast out devils: freely ye have received, freely give. 9 Provide neither gold, nor silver, nor brass in your purses, 10 Nor scrip for your journey, neither two coats, neither shoes, nor yet staves: for the workman is worthy of his meat. (Matthew 10:5-10 emphasis added)

The third appeal that God makes to the nation is made by the Holy Ghost in the Book of Acts. After the death, burial and resurrection of our Lord, Jesus again sends the twelve after His ascension with still the same message. The only difference now is that it is the Holy Ghost now appealing to the nation to repent of their sin of unbelief. To repent was to change their mind about who this Jesus of Nazareth really is.

> "12 And when Peter saw it, he answered unto the people, Ye men of Israel, why marvel ye at this? or why look ye so earnestly on us, as though by our own power or holiness we had made this man to walk? 13 The God of Abraham, and of Isaac, and of Jacob, the God of our fathers, hath glorified his Son Jesus; whom ye delivered up, and denied him in the presence of Pilate, when he was determined to let him go. 14 But ye denied the Holy One and the Just, and desired a murderer

to be granted unto you; 15 And killed the Prince of life, whom God hath raised from the dead; whereof we are witnesses. 16 And his name through faith in his name hath made this man strong, whom ye see and know: yea, the faith which is by him hath given him this perfect soundness in the presence of you all. (Acts 3:12-16)

Note that Peter is seeking to bring true conviction on the nation for their deed of having put to death their Messiah. What we must not lose sight of here though is that this is the Holy Ghost's appeal to the nation. Now though it is an appeal to trust in the resurrected Christ. Note as he goes on that this is the actual official offer of the kingdom to Israel.

"17 And now, brethren, I wot that through ignorance ye did it, as did also your rulers. 18 But those things, which God before had shewed by the mouth of all his prophets, that Christ should suffer, he hath so fulfilled. 19 Repent ye therefore, and be converted, that your sins may be blotted out, when the times of refreshing shall come from the presence of the Lord; 20 *And he shall send Jesus Christ, which before was preached unto you: 21 Whom the heaven must receive until the times of restitution of all things, which God hath spoken by the mouth of all his holy prophets since the world began.* (Acts 3:17-21 Emphasis added)

Note from this passage what would have happened if Israel would have repented (i.e. changed their mind about who the one they crucified really is). Had they, as a nation, genuinely repented, the following would have ensued:

1) Their sins would have been blotted out when Christ returned to earth (which would have happened shortly thereafter to establish the kingdom). This would have been Israel's national Day of Atonement. Israel, being a covenant people, has a defined Day of Atonement in which their sins nationally will be forgiven. Today we who are saved during the dispensation of grace each individually receive the atonement the moment we trust Jesus Christ as Savior (Rom. 5:11)

2) God the Father would have sent Jesus Christ back to earth to set up the kingdom. Had that happened, the present dispensation of grace would not have started.

3) God would have restored to Israel all of the things that He had spoken by the mouth of all His holy Prophets since the world began. The program regarding Israel and the Kingdom of Heaven set up on earth is called Prophecy because is is what the prophets have been talking about throughout the entire Bible up to this point in Acts Chapter 7.

Now let's draw our attention to Verse 23. "And it shall come to pass that every soul, which will not hear that prophet, shall be destroyed from among the people." (Acts 3:23) This is what John had warned Israel about in Matthew 3:11and 12

"I [John] indeed baptize you [Israel] with water unto repentance: but he that cometh after me [Jesus] is mightier than I, whose shoes I am not worthy to bear: he shall baptize you [Israel] with the Holy Ghost, and with fire. [12] Whose fan *is* in his hand, and he will throughly purge his floor, *and gather his wheat into the garner; but he will burn up the chaff with unquenchable fire.*" (Emphasis added)

The meaning of this purging of His floor is made clear by what John said in Verse 10 of Matthew Chapter 3: "And now the axe is laid unto the root of the trees: every tree which bringeth not forth good fruit is hewn down, and cast into the fire." This is serious business. The trees here are Israelites. When the Kingdom is set up, then all of Israel will be saved (Romans 11:26). That does not mean that God will somehow force unbelievers to believe and be faithful. It means that those who will not believe of their own free will are going to be purged from the nation. Only believing faithful Israelites will go into that Kingdom and the New Covenant will take effect through them.

The fire in Verses 10 and 12 of Matthew 3 is the Gehenna fire that we saw in our discussion in Chapter 3. Ultimately the purpose for the Tribulation Period is to purge unbelief from Israel and to get Israel saved as a nation. The apostle talks about this in Romans 11:26 and 27 saying "And so all Israel shall be saved: as it is written, There shall come out of Sion the Deliverer, and shall turn away ungodliness from Jacob: For this is my covenant unto them, when I shall take away their sins."

This witness of the Holy Ghost takes us back to what the Lord told the unbelieving scribes and Pharisees in Matthew 12: 31-32

> "31 Wherefore I say unto you, All manner of sin and blasphemy shall be forgiven unto men: but the blasphemy against the Holy Ghost shall not be forgiven unto men. 32 And whosoever speaketh a word against the Son of man, it shall be forgiven him: but whosoever speaketh against the Holy Ghost, it shall not be forgiven him, neither in this world, neither in the world to come."

The nation's rejection of the message from the Father given through John did not result in them being set aside nor did their rejection of the witness of the Son in Matthew Chapter 12. However, when they reject the witness of the Holy Ghost, (which did not come until the Book of Acts at Pentecost) things will change.

From Peter's message in Acts 3 to Stephen's message in Chapter 7 of Acts, it is the Holy Ghost witnessing to Israel that the one Israel crucified is their Messiah. However, Israel had an opportunity to repent of that deed until they stoned Stephen. Had they done so, the Tribulation period would have followed and run its course and then the Kingdom would have been established. Let's consider Stephen's pointed message to Israel:

> "51 Ye stiffnecked and uncircumcised in heart and ears, *ye do always resist the Holy Ghost:* as your fathers did, so do ye. 52 Which of the prophets have not your fathers persecuted? and they have slain them which shewed before of the coming of the Just One; of whom ye have been now the betrayers and murderers: 53 Who have received the law by the disposition of angels, and have not kept it." (Acts 7:51-53 emphasis added)

Stephen brought the indictment against the leaders of Israel. What Stephen sees as he looked up into heaven and what happened next is most significant to the rest of the Book of Acts and to life on earth for centuries to come after that. Note the next verse:

> "55 But he, being full of the Holy Ghost, looked up stedfastly into heaven, and saw the glory of God, and Jesus standing on the right hand of God, 56 And said, Behold, I see the heavens opened, and the Son of man standing on the right hand of God." (Acts 7:55-56)

Stephen sees Jesus standing at the right hand of God in heaven. This posture is significant because of what we read in Acts 2:32 from Peter's statement to Israel:

> "32 This Jesus hath God raised up, whereof we all are witnesses. 33 Therefore being by the right hand of God exalted, and having received of the Father the promise of the Holy Ghost, he hath shed forth this, which ye now see and hear. 34 For David is not ascended into the heavens: but he saith himself, The LORD said unto my Lord, *Sit thou on my right hand, 35 Until I make thy foes thy footstool.* 36 Therefore let all the house of Israel know assuredly, that God hath made that same Jesus, whom ye have crucified, both Lord and Christ." (Acts 2:32-36 Emphasis added)

Jesus was to sit at the Father's right hand until it was time for the Father to make His enemies His footstool. So what was to happen at this point (at the stoning of Stephen)?

The Seven Year Tribulation (the seventieth week of Daniel Chapter 9) was to come.

Israel was to be purged of unbelief by the Tribulation Period.

Armageddon would have happened at the culmination of the Seventieth week.

Jesus would have returned to earth to establish the kingdom.

But! That is not what happened. What did happen?

Jesus saved Saul of Tarsus who, at that time, was leading Israel's rejection of the resurrected Jesus Christ.

Jesus revealed the Mystery through Paul concerning the Dispensation of the Grace of God that we live in today.

Jesus temporarily sets Israel aside to reconcile the world – this made the whole world savable apart from Israel and the prophetic program concerning the Kingdom of Heaven.

All of the wonderful blessings that the world will enjoy in the promised kingdom have been postponed for over close to 2,000 years so far.

Most importantly, God started forming a new elect agency through which He will work in the world to redeem men. He started the Church the Body of Christ and began the dispensation of the grace of God. Saul of Tarsus could now be saved in spite of having committed the unforgiveable sin of blaspheming the Holy Spirit because God started a dispensation in which there in no unpardonable sin.

An Un-prophesied and Unprecedented Change in the Geopolitics of the World

The offer of the Kingdom to Israel was withdrawn. The reality of this is the fact that God does not have His Nation on earth today. Rather, what the apostle calls "this present evil world" began (Galatians 1:4). For nearly 2000 years now there is no nation on earth that could claim to be God's nation. Israel could have been, should have been, and would have been that nation but that is a lost opportunity (but only temporarily).

Though God does not have His nation in the earth today, He does have His people on earth. God did something totally un-prophesied and unprecedented. He interrupted His prophetic program and His dealings with His nation of Israel and temporarily set that nation aside as the elect agency by which He works in the world. Instead, He started a new and different elect agency. He started a Gentile church. This Gentile church is called out from the Gentile masses - which now includes Israel for that nation is today regarded by God as just another Gentile nation.

The Preaching of the Cross as Good News

It is a startling discovery to the observant Bible student that, if he were to go verse by verse through the Bible starting in Genesis 1:1, he would go all the way through the four gospel accounts and through the Book of Acts before he would come to the preaching of the cross as "Good News." The depth of the riches of all that was accomplished on the cross was a part and parcel of the mystery that the Lord Jesus Christ revealed to the world through the apostle Paul. God interrupted His program of prophecy to reveal what is called "the Mystery." God chose an unlikely candidate to be the revealer for such a blessed message – He chose the one who had been leading Israel's rejection of Christ, Saul of Tarsus who became Paul the apostle of the Gentiles. Observe Paul's statement regarding this message of grace:

Ephesians 3:1-12 (KJV)
[1] For this cause I Paul, the prisoner of Jesus Christ for you Gentiles, [2] If ye have heard of the dispensation of the grace of God which is given me to you-ward: [3] How that by revelation he made known unto me the mystery; (as I wrote afore in few words, [4] Whereby, when ye read, ye may understand my knowledge in the mystery of Christ) [5] Which in other ages was not made

known unto the sons of men, as it is now revealed unto his holy apostles and prophets by the Spirit; [6] That the Gentiles should be fellow-heirs, and of the same body, and partakers of his promise in Christ by the gospel: [7] Whereof I was made a minister, according to the gift of the grace of God given unto me by the effectual working of his power. [8] Unto me, who am less than the least of all saints, is this grace given, that I should preach among the Gentiles the unsearchable riches of Christ; [9] And to make all *men* see what *is* the fellowship of the mystery, which from the beginning of the world hath been hid in God, who created all things by Jesus Christ: [10] To the intent that now unto the principalities and powers in heavenly *places* might be known by the church the manifold wisdom of God, [11] According to the eternal purpose which he purposed in Christ Jesus our Lord: [12] In whom we have boldness and access with confidence by the faith of him.

The church which is Christ's Body is composed of all who come to faith in the redeeming work that Jesus Christ accomplished on the cross whether they by Jew or Gentile. All who come in faith are "justified freely by his grace through the redemption that is in Christ Jesus: Whom God hath set forth to be a propitiation through faith in his blood, to declare his righteousness for the remission of sins that are past, through the forbearance of God; To declare, I say at this time his righteousness: that he might be just and the justifier of him which believeth in Jesus." (Romans 3: 24 – 26). This justification is apart from the deeds of the Law – which has now been taken out of the way (Col. 2::14). Today anyone can have their sins forgiven and be reckoned by God as righteous (fit to be in God's presence) by simple faith in the good news that Christ died for our sins according to the scriptures, and was buried and rose again the third day according to the scriptures (1Corinthians 15:1-3). When a person believes that simple message, that person is baptized by the Holy Ghost into the Body of Christ (1Cor. 2:13) and sealed to eternal life (Eph. 1:13).

The Church which is Christ's Body is the subject of the body of doctrine that we know of as the Pauline Epistles. It is what Paul calls "the preaching of Jesus Christ according to the revelation of the mystery" (Romans 16:25). In these epistles the body of Christ is presented as if it were a virtual man that has Jesus Christ as the head and the corporate collection of all believers in the world as the body. This one new man actually is at work in the world today to "edify itself in love" (Ephesians 4:15 and 16).

If God does not have a nation in earth today that is His nation, how does He carry on His work of redemption (i.e. saving lost people) today? He does it through the new agency of believers (the Church which is His Body) as they individually live the Christian life and more so as they function together in local churches. The local church is what Paul calls "the house of God, the church of the living God, the pillar and ground of the truth." (1Timothy 3:15)

Geo-politics of the World Today

So then we ask how the geo-political structure of society fits into what God is doing in the world today. Obviously, God is interested in His of work saving the souls of men going forward in an efficient manner. That requires peace and tranquility in the world and it also requires sufficient freedom that people can choose to believe and live out their faith. We see this desire on God's part in 1Timothy 2:4 but I quote the entire passage:

[1] I exhort therefore, that, first of all, supplications, prayers, intercessions, *and* giving of thanks, be made for all men; [2] For kings, and *for* all that are in authority; that we may lead a quiet and peaceable life in all godliness and honesty. [3] For this *is* good and acceptable in the sight of God our Saviour; [4] Who will have all men to be saved, and to come unto the knowledge of the truth. [5] For *there is* one God, and one mediator between God and men, the man Christ Jesus; [6] Who gave himself a ransom for all, to be testified in due time. (1Timothy 2:1-6)

Based on this verse we understand that God obviously desires that we be able to lead quite and peaceable lives. His interest is that all men be saved and then to come to the knowledge of the truth. God is not working with nations at large today but with individuals. All people individually have a choice to make as to their eternal destiny. It is not tied in any way to the nation they hale from or in which they might have citizenship. So too, it is not based on the person's past successes or failures he might have in his spiritual experience. One's eternal destiny is keyed to one's choice as to what they believe about whom that was on the cross of Calvary and what did He accomplish there for them. The believer, at the moment he or she trusts Jesus Christ as Savior, instantly becomes a citizen of heaven (Philippians 3:20). However, he is also a citizen of some country on earth. Therefore, the Word of God does give some direction as to how to live as one who has such dual citizenship.

God is doing only one thing during this dispensation of grace. He is calling out the Church the Body of Christ from the lost masses of humanity. God has an eternal purpose for the Body of Christ – a destiny that is eternal in the heavens (2Corinthians 5:1). It must be remembered that that destiny is different from the destiny of redeemed Israel in the Old Testament, in the gospel era, in the early chapters of the Book of Acts or in the future kingdom.

There are people in every country on earth today who are being justified by faith in Christ and become members of the one true church – the Body of Christ. God does give instruction regarding believers in their relationship with the civil authorities. He says: "Let every soul be subject unto the higher powers. For there is no power but of God: the powers that be are ordained of God." (Romans 13:1)

So what does that mean "the powers that be are ordained of God?" We have to go back to the time of the flood of Noah and the Tower of Babel to find information on how God ordained human government and how government ought and ought not to operate. What happened at Babel was mankind joining forces with Satan in an effort to create a culture that excluded God and actually sought to prevent Him from enjoying His creation. Man was there at Babel in league with Satan trying to foil God's eternal purpose. There at Babel we see a one world government represented by the city and a one world religion represented by the tower whose top might reach unto heaven. I think also we see a one world economic system represented by Nimrod who was the great hunter before (i.e. instead of) the Lord. This was the first manifestation of what we today call globalism. God expressed His strong displeasure for this globalism by the confusion of the languages of the population then so that men had to separate from each other to establish separate and sovereign countries. He will not have a one world government until He sets it up through His nation under the reign of His Messiah.

The Kingdom of Heaven in Abeyance

There is today a push for a one world government as though man has been trying to reestablish that system that was dismantled by God back at Babel. Having separate sovereign free nations provides for the free expression of faith on the part of believers especially in countries that respect freedom of speech and freedom of religion as America does. The founding principle of America is that man is endowed by his creator with certain unalienable rights as life, liberty and the pursuit of happiness.

The establishment of sovereign free nations provides for the protection of mankind in that if the governmental structure of a country or society becomes corrupted and intolerant of the free expression of faith in God, one can simply cross a border to get free of it. The founding fathers of America, in order to provide for protection of freedom to worship as one pleases, saw fit to prevent the government from establishing a state religion or to prevent the free exercise of it.

America is not a Theocracy – the direct rule of God over the nation. There is no nation on earth today that is a Theocracy and there will not be one until Jesus Christ returns to establish His kingdom. Israel would have been that theocracy but lost that possibility by rejecting her resurrected Messiah and thus abdicated her responsibility to be His nation in the earth.

One day, the dispensation of grace will end with the catching away of the Church the Body of Christ to heaven (1Thess. 4:17 and 1Cor. 15:51). God will then pick up His dealings with Israel where He left off with them. The portion of the Bible beginning with the Book of Hebrews through the Book of the Revelation will then provide the nation the information by which the promises that God made with Abraham, Isaac, and Jacob will be realized by the establishment of the Kingdom of Heaven.

This study in Matthew's gospel is the third book in the author's "Prophecy Series." Bible prophecy consists of essentially the entire Bible outside of the Pauline Epistles. The author has a series of four books in what is called the Prophecy Series. The first of this series is "*A Study in the Book of Daniel – the Kingdom of Heaven in Prophecy.*" The third in the series is *A Study in Hebrews – Israel and the New Covenant.*. The fourth and last in the series is *A Study in the Revelation—the End Times Fulfillment of Bible Prophecy*. The Pauline Epistles comprises the realm of Bible doctrine called "the preaching of Jesus Christ according to the revelation of the mystery." While prophecy concerns a kingdom that will be set up on earth under the reign of Jesus Christ as Israel's Messiah, the mystery concerns the Lord Jesus Christ as the head of the church which is Christ's body – a Gentile church. For the Bible student who desires to go deeper into a study of the mystery, the book *More than Conquerors – a Study in the Book of Romans,* and the book *You and Your Creator – A Study in God's Eternal Purpose for Man* by this same author will provide in depth study in how we who live in the present dispensation of the grce of God are to live as members of the church which is His body.

The Bible student is instructed to study to show himself approved unto God by "rightly dividing the word of truth." (2Timothy 2:15) Appendix 2 below lays out in graphical and table form the New Testament Rightly Divided. Appendix 1 (Table 8) below shows the sequence of the flow of events from past history into future prophecy on how God plan for the ages unfolds in time. You will notice in this flow chart that we today are living at a time that is the balancing point between Prophecy and the Mystery. I encourage you the reader to study these two illustrations in some depth. My prayers are with you that you may profit greatly from you study and enjoy the riches of God's grace to you.

Michael J Tiry, Author

Appendix 1

For by him were all things created (Col. 1:16)
He is before all things, and by Him all things consist

All things subdued unto Him (I Cor. 15:27)
All things gathered together in Christ (Eph. 1 10)

History – God's record of the past

Prophecy – God's story of the future

Declaring the end from ancient times (Isaiah 46:20)
I have declared the former things from the beginning (Isaiah 48:3)
In the latter days ye shall consider it perfectly (Jer. 23:20)

History	Prophecy
rst rebellion – Satan and angels ; Ezek. 28:140 rst judgment – chaos (Gen 1:2)	The final rebellion – Satan and men The final judgment – fire (Rev 21:8)
arth made ready for man 1:3-31)	The Earth a perfect habitat for man (Rev 22:1-7)
ubjection to Satan 3:1-19)	The subjecting of Satan (Rev 20:10)
rsal rebellion (Gen 6:1-7) nent by water (Noah –Gen 6:8-2 arth purged by water (Gen 7:17- nments setup (Gen 9:5-7)	Universal rebellion (Rev 20:8) Judgment by fire (2Pet 3:7) The foor purged (Mat 3:12) Kingdom setup Perfect Government
f Israel (Gen 12:1 thru Duet.) ing on Israel (I and II Sam) nsion in Israel (I & II Kings)	Restoration of Israel (Rev 5:10) Judgment of tribulation Repentance of the nation (Rev 7:4)
mes of the Gentiles begins Ezra, Neh.)	The times of the Gentiles ends (Lk 21:24; Rev. 11:5)

ry of Christ
    The Truth
    His rejection and death
    His resurrection and ascensic
	Ministry of Anti-Christ
	    The Lie
	    His reception and reign
	    His destruction and doom

pirit poured out 2:17) nd coming in view all of Israel	The Spirit again poured cut (Rev 19:10; 22:17) Second coming in view Rise of Israel

Appendix 2 -- The New Testament Scripture—Rightly Divided

The New Testament scriptures start with the account of our Lord's earthly ministry in the four Gospels of Matthew, Mark, Luke and John. Following that is the Book of Acts. Then we have what is called the Pauline Epistles (Romans through Philemon). Finally we have the Hebrew church Epistles of Hebrews through the Revelation. That is how we find them laid out in our New Testament. That is actually how the themes of the books unfold in time. The earthly ministry of our Lord Jesus Christ is presented first regarding His ministry to the twelve apostles of Israel. The book of Acts continues with the ministry of the twelve to the nation until mid Act when we find a marked change with the saving of Saul of Tarsus and his call to be the apostle of the Gentiles. The New Testament then has the Pauline Epistles containing a markedly different focus. There the focus in not on Israel but rather it is a broad based outreach to the lost masses of humanity. The elect agency that we find in the Pauline Epistles is no longer the nation of Israel but rather the church which is Christ's Body and the focus is on the dispensation of the grace of God. The apostle Paul calls the message in these epistles " the preaching of Jesus Christ according to the revelation of the mystery." The Book of Romans presents the foundational doctrine for the mystery while the Book of 2Thessalonians presents the conclusion of it with the catching away of the Body of Christ to its eternal home in heaven. The Book of Hebrews then presents the foundational information to Israel that will equip the nation with the doctrine on how the cross pertains to their program of redemption as God picks up His dealings with them again. Hebrews through the Revelation then takes Israel through the Tribulation Period that follows the dispensation of grace and into the promised Kingdom of Heaven.

Half of the New Testament scriptures are about Israel and God's plan for that nation while the other half is about the Church which is Christ's Body – a Gentile church. The body of doctrine that pertains to Israel is called Prophecy. It is called prophecy because it is what " ...God hath spoken by the mouth of all His Holy Prophets since the world began" (Acts 3:21). The other half of the New Testament scriptures (the portion written by Paul, the apostle of the Gentiles) is called the Mystery because it is the body of doctrine that our Lord kept secret until He revealed it to us through Paul for us who live in this present Dispensation of Grace. Paul refers to it as " ...The mystery which from the beginning of the world hath been hid in God who created all things by Jesus Christ" (Eph. 3:9). When Paul, the apostle of the Gentiles ,tells us to study to show ourselves approved unto God and be workmen who need not to be ashamed, he is talking about rightly dividing the word of truth – Making the distinction between Prophecy and the Mystery.

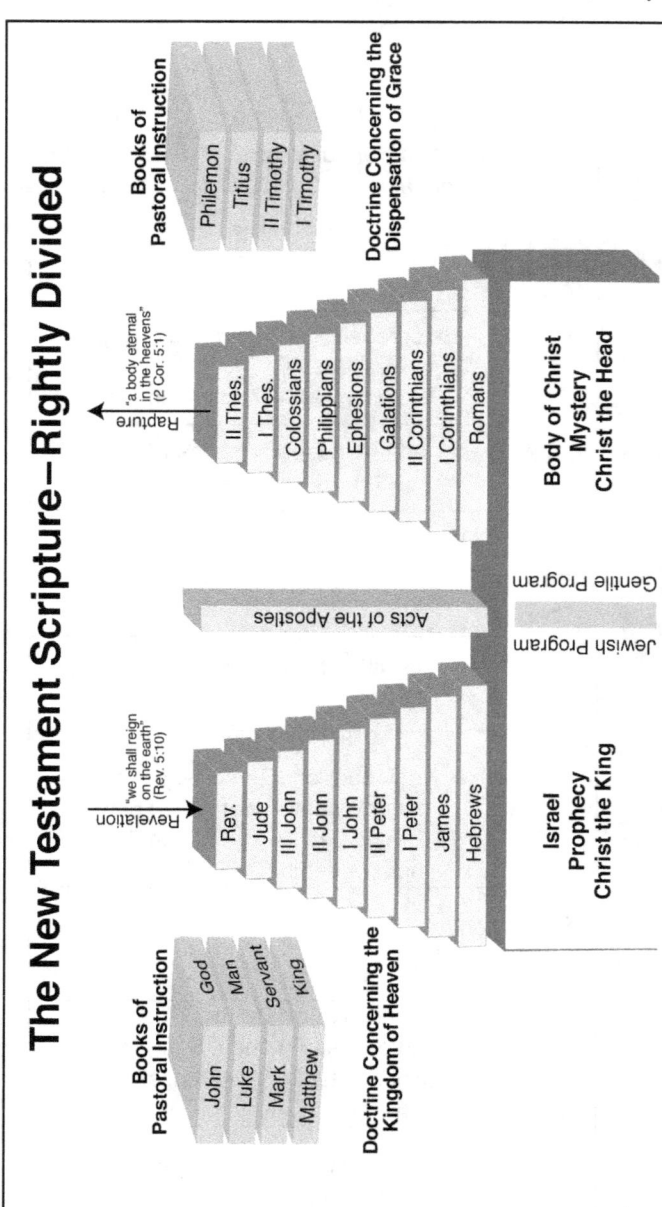

The New Testament Scripture–Rightly Divided

Books of Pastoral Instruction

Philemon
Titus
II Timothy
I Timothy

Doctrine Concerning the Dispensation of Grace

Rapture — "a body eternal in the heavens" (2 Cor. 5:1)

II Thes.
I Thes.
Colossians
Philippians
Ephesions
Galations
II Corinthians
I Corinthians
Romans

Body of Christ Mystery Christ the Head

Acts of the Apostles

Gentile Program

Jewish Program

Revelation — "we shall reign on the earth" (Rev. 5:10)

Rev.
Jude
III John
II John
I John
II Peter
I Peter
James
Hebrews

Israel Prophecy Christ the King

Books of Pastoral Instruction

God
John
Man
Luke
Servant
Mark
King
Matthew

Doctrine Concerning the Kingdom of Heaven

The central person in the Bible is our Lord Jesus Christ. He is the creator of all things in heaven and in earth (Col. 1:16). He is also the one who will reconcile everything in heaven and in earth back to Himself (Col. 1:20). There are two programs by which He will do that. Prophecy is the program by which He reconciles the earth to Himself. The Mystery deals with His reign in the heavens. Point by point the two program are different. The table on the facing page points out those differences. When we note the significance of the differences, we begin to understand how important rightly dividing the Word of Turth is to understanding the Bible

Table 9	Prophecy	Mystery
Purpose	That Christ reign on earth (Zech. 9:9-11)	That Christ preeminent in all things (Col. 1:18)
Goal	A Kingdom on Earth (Jer. 23:5)	A Body reigning in heaven (2Cor. 5:1; 2Tim. 2:10-12; Eph. 1:23)
Elect Agency	Redeemed Israel (Ex. 19:5 & 6; 1Pet. 2:9)	The Body of Christ (Col. 1:18, 24)
Relationship to Christ	Christ the King (Isa. 9: 6 & 7)	Christ its the Head of the Body (Eph. 1:21-23; 5:23)
Blessings to the Gentiles	Through Israel's rise (Gen. 22:18; 26:3 &4)	Through Israel's fall (Acts 28: 27-28; Rom. 11:11-15)
Relationship of Jew and Gentile	Israel Supreme (Isa. 60:1 – 3)	Jew and Gentile on the same level (Rom. 3:9; 10:12; cf. 11:30-32; Eph. 2:16-17)
View of Nations	Mainly concerns nation (Isa. 2:4. Ezek. 37:21 – 22)	Concerned with individuals (Rom. 10:12 – 13; 2Cor. 5:14 – 17)
The nature of Blessings to Men	Blessings both Physical and Spiritual on earth (Isa. 2:3; 11:1-9)	All Spiritual Blessings in Heavenly Places in Christ (Eph. 1:3-13; Col. 3:1-3)
View of the Lord's presence on earth	Concern's Christ's presence on earth (Isa. 59:20; Zech. 14:4)	Explains His present absence from the earth (Eph. 1:18-23)
Means of Salvation	Faith demonstrated by works (James 2:14-22)	Through Faith alone (Rom. 3:21 – 26; 4:4 & 5; Eph. 2: 8 & 9)
Relation to the Law of Moses	The Law remains in effect (Mat. 2:20 cf. 23:2; Acts 21:20)	The Law taken out of the way (Eph. 2:14-16; Col. 2:14)
Structure	Concerns God's Nation in the earth (Dan. 2:44; Mat. 6:10)	Concerns a body – a living organism (1Cor. 12:12 & 13; Eph. 4:12 – 16)
Miraculous signs and wonders	Required as evidence of faith (Mark 16:16)	Replaced with unfeigned love (1Cor. 13:8)
Apostleship	Twelve apostles, 12 thrones, 12 tribes (Mat. 19:28)	One apostle to one body (Rom. 11:13; Gal. 2: 8 & 9; Eph. 3:1-13)
Commission	Preach and baptize (Mat. 28:19; Mark 16:16)	Preach without Water baptism (1Cor. 1:17, 2Cor. 5:19 – 21; 1Cor. 12:13 cf. Eph. 4:5)
View of the Lord's Return	His return to the earth to Reign (Acts 1:11 cf. 2:36)	Return to the air to catch the Body of Christ away (1Thess. 4:17)